RESERVATION

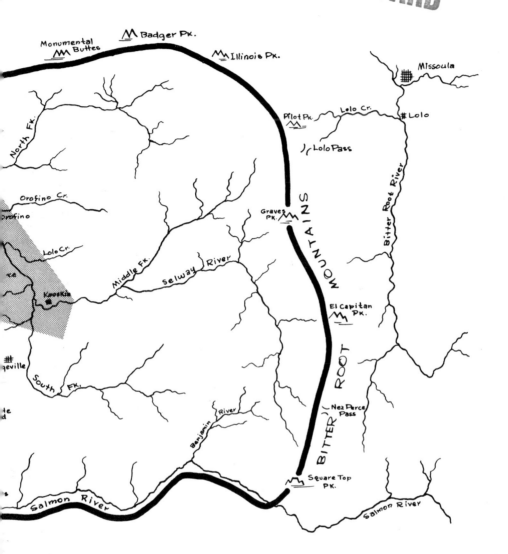

Reservation Boundary by Treaty 1855 (Interpretation by Judge E. V. Kuykendall, Pomeroy, Wash.)

"Nor shall any white man excepting those in the employment of the Indian Department—be permitted to reside upon the said reservation without permission of the Indian Tribe . . . " (Excerpt from the Nez Perce Treaty of 1855.)

Reservation Boundary by Treaty 1863. (Negotiated Washington, D.C., but never signed by Chief Joseph or any other lower Nez Perce chief and never recognized by them.)

"I am the man to tell you what you must do. You will come on the reservation within time I tell you (30 days). If not, soldiers will put you there or shoot you down!" (Words of General O. O. Howard to Nez Perce Chiefs—Conference Lapwai May 3, 1877—ordering Nez Perces upon reservation shown by SHADED AREA. (*Yellow Wolf: His Own Story*—Page 40.)

HEAR ME, MY CHIEFS!
Nez Perce History and Legend

Courtesy E. A. Brininstool

CHIEF JOSEPH

HEAR ME, MY CHIEFS!
Nez Perce History and Legend

By
L. V. McWHORTER

EDITED BY
RUTH BORDIN

Photographs are reproduced from originals
in the L. V. McWhorter Collection,
Washington State University Libraries,
Pullman, Washington.

THE CAXTON PRINTERS, LTD.
Caldwell, Idaho
1986

First Printing September, 1952
Second Printing October, 1983
Third Printing January, 1986

COPYRIGHT 1952-1980 BY
THE CAXTON PRINTERS, LTD.
CALDWELL, IDAHO

International Standard Book Number: 0-87004-310-2

Printed, lithographed, and bound in the United States of America by
The CAXTON PRINTERS, Ltd.
Caldwell, Idaho
145712

DEDICATION

For Camille Williams, Yellow Wolf, Peopeo Tholekt, Many Wounds, Black Eagle, all deceased, and to all others living or dead, without whose part this history could not have been written.

ACKNOWLEDGMENTS

THE CALENDARING OF THE McWHORTER MATERIALS pertaining to the Nez Perces was initiated by Mrs. Oswald Berg, and later continued by Robert Whitner, who, in addition to performing his technical duties, also made a careful study of McWhorter's historiography.

Services of a varying nature were performed by the following, to whom the editor wishes to extend her appreciation: Mrs. E. L. Avery; Miss Elizabeth Taylor; Miss Catherine White; Dr. Stewart Hazlet, dean of the graduate school; Richard Whittemore; the Friends of the Library of the State College, particularly Joel E. Ferris; Mrs. Anne McDonnell; Thomas Teakle.

Likewise it is desired to acknowledge the courtesy of the various groups and organizations who have permitted quotations from their publications:

The Washington State Historical Society, for permission to quote from *Building A State,* and from Eugene Wilson's manuscript, "The Nez Perce Campaign."

The Montana Historical Society, for permission to quote from *Contributions to the Historical Society of Montana,* II, IV, VII; and from J. B. Catlin's "The Battle of the Big Hole," contained in the *Historian's Annual Report, Society of Montana Pioneers, 1927.*

The State Historical Society of North Dakota, for

permission to quote from Volume I of the Society's *Collections*.

The State Historical Society of Idaho, for permission to quote from the fifteenth and seventeenth *Biennial Reports of the Board of Trustees of the Idaho State Historical Society*.

To Appleton-Century-Crofts, Incorporated, for permission to quote from Thomas B. Marquis' *Memoirs of a White Crow Indian*, and Hugh Lennox Scott's *Some Memories of a Soldier*.

The Abingdon-Cokesbury Press, for permission to quote from A. S. Atwood's *The Conquerors*.

The Longmans, Green, and Company, for permission to quote from Flora Seymour's *The Story of the Red Man*.

The Houghton Mifflin Company, for permission to quote from Hazard Stevens' *Life of Isaac Ingalls Stevens*, and from James McLaughlin's *My Friend, the Indian*.

The Lowman Hanford Company, for permission to quote from Ezra Meeker's *Pioneer Reminiscences of Puget Sound*.

To the MacMillan Company, for permission to quote from C. J. Brosnan's *Jason Lee, Prophet of the New Oregon*.

To J. P. Morgan and Company, for permission to quote from Edward S. Curtis' *The North American Indian*.

To H. S. Howard, for permission to quote from O. O. Howard's *Famous Indian Chiefs I Have Known*.

To Robert Bailey, for permission to quote from *River of No Return*.

TABLE OF CONTENTS

LIST OF ILLUSTRATIONS

LIST OF MAPS

INTRODUCTION

IN MANY RESPECTS THIS NARRATIVE IS EXCEPTIONAL, if not absolutely unique. It is Indian history, told from the Indian point of view, and depends largely upon Indian sources. Although the final product has had the benefit of scholarly attention, it remains folk history in most of its essential aspects. To the extent to which the culture of the red men of the Pacific Northwest is revealed, without any attempt to evaluate it in the white man's terms, it will serve the anthropologists and kindred social scientists even more than the historian. The latter, however, requires this background so that he may understand the conduct of the Indian, particularly in his relation to his conquerors.

Many may contend that, in times such as these, it is more important to study the dominant races and the minority or subject groups whose problems now agitate the world. Possibly so, but the history of the American Indian relations and United States policies should bring home the lesson that ignorance of the nature and character of other peoples, as much as greed and wanton aggrandizement, has led to conduct disastrous to the weaker contestants, and proved to be needlessly costly in terms of human life and suffering. The history of Indian-white relationship, furthermore, should dispel the pat assumption that participants, eyewitnesses, or those in responsible charge, are reliable sources per se. On the contrary, the person "who was there" is too often the one least competent to observe a situation, because of the fact that, by sitting in on it, he is not in a good position to get sufficient perspective.

Furthermore, the perfectly sincere well-wisher has, because of the smug complacency which all too frequently characterizes the type, on occasion perpetrated the greatest injustices and pronounced the most fallacious judgments. Soldier, Indian agent, missionary, and settler, alike showed, time and again, that they did not understand the Indian. This was due to the fact that they were prone to appraise the natives' society, culture, and religion by white standards. McWhorter believed firmly that those who chose to sit in judgment on the alleged heathens were themselves conspicuously lacking in true spiritual depth and profound ethical tradition.

Most obvious was the lack of comprehension of the Indian's noncoercive society. Had those who had to deal with the original inhabitants understood Indian society, in which tribal authority could not bind individuals, as white men's jurisdiction bound its subjects, they, possibly, might not have visited upon entire tribes vigorous reprisals for the overt acts of individuals. Indians could well have testified to the brutality of the incongruous "guilt by association." Not only were injustices perpetrated, but grossly distorted historical interpretations have resulted from viewing Indian problems through faulty social prisms.

Had the white man not read his concept of civil and military leadership into the Indian pattern, the absurd mistake of portraying Joseph as a military genius would not have been perpetrated. Any one who read McWhorter's *Yellow Wolf: His Own Story*, must have asked himself—"Where was Joseph during the great trek toward Canada?" This new work will jolt those who have portrayed the truly great chief as the "Red Man's Napoleon." He just wasn't; he was something much more—the leader of a great people in crisis, seeking freedom as they regarded it. Now, as never before, the world needs the inspiration to be drawn from the leadership exercised by the great Nez Perce. Joseph, therefore, was, and still is, important.

McWhorter gathered the data, but did not write the chapters which deal with the trans-Rocky Mountain retreat. Ruth Bordin, who wrote them, is not a debunker; she had no stake in the matter, except to reveal the actual situation as accurately as possible. Joseph loses nothing in stature by being portrayed as a great leader seeking peace for his people. Unlike the white statesman, who, because of his position as titular head of a state is also commander in chief of its armed forces, an Indian chief who might lead in negotiations was not necessarily in charge in the field. Neither the author nor the editor found any evidence that Joseph was, in any material way, responsible for the tactics and strategy employed on the famous retreat, which has been applauded by writers on military affairs. Whether the success of the natives, in eluding the forces sent against them, should be attributed to their military genius, or to the incompetence and ineptness of their pursuers, is a matter which each reader may determine for himself.

This book is Indian history, not merely because it tells the story from the Indians' point of view, but, likewise, because they participated in preparing the story. Their contribution went beyond casual interviews and scraps of testimony. They gathered testimony and recorded data; at McWhorter's request they checked and re-checked the facts; they read the first drafts of many chapters; and they evaluated the conclusions. Among the author's partners were some who had been warriors in the campaign of 1877; others were with the retreating party, but as noncombatants—among them were some who were then in their childhood; others were relatives or friends of participants; and some were tribal historians who had gathered and preserved their history —Indian-fashion. Though it must be acknowledged that the author relied almost entirely on the participants in the war and the descendants of the war party, it may be said, in extenuation, that there has seldom, if ever, been such a rich harvest of historical information from Indian sources. Unfortunately McWhorter did not live to write his own acknowledgment of the services of his Indian colleagues. Any selection made by others is likely to omit some deserving collaborators, and would be even more defective if an attempt were made to differentiate in the amount and value of the services rendered. The following were the most frequent correspondents of the author, and deserve the enduring gratitude of all who will enjoy the book: Camille Williams, Black Eagle, Two Moons, Peopeo Tholekt, Yellow Wolf, Many Wounds, Wottolen, Wounded Head, and Silas Whitman. Even those without knowledge of Indian society will understand that many of these men have already joined the author in the happy hunting ground.

Acknowledging without stint the extent and significance of the Indians' share in this monumental achievement, it should nevertheless be borne in mind that McWhorter was the spearhead of the project, that he directed the search for sources; and that the

synthesis, interpretations, and writing were to have
been his responsibility—which he fully assumed until
his death.

Another factor accentuated the Indian flavor of
his new history. McWhorter had identified himself
so completely with the life and causes of his native
friends that he virtually became one of them. He
was adopted into the Nez Perce tribe. Some members,
among them Yellow Wolf, even acknowledged him
as a full blood-brother, and Yellow Wolf formally
designated him as such. To some of us who were so
fortunate as to have known the author, he seemed to
have acquired the deportment, if not the appearance,
of an Indian. He had the dignity of bearing, the
serenity, and the note of sadness in his voice. Even
when he gave vent to his indignation over the injustices perpetrated against his fellow men—and on
such occasions he could employ very colorful language
—his voice never acquired the harshness or shrill
quality which is likely to attend angry expression.
Something he stressed, in the conversations he had
with the writer, was that the Indian language contained no words of profanity—that the most severe
term of opprobrium that could be applied to another
person was "bad man."

Having a profound respect for the Indian's religion, and particularly his ethical code, the author
resented what he regarded as the Christian missionaries' smug complacence in assuming that the
Indians were spiritually inarticulate. From his point
of view, the missionaries were thoroughly incompe-
tent to deal with their spiritual and ethical superiors.
Let us not be deceived by McWhorter's bitterness in
this matter; he had no quarrel with Christianity,
but felt that some of its disciples violated the admonition—"Judge not, that ye be not judged." He

had a great respect for the "Dreamer" cult; how near he came to accepting it is not clear.

There can be little doubt that McWhorter was qualified to interpret the spirit of Nez Perce culture. His deep regard for the great ethical values which, he felt, could be nothing less than the spiritual experience and achievement of a mature people, and his conviction that all mankind could profit by the Indians' way of life, qualified him to transmit their folklore to posterity. His formal schooling, which ended when he was twelve, certainly did not foreshadow scholarly achievement. Few self-taught men have been as successful as he was in acquiring a broad culture, and an abiding interest in history and folklore. Numerous short papers, pamphlets and tracts, besides three substantial books, reflected his careful scholarship and vigorous style, and paved the way for this, his posthumously published magnum opus. He built his studies upon a foundation of a fearless intellectual integrity and an eagerness to let the truth be known. Aware of his conscious bias, he, probably, did not recognize so easily his subconscious predilections. There never was the slightest effort to disguise his prejudices; his righteous indignation never became self-righteousness.

Eager to marshal all the facts, he was equally concerned with giving dissenters the opportunity to present their versions. So he offered them the opportunity to include their statements on particular matters in his book. Fully aware that his account would arouse strong reactions, he was never apprehensive about this circumstance. However, he definitely was not a debunker. This book is a labor of love in which the author was more concerned with telling the truth as he saw it than with refuting previous versions. He was contemptuous of most former writers on the subject and on occasion struck out boldly against his predecessors, yet he was more concerned about revealing what he considered the real facts. He thought so little of his precursors that he gave them very scant attention. Had he been in the slightest degree a publicity-seeking sensationalist he would probably have rushed into print against them, instead of devoting thirty years to the most painstaking research, thus delaying the final draft so long that it had to be published posthumously.

Next to intellectual honesty and curiosity, McWhorter's greatest attribute was his diligence. In his persistent search for the facts and determination to ferret out all the pertinent detail, he almost approached antiquarianism. Not that there can ever be too close a check, on the score of accuracy, but on occasion his preoccupation with minutiae constituted the chief factor in delaying the progress of his research. Whereas he was extremely painstaking, he was not systematic. He never developed a uniform system of note-taking or adopted a standard note form. Notations were made on every size and shape of paper. They were organized very well when they were given into the custody of the State College, and had been placed in file folders according to the chapters determined by the author. There was, however, likely to be more than one fact to a card, and his correspondence with collaborators reveals that on occasion important items had been misplaced or lost. Sometimes the information had to be solicited anew.

At the time of McWhorter's death forty-eight chapters, which now comprise the first twenty chapters, of a good first draft had been completed. The pattern of organization and the tone of the book had been set. His family was eager that the work be completed and that it retain, with as great a degree of fidelity as was possible, the author's conclusions and style. This was desired particularly for those chapters which McWhorter had completed. As to these, only the obvious errors of fact, and mistakes of grammar or spelling, and the most striking inelegancies in construction were to be corrected. In exploring the means towards this end, Mr. V. O. McWhorter, representing the family, consulted with Dr. E. O. Holland, then president of the State College of Washington. The latter suggested that the author's partially completed manuscript, notes, and collected sources be placed in custody of the State College, and that it, subject to the approval of the representatives of the McWhorter estate, designate a qualified historian to edit and complete the book. It was a fortunate circumstance which made Mrs. Ruth Bordin available for this assignment. Her Master's degree and additional training at the University of Minnesota had not stressed American history, much less the history of the West; but her thorough grounding in historiography and critical methods, as always, paid dividends. Those of us on the staff of the Department of History and Political Science at the State College were pleased and amazed by the alacrity and scholarly acumen with which she took hold of her assignment. In a remarkably short time she had mastered her background material, and, no less gratifying, she caught the spirit of the original author and his collaborators. She made persistent use of maps. Whereas she retained the chronology and organization of the original draft, she combined short chapters into more workable units and placed certain Nez Perce legends, which were strikingly similar to others, in an appendix, rather than leaving them in the text. She studiously retained her predecessor's conclusions in his portion of the first draft, and, by eliminating only grammatical inelegancies and a few needlessly blunt expressions, succeeded in retaining the flavor of McWhorter's writing.

The heuristics for the entire book had been substantially completed by McWhorter, but the intrachapter organization, interpretation, and writing of Chapters XXI to XXX are entirely the work of Mrs. Bordin. Naturally, the reader may expect an abrupt break between the sections of a book written by two persons who had never seen each other. However, to those of us who have read the manuscript, it appears that despite different vocabulary and sentence structure, the editor-coauthor sustained remarkably well the flavor and spirit of the original approach. Perhaps the final product has gained by the dovetailing and blending of the research of an intelligent, diligent, and inspired layman with the scholarship of a disciplined, imaginative, and academically trained mind. The friends and admirers of Big Foot* and the State College of Washington will share with the McWhorter family a deep sense of gratitude to Mrs. Bordin for her able performance of her difficult but, as she has acknowledged, not unrewarding assignment.

All in the least familiar with the preparation of this book would acknowledge that credit must go chiefly to the author and his Indian co-workers and to the editor, yet it would be difficult to exhaust the list of those who shared in this significant venture. The McWhorter family must be commended for the faithful way it carried out the wishes of its departed

---

* This was the name with which McWhorter signed many of his letters to me. His son told me that this was his father's Yakima name and that the Nez Perces called him *Hemene Kawan*, meaning "Old Wolf."

leader. His son, V. O. McWhorter, particularly, worked meticulously to provide safe custody for his father's material, to assure its adequate processing and to secure competent talent to edit and complete the manuscript. Time and expense were no factors in these matters. By placing the author's library, manuscripts, and personal papers bearing upon his researches in the library of the State College of Washington, and making them available to mature and responsible scholars as soon as this book has appeared, the family has made scholars of the future its debtors. Dr. E. O. Holland, who, as president of the State College of Washington, and subsequently as president emeritus, was always eager to perpetuate the best traditions of scholarship in the Pacific Northwest and to preserve the products of its creative genius, gave unstintingly of his time and effort to facilitate the administrative procedures necessary to secure the talent and muster the support necessary for the completion of the project.

And, as always previously, the Caxton Printers, Limited, have responded to the opportunity to supply students and the public with important books on the history of the Pacific Northwest.

State College of Washington
Pullman, Washington,
March 14, 1951.

DR. HERMAN C. DEUTSCH
Department of
History and Political Science.

HEAR ME, MY CHIEFS!
Nez Perce History and Legend

CHAPTER I

THE NEZ PERCE PERSPECTIVE: LEGEND AND HISTORY

THE ORIGIN OF THE VARIOUS RACES OF MANKIND HAS long been, and will continue to be, a topic of absorbing interest. The complexity of prehistoric artifact and sculpture, the often striking affinity in the legendary lore of widely dispersed primitive peoples, point convincingly to the one path up which the mind of man has ascended through the ages the world over. Just as any one species of the animal kingdom, however much a denizen of widely separated continents, evinces an astounding sameness of characteristics, so with the human race. If one nationality has outstripped another intellectually, it can well be attributed to environment rather than to any favoritism of the Creator.

How the American Indian came about has been a theme for speculation by the theologian, the anthropologist, the ethnologist, the archaeologist, the antiquarian, and the romancer, with nothing concluded beyond the fact that Poor Lo is here! Barring a few exceptions the evolution of the various tribes, with their multiplicity of languages (despite a striking unity of racial traits), cannot be traced. Too often this delving into their origins has been conducive to confusion worse confounded.

On the antiquity of his tribe, the Nez Perces, Howlis Wonpoon [War Singer] known as Camille

Williams[1] a native linguist and interpreter, comments:

> On the North Fork [of the Clearwater] River a few miles below Bungalow Ranger Station, Idaho, the footprints of a human being are plainly seen, sunken into the basaltic rock formation. The tracks are those of a man running upstream as if in pursuit of something, probably game.
>
> These footprints were made in a soft surface. How long since the change into hard basalt took place nobody knows. That man was older than the stone itself.
>
> On the Snake River there are stony tracks of a woman and child. Also tracks at a bathing place near Fir Bluff, today a solid rock formation. I was told that there is a single human track on a loose rock above Wawawai lower down the Snake River. Of course all these we naturally regard as of Nez Perce origin.
>
> An old story handed down through many generations tells that there was a flood in earlier days and that Yamustus [Steptoe Butte] stood above the sea and many Indians were there saved from drowning. This probably did occur thousands of years ago for sea deposits are found in many high places.

The riddle is that of the Sphinx!

In a wild country of rolling hills and sweeping prairies, beautiful valleys threaded with silvery streams gushing from canyon-gutted mountains, through whose craggy pinnacles the wind ever sings canticles to the gods, were found the Nez Perce people. Tall and stately, intelligent and pleasing in address, brave, though inclined to peace, they were the wilderness gentry of the Pacific Northwest. As warriors they had no equal aside from the unsurpassed Comanches.[2] Along with the Flatheads, close-

---

[1] [Camille Williams was one of L. V. McWhorter's closest collaborators among the Nez Perces and worked with him constantly after 1937 in the preparation of this volume as contributor and interpreter. Ed. note.]

[2] The Comanches were a southern offshoot of the Shoshonean stock of Wyoming, and were at home on the Platte River, as well as in

ly allied to them by marriage, one man was reckoned the equal of three Blackfeet.[3]

Of the traditional origin of the tribe and its early growth, Wottolen [Hair Combed Over Eyes], a blind old warrior and noted native historian, said:

> There are two places up Salmon River. Only two spots where the people lived. None were here on the Clearwater; none on Lapwai or Snake rivers; Kakayohneme Creek is one place. The other is about fifteen miles above the mouth of Little Salmon River. It is called Tannish [Cut-Out Trail]. This most wonderful passage among cliffs along Salmon River is not the work of man's hand. It is natural all through. Just as it was before the human race existed on this continent, I suppose. It was there before the white men swarmed over the mountain, taking from us our homes. But no one knows how many centuries back was the beginning.
>
> The first generations of Nez Perces grew up at those two places I have named. I do not know how many snows back of that time. The buffalo was hunted on the head of the Salmon. The people would go there for meat and hides during the summer moons. Next few snows they go a little farther east. Following snows they go still farther east, and to the north. After a time they reach the Yellowstone River. There they hunt, for the buffaloes are many. Finally they come to [now] Helena, Montana. There they find people. This tribe proves an enemy to the Nez Perces. After this they fight. The Bannocks, the Blackfeet, the Crows, the Cheyennes, the Sioux [Assiniboins]. All these tribes living in that country became enemies of the Nez Perces.

Kansas, Oklahoma, and Texas, and even in Chihuahua, Mexico. They fought the Spaniards for two hundred years, and were always friendly with Americans, but became bitter enemies of the Texans, who usurped their last hunting grounds. They were famed as buffalo hunters, and were reckoned the finest horsemen on the plains. (F. W. Hodge, ed., *Handbook of American Indians North of Mexico* (Bureau of American Ethnology, Smithsonian Institution, Bulletin 30. Washington, D.C.: Government Printing Office, 1907), I, 327-29.)

[3] Rev. Samuel Parker, *Journal of an Exploring Tour Beyond the Rocky Mountains* (Ithaca, N.Y., 1842) p. 237.

ice. *Koosolatt*
known; an a
shoulder, neck
belly of the gri
has been witn

The bones o:
found in the S
therefore such
of breaking tl
That is one st
back generatic

No Indian
reached the Ye
first Blackfeet
not their prop
by Nez Perces
different tribe
telling each o
Blackfeet alw
knee, or betwe
name, therefo
another sign r
closed hand a
Perces as the
and forefingei
tion, denoting
in decorating l

But the Ne
Iskoikenic [Sc
of the Nez Pei
them. They w
the French, v
war. They sl
and villages.
stealing horse
as Wyoming

walk down the river a way, then return back home. He kept going farther and farther, and finally came to White Bird Creek. He went to the top of White Bird Mountain, and was surprised to see a fine prairie far below him. He went there, and discovered smoke toward Clearwater River. Heading for it, and reaching the breaks of the river, he saw many tepees. He descended a way, and sat down about one quarter mile from the village. He was seen, and the Indians began asking one another who could be absent among them, and soon learned that no one was absent.

Two or three men then went to see who the stranger could be. When they spoke to him he answered in Nez Perce, and was taken to the village and given food.

He told them where he came from, and how the Salmon River Nez Perces had been buried and destroyed by the greatest of snow slides, as had been told him by his parents. Some days later a company went with the young man to Hot Spring, and brought the family to live with the Clearwater people.

After the Clearwater band grew to several hundred, some of the families moved to the Salmon River. . . .

A LEGEND OF THE *TASSHEA*

Many of the Nez Perce legends betray a hoary antiquity and the following is one of the oldest found among the Nez Perces. It is given here as told by War Singer.

It must have been centuries back that a strange happening came to the Snake River band of Nez Perces. One winter, while moving camp as customary, all were traveling afoot up the river on the ice. Some were dragging their belongings, while others carried bundles on their backs. Just as they turned to land and camp, they noticed two large horns standing up through the ice. Supposing the monster animal was dead, they took sharp-edged rocks with which to chip the horns off at the ice level. The horns would be useful, made into needed implements. With the cutting rocks they pounded the horns at the ice level, while all not so engaged stood close around

watch
throu
surge
about
down
jumpe
The
who h
young
tell a
likely
the ne
The
distric
his ch
but th
time t
as the
was a
and tk
the pl
monst

Rem

It is
might
what t
name
But n
eight
moved
monst
Kooso
Bitter
north.
would

Perces had more fights with the Blood and Piegan Blacklegs than with any other tribe. They would never keep peace. It was broken by them on several occasions. Only one minor band of the Blacklegs was friendly to the Nez Perces. Its members were called the "Small Blankets." All of the same tribe, they lived in widely scattered districts, some of them in Canada.

§

The older members of the tribe all subscribed to these ideas of the traditional dawn and early habitat of the Nez Perces. Wottolen, whose memory antedated the coming of the missionary, Spalding, has summarized tribal beginnings, the development of buffalo hunting, and his people's increase, thus:

It is not known for how many snows our first generations hunted buffaloes only at head of the Clearwater and Salmon rivers. Hunted for meat and hides all during summer and autumn moons. Then for next few snows they went little farther from their homes, moving toward the sunrise. Then for next few snows they go little farther. Next snow still farther, bearing north. Always finding better hunting as they traveled. Moving on, they came to Yellowstone River. Here was best buffalo hunting.

Where Helena, Montana, now stands they found first people. These people became enemies, after that they fought. Every snow was fighting. Stole horses and scalped each other. This enemy people were Blackfeet. Then came Crows, Cheyennes, and all tribes. Sioux were last of all tribes to fight Nez Perces.

But the Nez Perces had increased. Were now too strong to be whipped. If the white man cannot believe this, let him ask those tribes. They will tell him as I am telling.

After many, many snows fighting, peace was made with Crows and Blackfeet. The Nez Perces in meantime had grown numerous. They spread over lower Salmon, parts of Snake River, its water, and all of Clearwater River country. Had many horses, good horses. These were traded

to their late foes for buffalo robes and untanned hides. Nez
Perce horses were noted runners.[4]

The Nez Perces are the principal branch of the
Shahaptian linguistic family, but it is no more than
conjecture how they obtained their name.[5] There is
nothing in their tribal lore and traditions indicating
that nose-piercing in any form was ever practiced
among them. This misnomer is similar to the Flathead designation for Selish, where no deformation
of the infantile cranium can be traced, and the reason
seems inexplicable.[6] But a kindred case in a con-

---

[4] [It is believed that the Nez Perces obtained the horse about 1710-20.
See Francis Haines, "The Northward Spread of Horses to the Plains
Indians," American Anthropologist, 50:3 (June, 1938). (Ed. note.)]

[5] The sobriquet, "Nez Perce," as applied to the Indian tribe of that
name is probably a misnomer. Quoting a recognized authority:
"Nez Perces (Pierced Noses). A term applied by the French to a
number of tribes which practiced, or were supposed to practice, the
custom of piercing the nose for the insertion of a piece of dentalium.
The term is now used exclusively to designate the main tribe of the
Shahaptian family, who have not, however, so far as is known, ever
been given to the practice. (F. W. Hodge, op. cit., II, 63)."
The following clues may be applicable to any of the numerous tribes
so named by the French. "The governor and Council of New York
directed in 1687 that an inquiry should be made among the Five
Nations of how long since they first traded with the farther Indians
and the Indians with the straws or pyres through their noses. . . ."
(New York Council "Minutes" MS., V, VI, p. 5).
Again, LaSalle, in 1689, was presumably given a Nez Perce slave
as a present by Ontario Indians. (Berthold Rernow, The Ohio Valley
in Colonial Days, (Albany, 1909), pp. 55-6.)

[6] The Flatheads were a branch of the Salishan family to which
they gave their name, "Salish," more properly "Selish," interpreted,
"people." How they ever came by the uncouth cognomen, "Flathead,"
is purely hypothetical. Quoting Hodge, "A more popular designation
for the tribe is Flathead, given to them by the surrounding people,
not because they artificially deformed their heads, but because, in
contradistinction to most tribes farther west, they left them in their
natural condition, flat on top." (F. W. Hodge, op. cit., II, 415). By
the same authority, "Curiously enough the people now known in
official reports as Flatheads—the Salish proper (q.v.)—never flattened
the head. Dawson implies . . . that they were so named (Tetes-Plates)
by the first Canadian voyageurs because slaves from the coast with
deformed heads were among them." (Ibid., I, 465.)
If the French voyageurs saw deformed heads among the prisoners
held by the Selish, they were looking upon the elite of an enemy tribe.
To illustrate, an accomplished Wasco woman gave the writer the
following account of this comparatively recent custom.
"Only the heads of the chief's children were flattened. This was to

Clark, 1805, at which time the leading chiefs met in friendly council with the strangers. We are told:

... The upper village on the Snake was entirely destroyed with the exception of two women and one man. On the same river, near Asotin, lived a boastful man named Skin-a-way, who led out a band of six or seven hundred of his brethern against the Snakes, and not one ever returned to tell the tale.[8]

OF EARLY NEZ PERCE FORAYS

On this score Williams, the interpreter, writes:

I think that these two stories have been turned around from the two following incidents. Two Nez Perces were killed by Snake Indians, not Shoshones, when on a friendly visit to the Snake camp. When the Nez Perces heard of this, the father of one of the killed notified the different villages or districts. They all gathered in camp at a meadow, now a lake, called Peysomknaceen at Winchester, Idaho. There the Nez Perce warriors were formed and started for White Bird Creek, where they were joined by others, and two leaders chosen.

While going up Little Salmon River, one of these leaders fell from his horse. They all stopped and waited until he would tell them whether they were to be successful when meeting up with the enemy Snakes. When the leader, who was a prophet, got up he told them that three warriors would not be returning home. That they would lose three warriors, but more blood would flow on the enemy side.

Next day scouts sighted a Snake tepee. An attack was made and all the men killed. Two women were spared. One young Nez Perce warrior was killed.

The following day a large Snake camp was attacked. The Snakes were driven across a river with

---

[8] Kate C. McBeth, *The Nez Perces Since Lewis and Clark* (New York, 1908), pp. 16-17.

considerable losses. One Nez Perce was killed, and a Snake warrior, a member of their band who fought with them, was found standing with one foot in the water, leaning on his spear. They first thought that he was alive, but there was a bullet hole between his eyes. That made the three warriors predicted to be lost on the Nez Perce side.

Regarding the six or seven hundred warriors [as told by McBeth] who never returned, that is a large body to be entirely lost track of. "Skin-a-way" is a new name to me. I do not know any English meaning for it.

I never heard of any Nez Perce war party being wiped out by any tribe. The most ever killed at one time was thirty, including a white man, done by the Blacklegs. This happened along the boundary line of now Idaho and Montana, as I have told you.

At one time half of a war party of two hundred and sixty-six Snakes were killed by the Nez Perces. The count of the enemies was made by one of two scouts, above Rapid River, branch of the Little Salmon. They were lying in a stone cave, which can still be seen, watching the trail along the opposite side of the river.

One of the scouts raised up, when, at that time, that moment, Snake warriors came in sight traveling down the trail on foot. The standing scout did not dare move. He stood as a rock, for he was seen by the enemies, who stopped, looking closely. Probably they thought him a stone, for soon the band moved on, passing out of sight. The scout lying flat counted them as they walked by. He warned his partner to remain motionless for awhile. Some of the enemies might be concealed somewhere and sure enough they were. After a time two Indians came out from hiding and followed after the others.

When sure that all enemies were gone, the scouts left their rock shelter and, passing back over the ridge, recrossed the main Salmon on a raft they had left there the day before. Finding their hobbled horses, the next day they reached Weippe meadow, where the tribe was having a big gathering. They told the news of how the enemy Snakes intended attack on any Nez Perce found.

On this same day, or possibly a few days later, two men and a Snake Indian slave left Weippe for the Clearwater, to bring provisions. The Snake slave was taken to help with the packing. When descending Kamiah Hill, they met this same band of warring Snakes, and all three were killed. Their dog ran back to Weippe, by which friends knew what had happened.

The Nez Perce warriors hurried to pursue the enemies, and came near them on the summit of the hill or mountain south of Kamiah. They followed them until daybreak, when the battle began at Red Rock Spring. The Nez Perces were too many for the enemy and there was a running fight. With the Nez Perces was a Snake slave who interpreted all of the commands or instructions that the Snake chief called out to his warriors. He was telling them to head for a rock that they had seen when passing there earlier, and of which they well knew.

The Nez Perces misunderstood and thought it was Rock Canyon that the enemy was heading for, and so kept on the west side of the Snake, to prevent them from going there. But they soon found that they were heading for a cave on Cottonwood Creek, about a mile from its mouth. It was a running fight of some five miles, and the bravest man of the Snakes was captured alive when his horse stepped into a badger hole. He was riding a horse stolen from the Nez Perces.

A large number of the Snakes took refuge in the cave. A big fire was kindled in its entrance and all were either smothered to death or smoked out and killed. From that time this cave has been called *Sapachesap* [Drive-in].

This ghastly tragedy took place the same or following year of the passing of Lewis and Clark through the Nez Perce country.

The Snake warrior who was captured had his body encased in armor constructed of young growth syringa sticks, so hard and smoothly polished that an arrow could not penetrate it. He had a knife but did not attempt using it against his captor. When this Nez Perce grew old and feeble, scarcely able to get on his feet, he would grow mad because the "cowardly Snake" had not used his knife on him so that he would have been killed rather than live to grow so old, weak and feeble.

[Different members of the older Nez Perces have told me of this cavern, which I have never seen, and its ghastly history. In the running fight and the appalling holocaust at this underground chamber, half of the enemy band, estimated at over two hundred, lost their lives. None of those trapped escaped, but at this late day only the shadow of these former great events is dimly seen.]

§

CHAPTER II

EARLY TRIBAL WARS: THE ERA OF RED BEAR

WOTTOLEN TELLS OF RED BEAR

AMONG THE TRIBAL NOTABLES WHO CANOED DOWN THE Clearwater to meet Lewis and Clark where Lewiston, Idaho, now stands, was Hohots Ilppilp [Red Grizzly Bear], in time abbreviated to Red Bear. Wottolen [Hair Combed Over Eyes], a grandson of this renowned warrior, chief, and prophet, contributed the following, his son, Many Wounds, interpreting.

Red Grizzly Bear was a chief famous among the tribes. His bravery as a warrior was attested by the eighty wounds he carried, received in battles. From these scars, in later years, he was known as Many Wounds. He knew and took part in all the wars of his day. Always a leader, when foraying he went ahead of his band; no one ever traveled in front of him.

Whether night or day, on foot or on horseback (I cannot explain the mystery) some kind of foresight was with him. Even if an enemy were at a distance and invisible, Many Wounds would drop into a trance of prophecy, and while thus sleeping he beheld all enemies passing before him. Everything pertaining to the enemies: the kind to be met, whether the meeting would be that same sun or the next, the number of scalps that would be taken and the kind of horses they would secure. This happened a number of times. Of most wonderful strength, he used principally his

right hand and arm in battle. He was known everywhere west of the great mountains [Rockies] even
to the big waters [Pacific].

Chief Red Bear first learned of white people
through a girl of his band living on Tamonmo.[1] When
small she was stolen by the Blacklegs in the buffalo
country, who sold her to some tribe farther toward
the sunrise. In time she was bought by white people,
probably in Canada, where she was well treated. It
is a long story; how in time, carrying her little baby,
she ran away and after several moons reached the
friendly Selish, who cared for her and brought her
in a dying condition to her own people at White Bird.
Her baby had died on the way. She was called Watkuweis [Returned from a Faraway Country].

She told of the white people, how good they had
been to her, and how well she liked them. When the
first two white men, Lewis and Clark with their followers, came, Watkuweis said to her people, "These
are the people who helped me! Do them no hurt!"

This was why the strange people had been received
in friendship.[2] There had been a prophecy about Red

---

[1] *Tamonmo:* ancient name of the Salmon River, meaning 'unknown.'

[2] The seriousness with which the Watkuweis story is accepted by
responsible members of the Nez Perce tribe is amply attested in the
following contribution by Many Wounds, May 7, 1930:

"In the buffalo days a girl was missing from a Nez Perce hunting
camp in Montana. In after snows, when she came back to her own
people, she told her story to Chief Red Bear, to whose band she belonged. Told how she was sold by an enemy people to a different
tribe, where she was a slave. Then she was sold to white people, who
kept her as one of their own kind. This story soon spread through
all the Nez Perce nation.

"Our oral history says that she received a baby, then escaped to
return to her own country. When about halfway on the trail, the
baby died and she buried it. She was by blood a Bannock but was
reared as a Nez Perce from before her memory. She was given the
name *watkuweis* which means 'returned' (from being lost).

"She told history about the whites and every Nez Perce listened
on that day. Told how the white people were good to her, treated
her with kindness. Her story opened much friendship for the future.
It was worth good to both whites and Indians.

"That is why the Nez Perces never made harm to the Lewis and

Bear and a new people, which was thus fulfilled in 1805. He met the strangers. They first have a smoke. If no smoke, then they must fight. Red Bear made presents of dressed buckskins, and they gave him beads and a few other articles. They afterwards found the white man's gifts to be cheap.

The canoes made by Lewis and Clark to descend the Snake and Columbia rivers were made from five yellow pine trees given them for the purpose by Chief Walammottinin [Hair or Forelock Bunched and Tied]. The explorers first met him when fishing in the Kooskooskie Smaller River, now the Clearwater. It was in this chieftain's care that they left their horses and cached goods, all of which they found in the best of condition upon their return the following year.

After visiting the explorers, Red Bear returned to his home near the mouth of White Bird Creek, Salmon River. When he died, he left good council, good instructions for his people. The whites owe honor to his memory.

My father, Chief Black Eagle, was the son of Chief Red Bear, Sr., who met Lewis and Clark. I am his grandson. I have seen one hundred and four snows [1926].

Clark people in 1805. We ought to have a monument to her in this far West. She saved much for the white race.

"I feel proud about her. I should call her peacemaker between Indian race and white race! We must remember her fine qualities and wonderful long trip only to die at home."

The following comment was made by interpreter War Singer. "*Watkuweis* means any person or domestic animal that returns from a different district or country. Thus *watkuweis* or *watkuese* means 'returned from a far country.' She called the whites, *Allimah* [From Near Water]. This was because they had first come in boats from the sea, as she had learned in Canada. Thus Watkuweis saved the lives of those early white explorers at the Weippe. She told her people that the whites had given her good treatment after she was sold to them."

For similar versions of the foregoing see Kate C. McBeth, *op. cit.*, pp. 24-25. *Also*, Eliza Spalding Warren, *Memoirs of the West* (Portland, 1917) p. 7.

Chief Red Bear, most famed of his generation and the youngest of six brothers, grew up under the rigorous, Spartanlike schooling universal among the tribes. From the time he was about ten years of age, he swam across the Salmon River and back (at a point a short distance above the mouth of the White Bird), every morning for five consecutive winters.[3] Wottolen continued:

It was during the days of youthful training and development that Red Bear went on foot to Slate Creek[4] to look for flint arrowheads where there had been fighting. It was morning and he stayed until late evening. Starting for home he had gone a good distance when it grew dark. He lay down by the trail and slept. In a dream he beheld a great, blood-stained grizzly bear approaching. Awakening, he sprang to his feet, but no bear was to be seen. Silently he resumed his buffalo robe and dozed off, only to be aroused a second time by the same fearful vision, which vanished as he leaped erect. He again lay down and as he drowsed the monster bear appeared for the third time. This time the boy did not awaken entirely, and a voice spoke to him:

"Do not be afraid. You see my body. Blood is all over it. When you become a man, when you go to war and do fighting, you shall receive many wounds. Wounds shall cover your body. Blood like this from my body will course down your limbs. But you will not die. After these wars, and fights, because of your wounds and bloodstains people will call you *Hohots Ilppilp* [Red Grizzly Bear]."

When this boy had grown to young manhood, and had received arrow and spear wounds in battle, he told his father and the people about seeing the blood-

---

[3] Five is a mystic number in the Dreamer religious cult.

[4] *Eausninma* is the Nez Perce name of Slate Creek, Idaho. *Eaus* is an old term almost forgotten by the tribe. Ninety-four-year-old (1936) Phillip Evans says it means the oar or pole used in poling boats, not the flat oar.

reddened grizzly bear, and what it had said to him. From that time he was known as Red Bear, and was made a chief. He was a strong brave warrior.

After taking his name the new chief never used a gun in battle. There were only a few fire-rock [flint-lock] guns, and ammunition was scarce. He had a club made from the hard heavy syringa found growing along the canyon streams. It was nearly arm's length, and entirely unlike the stub-handled, stone-headed war club of the foot warriors. With this tied to his wrist by a thong loop, he would rush into battle. The Bannocks all learned to know and fear him.

At one time when going up Little Salmon, at a place now called Riggins, he discovered a war band of Snake or Bannock Indians coming toward him on the trail. There was a small creek with large rocks intervening. He hid his gun and secreting himself, he waited the advance of the hated enemy. They were out for fighting or stealing horses. When they drew near, Red Bear sprang from hiding and downed the foremost warrior before his presence was fully known. In the confusion he killed others of the startled foe, who recognizing their unconquerable enemy, swam the Little Salmon to safety.

Other similar exploits are also ascribed to Red Bear. He bore eighty distinct scars received in conflict, from which, in later years, he was known as Many Wounds. In comparison, the great Chief Red Cloud of the Sioux had to his credit eighty coups for as many distinctive deeds of personal valor in battle.[5]

§

Such was the "Bloody Chief," who spoke in council with Dr. Elijah White, first United States Indian agent to enter the Pacific Northwest, taking office in 1842. Of this Nez Perce chieftain Dr. White says:

---

[5] Hodge, *op. cit.*, II, 359.

Soon the Bloody Chief arose—not less than ninety years old—and said: "I speak today, perhaps tomorrow I die. I am the oldest chief of the tribe; was the chief chief when your great brothers, Lewis and Clark, visited this country. They visited me, and honored me with their friendship and counsel. I showed them my numerous wounds received in bloody battle with the Snakes; they told me it was not good, it was better to be at peace; gave me a flag of truce; I held it up high; we met and talked. We never fought again. Clark pointed to this day, to you and this occasion; we have long waited in expectation; I can say no more; I am quickly tired; my voice and limbs tremble. I am glad to live to see you and this day, but I shall soon be still and quiet in death."[6]

Red Grizzly Bear, whose name appears twelfth in the list of the signers of the Treaty of Walla Walla, June 11, 1855, there spelled "Ha-ha Still-pilp," was a son of the senior Chief Red Bear, or Many Wounds, the "Bloody Chief" of Dr. White's council. The eldest son of Red Bear was Koolkooltom, Sr., Selish for "Red Arrow Point." He was a mighty warrior and a great prophet. He led in fights against the Cheyennes in particular. Another son, Koolkooltom, Jr., lived at White Bird and was wealthy in cattle. Not a warrior, but a prophet, he inherited his father's mantle. He died on the Salmon River before the 1855 Treaty. His son, who took his illustrious grandfather' name, was a scout for General Howard against his own tribe in the conquest of 1877, but he did not enlist under his ancestral name. Blacktail Eagle, who will figure in these pages, was the youngest son of Red Bear, Sr. Another son was Black Eagle, the father of Wottolen, who has already been

---

[6] A. J. Allen, *Ten Years in Oregon; Travels of Doctor E. White and Lady* (Ithaca, N.Y., 1850), p. 185.

O. D. Wheeler, in his *Trail of Lewis and Clark* (New York, 1926, third edition), p. 267, gives the name of this famous warrior as "Red Flute," an obvious error. *Sappoomeus* is Nez Perce for "flute," and *ilppilp* is "red."

quoted. The ancestral name, Black Eagle, is carried by Wottolen's only son at this writing.

An occurrence, which took place in historic White Bird Canyon, centers around Red Bear's deadly hatred of the Bannocks or Snake Indians. The story is given here as it was told the author by Wottolen, who had heard it often from his aged grandfather.

When my grandfather, Red Bear, Sr., was a small boy, his father, Chief Pah Wyanan [defined as "belonging to Wyanan," located on the north side of the Snake River above Wawawai] and his two wives, one of them mother of Red Bear, were surprised and killed by Bannocks as they were returning home with supplies taken from their individual *wecas*,[7] located on an upland flat with a great many others of like kind.

When on the way to the *wecas*, opposite Hauun ["Sinking" or "Sliding-down Earth"][8] they saw through brush the naked legs of a young man fishing in the creek. They stopped there a short time, then went on toward their *wecas*. That was the last they were seen alive.

After the Bannocks killed these three people, they found the tracks of the young fisherman, and in a fight they wounded him in both his legs. But he was brave and succeeded in killing two of the enemy. He captured a bow, a scabbard of arrows, and a rawhide shield. He scalped the two dead Bannocks to prove his bravery.

Chief Pah Wyanan and wives were buried on highest of the two Cemetery Buttes, east of the field of *wecas*. My

---

[7] *Wecas:* These were primitive storage pits or caches, numbered by the score, occupying a bench or flat on the eastern slope of the dominant rock-crowned ridge or butte, the northern extremity of which marks the point where the troops were halted and turned back in the battle of White Bird Canyon, June 17, 1877. This butte is known as Wecas Pah ["Place of the Wecas"]. The well-preserved pits are now overgrown by rye grass.

[8] This strangely erratic phenomenon is observed in the first creek bluff. When the author was on the ground in the summer of 1932, a recent convulsion or disturbance of the earth's surface had left the bed of lignite coal exposed. A straight break, not unlike that made by a plow minus the moldboard, extended across the valley and into the mountain for miles either way. One of the Nez Perces prophesied, "This land will all sink, a judgment sent on the white people who took it from us like robbers."

grandfather, Red Bear, Sr., is buried about a quarter of a mile above the mouth of White Bird, opposite side of Salmon River. It was winter when he died. Too bad to cross Salmon, was why not buried on Cemetery Butte. My father, Black Eagle, was buried at Tolo Lake.

The following pre-Lewis-and-Clark tribal-war story, narrated by Wottolen, is a fair sample of the oral annals of these days. It was told in November, 1926, with Wottolen's son, Many Wounds, as interpreter. Black Eagle, its chief character, was the second son of Red Bear or "Bloody Chief," and was prominent in his day. A leader of war parties, he was denied a proud death on a battlefield.

Black Eagle and wife lived on west bank of Clearwater, between now Stites and Kooskia, about one and half miles from first-named town. A secret place, was long before discovered by Bannocks and Paiutes.[9] Between these tribes and the Nez Perces had been wars as far back as memory could reach.

In center of thorn-brush thicket Black Eagle's wife cleared a spot just room for their tepee. Nothing could be seen from outside.

It was about June time. All the people had gone to dig camas at Weippe, and Black Eagle and wife were living in this thorn-brush thicket supposed to be safely hidden from the enemy. They did not cook in the daytime. Smoke would be seen. It was only at night they cooked, when fire was hidden by the bush screen.

But the Paiutes were abroad. They climbed a high butte east of now Kooskia, between middle fork and Clearwater and watched down over the valley. They saw the fire at

---

[9] *Paiutes:* "A term involved in great confusion. In common usage it has been applied at one time or another to most of the Shoshonean tribes of w. Utah, n. Arizona, s. Idaho, e. Oregon, and Nevada, and e, and s. California." (Hodge, *op. cit.* II, 186). "The Bannacks were a Shoshonean Tribe," *(Ibid.,* I, 129).

The Bannocks were often referred to as Paiutes by the Yakima and kindred tribes, who held them in great respect as fighters. Paiutes proper were "Peaceable, moral and industrious, and highly recommended for their good qualities by those who have had the best opportunities for judging." *(Ibid.,* II, 187).

Black Eagle's lodge, and with crossed poles gauged the direction and located the lodge. Next morning, guided by the pointing-stick, they surrounded the thicket and, crawling like weasels, soon rushed in and killed both the Eagle and his wife, leaving them scalped.

The Paiutes came in considerable number, took every horse (sixteen in number) that Black Eagle had, and everything in the tepee. He had a large brass kettle for boiling salmon. A headman, he often gave dinner feasts. One of the Paiutes took this kettle, and mounting his horse, carried it on his back—[with] the bail looped over his shoulder. . . .

They crossed Camas Prairie, crossed the mountain to White Bird Canyon and followed up Salmon River to mouth of Little Salmon without meeting trouble. They followed up this last stream and before reaching Salmon Meadows, met a band of Nez Perce warriors. These were led by Koolkooltom, brother of Black Eagle. This young man was a prophet, and always foretold one sun ahead of any impending clash or battle with an enemy tribe. The morning before he had told his band what was ahead of them.

Seeing people coming up the trail with several horses which they thought the Bannocks had stolen from them, Koolkooltom posted his men as a trap. The Bannock chief was in the lead. He was leading a fine, blazed-faced horse, recognized as one of Black Eagle's. A warrior brought up the rear with the brass kettle swung by its bail to his back, the bail looped across his breast.

The first arrows missed the Bannock chief, but the next firing killed him. Then came the battle proper. The Bannocks were routed, many of them were killed. The scalps of Black Eagle and his wife, horses, and kettle were recovered, with the spoils of the battle marked by the scalps of the dead enemies, the Nez Perces returned to their village well avenged for the death of Black Eagle and wife.

THE NARRATIVE OF RED ELK

This occurrence took place during the early childhood of the youngest son of the Bloody Chief, also named Black Eagle, and the father of Wottolen. With what care and fidelity these tribal-hero war stories have been handed down through the decades, is well exemplified in the one here told by Red Elk, Many Wounds interpreting.

Koolkoolletchacoosman was chief. First he was a strong warrior, cunning, brave, and fearless. Then he became a chief. No cowardly man could ever become chief in any tribe. One evening Koolkoolletchacoosman called the people to a feast. Called all of his brave and prominent warriors. He said to them, "When the sun rises again, I leave you people. I want to make a visit. I shall go about three sleeps, afoot and alone. I am not asking any of you to follow me. I am going up the Salmon River, past Little Salmon, past Salmon Meadows, below Payette Lake. I will travel one sleep below this lake to Wallukitpah [descriptive of a crooked or winding stream]. I will stop to see what any enemy is doing there. I am going to locate my enemy's camp."

Chief Many Wounds, or Red Bear, was listening. He replied, "You will not go alone. I will go with you."

A younger brother of Many Wounds spoke, "I would like to go."

Kywis, a brave warrior, said, "I will go with you people."

Then Piyus Issucin [Snake Crown] spoke, "I would like to go help locate the enemy."

Another warrior, name lost, joined the band. Six warriors, all; they got ready and next morning started afoot. They take two or three pairs of extra moccasins each, and they take provisions according to their number. They arrive in the evening and locate the enemy. The enemy is camped on each side of Long Valley River. They are Snake Indians, and have stick-fish traps. There are many Snake Indians, catching plenty of salmon and drying them. Every season the Snakes come there to fish.

The two chiefs say nothing. The four young men talk. They are asking, "What shall we do if we attack? Will we succeed? Can we succeed or will we fail?"

The chiefs say nothing. The young men turn to Red Bear and ask, "What do you say?"

Red Bear then answered the young men, "I believe it will be harmless to us. I do not believe many are brave in the enemy camp."

Red Bear then asked the chief, "What do you think, Koolkoolletchacoosman? You are the leader."

The chief gave his answer, "I think is not dangerous if we attack the camp."

So all agreed to attack the camp. Do it the next morning early. Surprise the enemy.

The next question was of secret power. Koolkoolletchacoosman said, "I am going tell something about my power. When I was a little boy I was sent by my parents climbing up high mountains. A spirit of the Black Eagle gave me power. I saw it was a human being. The spirit told me, "When you go to war, any kind of war, you stand like a brave man. You will not be overcome by the enemy. Should you feel some danger do not be scared. Tell your warriors to call you 'Tipyahlannah Elassanin' [Black Eagle Making a Roar.]"

When this talk was made, Kywis was struck with the same power as belonged to Chief Koolkoolletchacoosman. Power given through the black eagle.

After the Chief had finished, Red Bear said, "Listen you young warriors! Early morning we attack the best we can. Go in every tepee. Use knife and *kopluts* [war club]—not our guns. Nobody halloo. The war whoop must be silent. Kill quietly the men. Not the women and children. Feel the hair. Women have theirs differently fixed."

Morning came and they attacked the Bannock camp. All followed the orders of Red Bear. Many tepees are entered; knife and war club alone are used. About half the camp thus passed, and then the gun. The enemy was alarmed, and then the fight with the gun. Light came. Only five of the Nez Perces fighting. One had been left behind. He was a Snake captive and would not fight against his people. He had hidden away but none knew it.

Now was a desperate fight. There were too many of the enemy, and the Nez Perces went to a hill. They ask, "Where is Piyus Issucin? Must be he is killed." Piyus Issucin, the captive Snake, had married the sister of Kywis, who was now crying. He said, "Let us go back and finish the fight!"

About sunrise they go again after the Bannocks, the Snakes. Chief Koolkoolletchacoosman was shot across the breast, and he drew it out. Many Wounds was shot in the left eye. They quit the fight. Going to their last camp they found Piyus Issucin. Then they knew he had not been in a fight.

They now started for home. Traveling two days, the brother of Red Bear, Many Wounds, died. They buried him there.

A little way from where they buried the young warrior, they had a fire. Koolkoolletchacoosman was sitting by the fire. Tipyahlannah [Eagle] came where the wounded chief sat. Koolkoolletchacoosman said to his Eagle *Wyakin*,[10] "This young man died. I will now die. I am to blame." Then while they were burying the dead warrior, the Chief took stones and struck his wounds. After that he did not live long.

---

[10] *Wyakin*. See L. V. McWhorter, *Yellow Wolf* (Idaho, 1940), pp. 295-300, for a discussion of this belief in a guiding spirit represented by birds, animals, and forces of nature.

The war party came back to Lahmotta,[11] which the white people call "White Bird Canyon."

Red Bear . . . was then made the leading chief.

§

The following account of the killing of a Bannock or Snake chief, by the Cayuse, was given by Chief Peopeo Tholekt, Nez Perce, who was well informed on the early history of the neighboring tribes. The story follows.

It was up in the Snake Mountains. The Cayuses came upon the encampment of the Snake warriors and defeated them. Chief Tamanmo was in his tepee when the attack occurred, and the enemies circled it and captured him. They tied his hands and feet together and tortured him. This was before the Indians had metal knives. They cut the chief's arms off at the elbow, and his legs off at the knee joints with flint knives. They scalped him and left him to die.

Tamanmo is the name of a place far up in the Snake mountains, and the chief killed was named Tamanmo.

To the foregoing, War Singer adds: "Tamanmo is the name of the Salmon River and the Snake chief must have been killed at its head. An old woman on the Umatilla Reservation told me a story that might be the same only turned around as to the killing."

Some Cayuse Indians were attacked in their own country [now Oregon] by Snake Indians and cruelly treated. After some time, the Cayuses decided to look for the killers as they knew whose band had committed the crime. When they entered [now] Idaho, their scouts discovered a man sitting on top of a butte. They surrounded him and took him alive. To their surprise he appeared to be the chief of the Snakes. He was hunting rabbits and izhkumsizlaklik

---

[11] The literal rendition of *Lahmotta* or *Lahmatta* is "restless," "tired," "bothered." It is a long, and in places a steep trail, leading into and out of White Bird Canyon and the traveling either way was laborious and fatiguing. See *Yellow Wolf*, p. 50ff.

[ground squirrels], and was watching for one to come out of its hole, when he was surprised and captured.

His hands were tied up. He was asked questions about the killings and he told truth about how the Snakes treated the Cayuses at the time they were killed. Every time he told of cruel deeds he did to the Cayuses, one of his fingers was cut off. When all had been severed, then next his wrists. He soon bled to death.

The Umatilla tribe used to live at mouth of Umatilla River, so that band was never bothered by the Snakes. The Cayuses were the real owners of the present Umatilla reservation. Of these early tribal wars, our interpreter again writes:

There is a place just east of the Idaho-Montana border line, a creek which empties into the Salmon River, where thirty Nez Perces, probably a few of them Flatheads, one white man, were killed in a battle with the Blacklegs or Schemers. Only one, a Flathead scout, escaped. Of the enemies killed, nothing is known further than that in the opening fight between three of their scouts and the same number of Nez Perce scouts, two of theirs fell but the third one escaped and gave the alarm.

After the scout fight, two of the Nez Perces rode away for camp, while the other one, the Flathead, was busy securing the two Blackleg horses. His own horse running away from him, went among some bushes, unseen by the enemy, so they supposed the two mounted Indians to be all there were, and thus the one escaped. He watched the fight from a distance and said the Blacklegs outnumbered the Nez Perces about ten to one. He also said that the Nez Perce powder got wet the night before because of a flood. Only the white man's powder was dry, which he had shared with the Nez Perces. He was the last man killed. Powder gone, he drew his knife but was shot dead.

My paternal great uncle, Wyatanatom Yokakt [Sun Chief] was among the killed. He was brother to my father's mother. Later my father took this uncle's name. Another of the killed was Tawis Geejumnin [Worn-out Horns]. He had made a trip to St. Louis with two other Nez Perces, one of whom died there. [In response to query.] It is hard to tell for what purpose they went. One Selish or Flathead Indian, maybe two, started with them, but it is known that one turned back after traveling with them for a week. This was shortly before the missionaries Spalding and Whitman came.[12]

---

[12] This was the renowned Nez Perce-Flathead quest for a "better religion," for the "Book of Heaven," for the "How to Reach Heaven." But the "How to Reach Heaven" was not pointed out to them at St. Louis, a city of ten thousand souls and five Christian denominations with as many churches. There was no Bible for them in their native language. These wilderness wanderers after knowledge had but pursued the phantom glimmer of a will-o'-the-wisp.

Whatever the incentive for the long journey with a fur trader's pack train, the stir of interest and excitement growing out of it in later years may be regarded as the creation of the fertile, though erratic and wavering mind of a visionary and vainglorious missionary.

A splendid resumé of this historic myth is to be found in Clifford Merrill Drury, *Henry Harmon Spalding*, (Idaho, 1936), Chapter 3. See also T. C. Johnson, "The Evolution of a Lament," *Washington Historical Quarterly*, Vol. II, No. 3.

CHAPTER III

LATER TRIBAL WARS: THE NARRATIVE OF TWO MOONS

AT THE CLOSE OF THE YAKIMA VALLEY HOP-PICKING SEASON in October, 1909, Lepeet Hessemdooks [Two Moons], then a chief of Joseph's band of Nez Perces camped at the writer's farm. Two Moons was then in his eighties, but he had been an actor in the drama of the later tribal wars, and he told many stories of his early deeds. While reckoned a full-fledged Nez Perce, Two Moons was really of mixed tribal lineage. His mother was a Nez Perce, while his father, Silskoo [Five Blue], was a notable Selish warrior, who "went through many arrows and bullets." But Two Moons' ancestry and heritage of the occult is better told in his own words which follow.

My grandfather's name was Two Moons, given him by the power of the sun and moon, the two. It was the spirit they sent, and he was one of the heirs to this spirit. And I have the power and strength of this spirit, the same as did my grandfather. It came to me as it traveled down through the family all along the generations.

The sun once upon a time appeared to my grandfather when a boy, and talked to him when he was asleep. It said to him, "Now my boy you are to be like me. Look at me! Nothing can touch me, nothing can harm me. I have great strength and power! Therefore, you will be like me. You will go through battles and the arrows of the enemy will not enter your body."

Wherefore, my grandfather was a warrior, and faced the arrows of the enemies, but no sign of a wound ever showed upon him. He received no hurt whatever in battle. He grew old and died without the enemy being able to inflict a scar upon his body.

To the query, "Through what means or channel was this power brought to you?" came Two Moons' rather emphatic reply:

This is a very big subject to speak about, and I did not think that I should ever be asked to tell. It is a great subject, and I could hardly reveal that which you ask of me, and still hold to that power, believe in it and use it should occasion ever again come to me. It is for the battle and the dangerous moments and hours to be talked about. I can call no words now to prove all things, but I am a man who must not reveal these things for only the telling.

On occasion just as I experience this power, I tell it. You can ask the Selish who were always our friends. Of enemies, ask the Crows, the Blackfeet, the Sioux, the Cheyennes, Bannocks, and other Snake tribes. I have entered battle with all these enemy tribes. Seeking my life, I have faced within close steps of death, but no sign of wound have I carried therefrom. I did not think you would ever ask me to tell you of this, my Power given by the spirits. It is a deep subject you have asked of me. A mystery not understood by whites.

I explained that I knew something of the rules and laws by which this spirit power was to be attained and preserved, but felt that he was never again likely to become engaged in any phase of warfare and therefore might be permitted to reveal something of that which ordinarily was to be kept hidden. But I suggested that he make his own decision, adding, "I do not want you to speak against your own heart! A warrior should not mistreat his protective spirit powers."

Two Moons replied:

I am glad you are not again placing the question to me. I cannot tell without committing the wrong. I have come through many battles with the help of this power and strength. I have a charm at home, given me when I was a little boy. During those dangerous times I always wore it around my neck. I did this when any battle was to be fought. I stripped my shirt and rolled down my leggings or took them off, and with exception of breechcloth and moccasins, rode into battle naked to meet the enemy. Wearing the charm about my neck[1] I have ridden where the bullets were like scattered hail, at which time this charm would talk to me. Convincing me that I was being protected. It brought me strong for the fight. Made me feel as a boy with his ball or marbles.

I often told other friends when we were placed in grave danger, that I would bring them through to safety. Do so by the strength of the *Wyakin* power accorded to me. I cannot—must not—talk idly of my Spirit Powers.

The old warrior spoke with a tinge of pleading and was assured there would be no further urging, to which he solemnly responded:

I am telling to you this much for the reason I want to love everybody, nor do I tell to anyone else. Some men talk to one man, then that man, and this man, and then lose them as friends. This is not good! I love all, the white and the red, and I want to die that way. But of this protective spirit power, I will tell

---

[1] The charm worn by Two Moons was made from the wing bone of a crane. "This bird in flocks flies circling high, near to the sun." It was most evidently a war whistle, an ancestral inheritance.

you what I saw in the Clearwater battle which I did not give in my story of our war with the whites.[2]

It was Sarpsis Ilppilp [Red Moccasin Tops]. The soldiers were in line of battle, and this great warrior rode in front of them. Not in the full spirit of his horse, but just galloping slowly along. The soldiers were firing at him as fast as they could load and shoot. One hundred soldiers, and the smoke from their guns rose like a cloud. Sarpsis Ilppilp came riding on out of range of the soldiers, up to where we were.[3]

Beginning with true life in this world, I will tell you how my time began as a warrior. You can see me now, and judge for yourself, that I look very old. There is trouble, wherein at this late life I cannot strengthen my early stories with witnesses to show that I am telling only truth and not more than the truth. My boylife mates and friends, my warmates, chiefs, and warriors, have all passed away. I am left alone! But all the truth I know, a true story, will I tell you.

First Warpath

The first experience I had in war once upon a time, we were camping, and our chief lost his own horses overnight. Every horse of the chief's was stolen! That very next morning this chief made known, "I will find my band of horses and see if I can get them back. Steal them back! At least a part of them."

[2] Two Moons and Wounded Head told their stories of the 1877 war to the author before they gave their tribal-war narratives.

[3] With this preliminary, the aged warrior, scrupulously clean, bathing in the river twice daily, and immaculate in every detail of his native dress, was ready to launch into his theme. Scorning a proffered chair, draped in a blanket he remained standing throughout the two days' interview, stopping for an occasional rest and smoke which he indulged in while sitting on the ground.

The chief got ready and I, a boy, said to him, "I will go with you!"

I was young. Thirteen snows of age. But the chief was a cousin of mine, and on that account I wanted to follow him. I would die with him in case he engaged in battle. Seven others joined to go.

We started that morning, tracking the horses. Tracking for two suns, we met the very Indian on the third day who stole the horses. Nine of us were following the trail, and the third day we went through a deep gulch. The chief was in the lead, and I next behind him. The others were coming, one by one, close after us. A short distance from the gulch, those very Indians with our horses were passing. The warriors back of the chief, and I were first to see the enemies ahead.

They were Crows. He held close and still. Those Crow Indians, enemies of ours, were crossing the gulch but did not see us. Our chief gave low command, "All get down from horses!"

We slid to the ground, still! The chief commanded we keep quiet till the Crows crossed the gulch. The chance we had to fight was to let them pass out onto the prairie. Then we could go after them! So we waited until they did get out on the prairie, where no timber or hills could shelter them.

Our chief, Lahpatupt[4] waited until the Crows passed out of sight. Then we went after them! There was one Indian we chased. I, a small boy, was riding a small pony, a swift pony, a good runner. In the chase, my horse being very fast, I became in the lead.

---

[4] The English rendition of this name was thus given: When the Indians kill game, as a buffalo, deer or elk, bringing it to camp, they cut out the great bones in the forearm and hind legs, crack that bone to get at the tallow (marrow) inside for food. They call that one break *tupt*, but when the bone is broken the second time, it is *lahpatupt*.

I went out on the prairie with the purpose to kill him
first, or capture the horse so to be mine.

But the Crow passed over a rise out of sight, and
when I came to top of this low rise, I could see no signs
of any Indian. I looked around, and the others coming
up, we looked all over a long distance. There was no
sign, until some one saw to one side a long-like washout, big enough for a horse to go in. There was where
he must have gone! We saw his head just showing
above the washout.

One of our men who could speak the Crow language
spoke to him and asked to what tribe he belonged.

He told in his own language he was a Crow Indian.
The chief called the sign to him, "Come to us! We
will not hurt you!"

The Crow motioned back the sign, "I am afraid of
you! I cannot come to you people! You will kill me!"

They talked more, and finally he came near, holding his gun ready to shoot. He had a few bullets in
his mouth for quick loading. We all sat down in a
circle, and smoked our pipes. We signed to him to
smoke with us, promising we were not going to hurt
him. But he told us, pointing to the sun, "From
where that sun stands you people will take my life!
That is what you are after! I am afraid!"

Several men stood up to him and tried to shake
hands with him. But he backed away, telling them to
stand back. I was the smallest in the bunch, for I
was very small when young.[5] Everyone who stood
up to shake hands with him would have a gun in his
hand. For that reason, he must have been afraid of
them.

I dropped my gun and went to him barehanded. I
signed to him, "Friend, shake hands! We are not
going to kill you!"

But he stood back and motioned reply, "Stand

PREWAR NEZ PERCE DREAMERS

The picture was taken on the land where they lived prior to the war of 1877

Courtesy V. Alonzo Lewis

The Old Spalding Mission, which stood near the bank of the Clearwater at Spalding, Idaho. It has since been moved and converted into a museum building.

away from me! You are a little man. Look a little small, but I am afraid of you! This very sun you people are going to take my head, my scalp!"[6]

The chief made the sign, "We will smoke now, the peace-smoke. Then we shall go wherever your camp, and camp as friends with all you Crow Indians."

The Crow answered with the sign, "Just over the mountain there, over the hill on Big Horn River, the Crow Indians, my band, are camping. Fifty lodges all pitched along the riverbank."

Again the chief signed, "We shall smoke, and then go and visit with you over there." But this Crow Indian would not believe us. He had seen our ropes and lunch packs tied to our saddles, and he motioned the sign, "You Nez Perces are telling a false story! I notice you have ropes and provision supplies with you. You people are out to fight or steal horses from other tribes. Therefore I cannot believe you!"

He stood ready to fight, wherein he stood down not in a way that he was anxious to make friends with us. He was ready to jump in case anyone sprang at him. Out from us a short distance he stood. We asked him to sit down and smoke with us, which he would not do.

First Scalp

The chief was sitting at the end of the circle, and I was next to him. He was nearly a large man. Eight of us were in that circle, and the ninth man was down in the gulch under that caved bank. He was afoot,

---

[5] Two Moons' height at the time of his narrative was four feet ten inches in his moccasins. He could just stand erect under the writer's outstretched arm.

[6] ". . . going to take my head" in this sense should be regarded as figurative. While there are instances where the head of an enemy was sometimes delivered, head-hunting was not practiced among the tribes. In Indian pictograph writing a headless human figure of course denoted a dead person.

and crawled behind the chief, the heavy man. This to get near the Crow Indian, as he stood in front of the chief. Of course he sneaked, and getting close, he shot the Crow in the forehead. He fell, landing in front of me. There was a chance for me to grab him! I was the first to get hold of him. I was the one who scalped him!

"How is the scalping done?" I asked.

"The cut is over the eyebrows, above the ears and on around the head. Then a jerk of the hair, the scalp comes off."

The author's question seemed to arouse an apprehension in the narrator's mind that his statements were being doubted, as he earnestly added, "The story I am giving you to write down is all true! But my early warmates gone, I cannot give you witness proof."

I told the interpreter to tell Two Moons that no part of his story was doubted, that Yellow Wolf and the other warriors had spoken well of him. That was why he had been asked to give his war life in his own words.

A Race for Life

That day we killed the Crow Indian, that same evening we started for the Crow camp as directed. We reached there that night. One of the warriors said, "We shall now slip into the enemy's camp and take their horses!"

But no one wanted to go. They feared the Crow warriors. My first war trip, I wished to make myself brave. Going to the chief I said to him, "I will go see what I can do."

A friend of mine, a short man like myself, now spoke, "I will go with you! That is why I came. To try to get some Crow Indian horses!"

We both went through the dark closer to the enemy's camp. Some were awake and discovered us!

They gave us quite a chase. On good fast horses we outran them. Getting with our party, we continued, riding hard until we came to a gulch. There we turned to the prairie, and the enemies made a head toward the mountain. They thought we were skipping for the mountain.

We traveled the rest of the night. Away from the camp, away from the enemies, until we reached the Yellowstone River. That morning we came to a small gulch, and the chief spoke the order, "We shall rest our horses and let them eat the grass."

We dismounted and took off saddles. Everyone was sleepy from riding the night. Everyone turned his horses loose to feed, then lay down beside the saddles and slept.

But this my first experience in war, I said to myself, "I will not let my horse go, neither do I want to die out here!"

The Surprise

I staked my horse on a long rope that he could eat. I sat down by my saddle and watched while the others slept. Their horses went to sidehill for grass and at same time the enemies were overtaking us, hundreds of Crow Indians.

I am telling you, I was wide-watching while my warmates slept. I was first to see the enemy Crows, riding swiftly down upon us. As they came in sight, I yelled the alarm for my mates to skip for their lives. They sprang up and ran for their horses, a short distance away. On account of staking mine in the grass, I was first one mounted and first one on the run. I took the lead, for my horse was fast, as stated when chasing Crows. He ran away with me. A racer,

I could not hold him. We made quite a distance, my warmates shouting as they came after me.

Back on our trail yelling their war cry, the Crow warriors gained fast. We approached a big hill, and doing this I judged about my horse. We would sure give out before reaching top of that hill. Running away had broken his wind. Could I have held him and just kept out of gun and arrow reach, escape would have been easy.

Climbing the steep grade I looked back. I saw our chief. He was on a mule. It must have been he could not get his horse quick. That mule was playing out on him. The enemies were close behind him, whooping wildly.

Death of Chief Lahpatupt

We reached the hilltop, passed over its ridge. We jumped from our saddles and ran down the slope. I came to a small gulch. My chief passing me, jumped across the washout. There, he was shot in the leg and crippled down. I passed him, turned down the gulch and skipping for my life. The other of my friends on horseback, keeping straight ahead, left me. Had I not turned aside they would have picked me up. Our chief fought but was soon killed. I heard the shooting but did not see. Alone and afoot, down the gulch I ran as fast as I could. I saw no brush, no timber, shelter from the enemies. Nothing but prairie! Open prairie with the short grass. Going on I came to a bunch of rosebushes, and there I hid.

All that sun I sat there, the enemies looking for me. Their horses near stepped on me in their searching. A pile of rocks short steps away the enemies dug through, looking for me. But I was all the time under the bush. My gun ready for the shooting, should I see the enemy take a look at me. I would fire and kill one of those Crow Indians first.

But the enemies did not find me. It was late fall and no leaves on that rosebush. Nothing there to blind their eyes. But somehow, maybe by the spirit, that I was not found in my poor hiding.

The sun went down and night drew on with a blanket of darkness. I was saved, and I skipped. Barefooted, with only breechcloth and shirt. No food for the hungry stomach. Growing colder, soon snow was falling. All night I traveled, and when came the morning snow was above my ankles.

Seven suns I traveled for home with the bare feet. Nothing to stop the hunger. My friend, it hurts my heart to tell you this story. It reminds me, and makes new the burns with the telling. All those friends of mine with me that day have long snows passed from life. The chief was there killed and today I am alone.

Besides myself, the seven of my warmates escaped and reached out to stop the hunger. To shoot might bring the Crow enemies. Arriving home I found my seven friends, warmates of mine who had escaped to safety. They thought me killed along with our chief.

When asked his age at the time, and what prevented the Crows from seeing him in hiding, since the rosebush was bare of foliage, Two Moons replied, "As I can judge, I had seen thirteen snows. As I have told you, I was making myself a brave warrior on my first warpath. It was by the strength and the power given in the promise of the Spirit, whereby I was able to remain unseen by the Crows. What I have told you was my first experience in war and fighting."

Stealing Snake Horses

Time went on and we made peace with the Crow tribe. Stopping with them at the Big Horn Mountain, we took a trip from there, looking for Snake Indians. Twenty-two Nez Perces, and twenty-two Crows agreed to go. Living with the Crows at that time, the war party numbered forty-four.

Traveling five suns, we discovered the enemy's camp. We watched from hiding until came the night. It was then, in the darkness, that we drew near to steal their horses.

Three men must be selected to go where horses were corraled. Three best warriors, well experienced, must go. They were our chief, Ealaot Wadass [Common Earth],[7] Pahkatos Owyeen [Five Wounds],

[7] The following, told by the interpreter, War Singer, is of historic interest. "I will add a few words to the story of Ealaot Wadass ["Good for Nothing Earth," or, "Useless Ground"].

"In the night fight with the Bannocks, no Nez Perce was shot; one Bannock was shot with an arrow when two of them rode a few rods toward the Nez Perce dugout. Kapsis Isskit [Bad Trail] used gun, Pahkatos [Five Wounds] used bow and arrows. Of these two Bannocks, the one using gun missed his aim, the arrow man hit his aim. The Bannocks turned their horses and the one wounded with the arrow fell off his horse, but the Nez Perces did not know as it was dark. One Nez Perce wanted to follow them afoot, but he was kept back or warned not to do it, as he might get shot by mistake. That is what saved the life of this wounded Bannock.

"The Bannocks first feared that a large force of Sioux was attacking them, when the noise and talk they heard of the careless Nez Perces when they were helping themselves to horses. They listened carefully to talk of these thieves. Then some Bannock knew it was Nez Perce language. So word was passed along that they are Nez Perces. The experienced man said, if they are Nez Perces, they must be about ten in number, as they knew Nez Perces never go in large bands to steal horses. And that was the truth.

"After the night fight, some miles away, the Nez Perces were overtaken. Then there was a running fight; three or four Nez Perces were afoot, but were good runners and got to the high point called Tipsuopa. This is where the leader, Ealaot Wadass, was wounded and one unknown killed. When the leader passed away, not long after that, his personal things were distributed among his friends. Among this was the shield, given to him by the head man of Buffalo Indians or Nez Perces. If, in any attack by a large force of any tribe, should Nez Perce camp be attacked, he was to take the lead in meeting the enemy. At that meeting the leader held the shield for awhile, walking back and forth in the long tent, deciding who he should give this shield to. He finally decided who he should put the shield on. Then he walked to a young man named Raktiel. But after this, there was no more attack on the Nez Perce camp. This same man lost his finger in Fort Misery fight with Major Mc-Conville in 1877. He was prisoner of war in Vancouver, where he died. I inherited the shield from my uncle, my mother's brother."

Wahchumyus [Rainbow], warrior of many battles. Rainbow said that he got his power from the air, the rainbow too giving him fighting strength, wherein, while seen, it could not be grasped. Thus his name was one of might and power.

Seven horses were brought from the corral by these great warriors. It was when they returned for other horses, that came the trouble.

The Snake Indians were awake!

They gave us a chase! They came after us hard for a little ways, when we dropped to a deep gulch. There, was fought a battle in the dark.

In the meantime the Crow Indians, our friends, had left. Skipped away from us! Just twenty-two of us fought that night with the Snake Indians, who numbered over one hundred.

Chief Ealaot, after the chase, had covered several miles to higher ground, was wounded and killed along with another light young warrior. The enemies circled us; closed around the gulch. Had us corralled. At last they ceased firing, and rested. They slept and rested on every side of us. It was to hold us there until the morning. Then we knew they would kill us all!

There are this time, 1908, at Lapwai Nez Perce reservation, those who know about this night battle. They know what I did. They could witness for me if here.

There was seen no way by which we could get out. Then at that moment, the very man that I am, I said to my friends, "Let us go out from this place! No use dying here in the morning. There is night for escaping."

The next leading man to our dead chief, replied, "How can you escape? Enemies on every side of us!

In every direction! Sleeping lightly while guards watch us."

"I know by what power I can get out! Those enemies will not know when I pass through their circle," I told him.

The leader studied. Finally he said, "Go ahead! Take us out if you can!"

The two dead men we now tied on their own horses. We would not leave them to be cut to pieces by the Snakes.[8] I went in front. Leading my horse, the first man following held to his tail. The next man the same way, all strung out. Going slow we so filed down the gulch, a washout through sand.

There was a little ways with no banks hiding, where entering a prairie. We passed there quietly, the enemies not noticing. No noise; no stumble-rocks for the horses' feet.

Every warrior had called his secret power.

That was one great thing I did, saving my people that night. We now rode swiftly the rest of the night. But the Snakes had missed us, must have found us gone soon after our escape, for just at sunrise they caught us. We had a battle there in the early morning. A big battle on horses already tired with running. With mad yellings, the Snakes attempted to head us and hold us in the open unprotected land. But their horses were also winded. They did not charge directly at us. They came alongside, a distance away, but could not pass us. Of course they rode hanging to opposite side of their horses from us, and sent arrows and bullets but none hurt us. We returned yell for yell and shot for shot. A couple of the

---

[8] Among the Seminoles, to leave a dead body on the field was regarded as a dishonorable defeat. See Joshua Giddings, *The Exiles of Florida* (Columbus, 1856) p. 334.

enemies and a few horses went down. Pressing on we reached broken ground and skipped into a deep gulch.

Battle Among the Rocks

Dismounting, we prepared to stand our enemies off. I ran to a big rock, to hide behind it and shoot from there. While thus shooting, my friends gathered rocks and built a sort of round circle and I got inside of it.

I was a small man, of course, and it did not take many rocks to cover me from the shots of the Snake warriors. In the meantime the Nez Perce warriors were making other rock trenches, and fast as made they shot from their covers. In a few moments this pile of rocks beside me was knocked down by bullets, then I had to hang onto the big rock I first came to.

While clinging to this rock, holding the gun on the right side, the barrel was hit with a shot, and the gun struck me on the head and knocked me flat. Seeing this, the warrior next side of me announced to his fighting-mates that I was killed. I could hear what he said, what he was talking about. I was just knocked out of senses for a few moments. When I came back to my mind, I said to them, "I am alive. I am not killed!"

Then I loosened my hand from about my gun. It was numb. I could not feel anything on account of the gun barrel being struck. When I opened my hand, little pieces of bullet dropped down into my hand, from where smashed on the gun barrel.

Snake Chief Killed

My hand becoming so I could use it, I fought with the rest of my warmates. The sun traveled on. During the fight a friend hiding beside me, spoke, "Look back! There is one coming right to us with his war spear and tomahawk! All fixed up representing himself a big chief, a big warrior!"

I had a very good gun, a dead-shot rifle, and turning I aimed at this chief, Snake Indian chief. My aim was good, and I killed him!

That was my work that day. To kill that chief! Two or three men are alive from that battle, living on the Nez Perce reservation, Lapwai, Idaho [1908]. They can tell the same story that I am telling you.[9]

This battle lasted from morning sunrise until evening sunset. Then the Snake Indians gave up and left us. Darkness coming on, we buried our two dead secretly in the rocks. Of course the enemy carried their dead away with them.

On a near mountain during the fight, were those friends of ours, the Crow Indians. They camped looking on from there. Watched us fight! It was not a very high mountain and they could hear us hallooing and shooting.

About three snows after this battle, we made friends with those Snake Indians, who came from southern Idaho to visit us. Camped at White Bird, they told their story of this fight. They asked how many Nez Perces were left from the fighting. No other Nez Perce warriors were killed but the two in the night fight. There were more of the enemy Snakes killed.[10]

This was the usual course after making peace, to talk over past battles, telling incidents of the fights. The Snakes found me. They used to call me Shoolimca Hato [Short Bull].

---

[9] This fight was near the old Crow Agency, on a butte called *Tipsas*, meaning "scraper," as it looks like a hair scraper from a distance.

[10] This daylight fight occurred near the old Crow agency, Montana, according to War Singer.

To the Rescue of a Beleaguered Tribe

Seven snows after this war with the Snake Indians, I went through another battle.[11] This time it was the Crow tribe we fought.

A few bands of Nez Perces were camping, hunting buffaloes on the Big Horn River, Montana. The Crows and Snakes got into a fight some thirteen miles east of us. We knew nothing of it until a Snake Indian woman came with the message that her people, a small camp, were about all killed. The Crow Indians had the best of the fight.

Eapalekthiloom Kawat [Piling Clouds, or Cloud Piler], was chief of this band on the Big Horn, and was present when the woman arrived.[12] At this time the Nez Perces and Snake Indians were great friends. It was for this reason the woman had to notify us of her people's dangerous trouble. Hearing her message, Eapalekthiloom Kawat called his announcement, "All you warriors! Get ready your horses! We shall go assist the Snake Indians."

We did go. I, Two Moons, was there myself. Each man took two horses. Not one went with only a single horse.

When we reached the battleground we found the Snake Indians all crying. Full of tears, for many had been killed. The number of our Nez Perce warriors was about sixty-five. The Crow Indians were great in numbers, the enemies we had to fight.

The Snake Indians were in such shape we had to fight hard. The Crows outnumbered us greatly.

---

[11] When Two Moons was asked if this meant continuous peace for seven years, he replied, "I am telling you of our best [major] wars only. Most every snow there was fight; much of it not hard. Horse-stealing and maybe a little war somewhere when hunting the buffalo."

[12] The coming of this woman had been foretold, but the prophecy was not understood at the time it was made, according to War Singer.

Chief Piling Clouds fought at one end of the battle grounds, while Chief Husis Moxmox Morhin [Yellow Head], fought from the other end.[13] Each had his best warriors.

Yellow Head had hardest fighting. He saved a number of Snake Indians, and killed some of the Crows. On account of his bravery we were all saved, as the Crows were afraid of him. It was when the Crows, a great number of them, chasing us a little ways and about to overpower us, Chief Yellow Head got down from his horse and drove them back. Held them until we recovered and came to his assistance. We then held them to nearly sundown, when Chief Yellow Head was killed. When he fell, it was then the Crows made a rush for us.

In the battle that ensued, Chief Piling Clouds and our best warriors were killed.[14] All the leading fighters fell; and I tell you, my friend, there I had the experience of battle.

We were now driven to the canyon where our next best fighter was killed. His name was Hiyatommon [Shouter]. Slow running, his horse about given out after crossing into the canyon, there faced with climbing from the foot of the hill, Shouter hallooed to the others, "Know this all of you! I am getting down to fight! Not that I want your assistance, but you must know I did get down to fight!"

With that this brave warrior slid off his horse, and faced the approaching enemies. Intending to use his bow and arrows, he found himself helpless. He had lost his bow! Only arrows were in his pack [quiver].

---

[13] Interpreter Whitman said, "Yellow Head was my paternal uncle. Many of us younger Nez Perces are of warrior lineage."

[14] See Appendix I, end of this volume for further information on the death of Cloud Piler. He was not killed at the battle of White Bird Canyon in 1877, as some accounts have indicated.

Seeing this, the Crows rushed him. Counted coup on him, then killed him.

Witnessing this, I, Two Moons, whipped my horse, skipping for my life. My horse also was fast giving out. Every Indian, Nez Perce and Snake, seemed about out of senses. They knew not that they were mixed up with Crow Indians, their enemies. A great number of Snake warriors were thus killed.

After running for my life, I caught up with a friend, a Nez Perce Indian. He was about at a stand-still, and yet whipping his horse, trying to get him to go. But his horse was done. Bullets buzzed about him. Passing him a short ways, I thought not to leave him, but to assist him. So I rode back to his side and reaching over struck him twice on the back with my whip. Struck hard, telling him, "Remember you are in battle. You must not go out of your sense! Come across to my horse! We will run for our lives!"

He did come across to my horse, and we continued on. But we could not, both of us together, make the horse run. He was too far gone. The Crows still pursuing, kept shooting at us. Finally my friend slipped to the ground and fired back at them. This checked the Crows. They quit the chase and turned back.

This was all of that fight, and we continued on home.[15]

---

[15] See Appendices II, III, IV, V, pp. 561-67; 568-77; 578-88; 589-93, end of this volume for additional accounts of tribal warfare by Two Moons, Husis Owyeen and others.

CHAPTER IV

LEX SCRIPTA MISSIONARUMS[1]

WE HAVE SKETCHED THE GROWTH OF THE NEZ PERCE from their traditional beginnings as a primal band of doubtful numbers to the numerous and virile nation found at the zenith of its power by Lewis and Clark in 1805. From that date the decline of the Nez Perces was inevitable. But the seed of actual disintegration was sown with the advent of a trio of major missionaries into the vast trans-Rocky Mountain area then mapped as Oregon. With the perverseness human being sometimes exhibit, these renowned carriers of the "message" eventually developed into active colonizers and traders, harbingers of tragedy and eventual war.

Jason Lee in Old Oregon

The Rev. Jason Lee who came in September, 1834, left no concrete and dependable record.[2] Under a

---

[1] [Found among the McWhorter papers was this explanatory note, "It is needless to say that the foregoing account of the early Protestant Christian missionaries was written from the point-of-view of the long-haired Nez Perces, those who have kept their native religion known as the Dreamer religion. They resent the white man's coming and the part the missionaries played in advertising in the East, from whence they came, the beauties and the richness of the Western country. Not all the Nez Perces feel so strongly on the subject." (McW NP 4/12) For exhaustive accounts of the same developments from the missionary viewpoint see Dr. C. M. Drury's excellent volumes, *Henry Harmon Spalding* (Caldwell, 1936) and *Marcus Whitman* (Caldwell, 1937), and C. J. Brosnan, *Jason Lee, Prophet of the New Oregon* (New York, 1932). (Ed. note.)]

[2] [The Fisk-Lee correspondence was discovered before publication of the Brosnan volume, much of it is reproduced therein, and throws considerable light on the Lee mission. (Ed. note.)]

Methodist diocese, he was appointed superintendent of the mission among the Flathead Indians, with two associates, Rev. Daniel Lee and Cyrus Shepard.[3] This was in response to the "Macedonian Cry" of the famed Nez Perce-Flathead delegation to St. Louis in 1831.[4] The Flatheads were then as now, in western Montana, but the new superintendent of their mission did not go near them when he chose a site for his new station. Proceeding to Vancouver, to meet his mission supplies which had been shipped around the Horn, he is said to have heard reports of the Flatheads which deterred him from pursuing his original purpose. The environment there was "too dangerous," for his mission work, and "that the Willamette afforded them a fine field, and that they ought to go there, and they would get the same assistance [from Dr. McLoughlin] as the settlers."[5]

On the other hand it has been averred that it was neither accident nor influence that determined Lee's mission site, but his own clear and comprehensive statesmanship.[6] The switch to the Willamette was of the Superintendent's own volition. This beautiful valley, a garden spot of the Pacific Northwest, with its many political and commercial possibilities, proved alluring. Perhaps the "call" to the Flatheads had been misinterpreted. Mayhap the hand that touched the pen of diocesan endorsement to the Flathead Mission was gloved.[7]

---

[3] Rev. A. S. Atwood, *The Conquerors* (Cincinnati, Ohio, 1907), p. 28.

[4] See Chapter II, pp. 29-30.

[5] Frederick V. Holman, *Dr. John McLoughlin* (Cleveland, Ohio, 1907) p. 55.

[6] H. K. Hines, *History of the Pacific Northwest* (Portland; 1899), p. 92; Holman, *op. cit.*, p. 56.

[7] John M. Canse, *Pilgrim and Patriot* (New York, 1930), p. 37. [Lee himself said of his change of plan, "It was among the real Flat Heads (Chinooks) that we located our mission, for it was left to us to locate where, in our opinion, after having surveyed the ground, we could do the most good. . . . We chose a central station,

The Willamette Indian population was small, a diseased and pitiable remnant of former native greatness, and perhaps the least susceptible to improvement of any in the trans-Rocky Mountain area. The visits of mariners along the coast had left, as had Captain Cook's syphilitic crew in the Hawaiian Islands, a veritable heritage of loathsome, wasting decadence, ghastly in its cankerous ravages of both body and mind.[8] Just prior to the coming of missionaries into the lower Columbia River country, villages and entire tribes had disappeared, vanished before a pestilence of the white man's induction which left the river shores strewn with the unburied dead.[9] And

---

advantageous for a principal station." (Lee, as quoted in Brosnan, *op. cit.*, p. 124). McLoughlin was at least partially responsible for their change of plans. He writes, "In 1834, Messrs. Jason and Daniel Lee . . . came with Mr. Wyeth to establish a Mission in the Flathead country. I observed to them that it was too dangerous to them to establish a Mission (there) . . . that the Willamette offered them a fine field . . . (McLoughlin as quoted in Holman, *op. cit.*, p. 55). (Ed. note.)]

[8] Gustavus Hines, *History of the Oregon Missions* (Buffalo, 1850), p. 210.

[9] Rev. Samuel Parker, *Exploring Tour Beyond the Rocky Mountains* (Ithaca, 1842), p. 191. As will later be shown, the Chinooks have a tradition of a prophet foretelling this disaster some three generations before it occurred. No adequate conception can be formed of the terror and suffering that must have been endured by the helpless people. At best the death estimate is conjecture.

A piteous tale of those plague-stricken years was told the writer by Anawhooee [Black Bear], a venerable Wasco woman of chieftainly descent, as revealed by her flattened head, while ascending the Columbia on a steamboat in the summer of 1911. The story follows:

"A small girl, I was with my parents and others in a canoe coming up the Che Wana [Big River] not far this side where Portland stands. A little girl of about twelve snows appeared on the bank and called to be taken with us. She said, 'I am alone. Everybody dead but me! Take me with you! I do not want staying here with the *mamaloos* [dead]!'

"But my parents and friends were afraid to take her on the canoe. Afraid of whatever had killed all in that village. Might bring death to our own village. That little, lonely child was left crying on the Wana's bank. I can never forget seeing her. Cannot forget her piteous crying. I was but a small child myself, but the remembrance of it never left me.

"There were many such cases along the Che Wana. Nobody knew what the sickness. The medicine men were helpless to drive the death trouble away. It was a white man's disease, brought by them, and then they took from us our lands."

the social and marriage relations of the simple, confiding women had been ruthlessly betrayed by members of a so-called civilized Christian race. Thus in the richest country, populated by the fewest Indians, and those few of the lowest receptive mentality of any section of the Pacific Northwest, the "Flathead Mission" was established, its name changed to read "Oregon Mission." Its location was some five hundred miles beyond the home of the Flathead Indian tribe.

Within four years after its establishment, the Oregon Mission metamorphosed into an active colonizer of lands to which the Indian title had never been extinguished. In March, 1838, Rev. Lee returned East solely to bring additional emigrants.[10] The saving of heathen souls was foregone, and the gospel wagon sidetracked as a thing of cumber. Mammon had invaded the synagogue, and its keepers grew busy laying claim to, and staking, from six hundred and forty to one thousand acres each of enchanting Indian domain.

Emigrants were brought in, and the colony expanded. Dr. John McLoughlin, factor of the Hudson's Bay Company at Vancouver, and the best friend the missionaries ever had, as well as the saviour of famine-stricken, starving American emigrants, fell victim to the trend of the times and, in 1829, laid claim to, and improved, lands and water power at the Willamette Falls as provision for his family and his declining years.[11] Under the joint occupation treaty

---

[10] [Brosnan does not agree. ". . . the Lausanne reinforcement was not primarily a colonizing enterprise, but distinctly a missionary expedition in character and purpose." (Brosnan, *op. cit.*, pp. 147-51). "But it is admitted that by 1838 Lee saw his enterprise as much as an adjunct to a new white civilization on the Pacific coast as a mission." (*Ibid.* p. 92). (Ed. note.)]

[11] Holman, *op. cit.*, pp. 23-103, 104; Allen, A. J., *Ten Years in Oregon* (Ithaca, 1850) pp. 200-201.

of 1818 between Great Britain and the United States, McLoughlin was entitled to take up Oregon lands as a British subject. Of this property he was shamelessly despoiled, plundered by the very mission element whom he had befriended.[12] And the "White Eagle," the "Father of Oregon," died a broken-hearted old man. In the process of saving Oregon for the United States, the loyal American buccaneers killed the "noblest Roman of them all."

What the Flatheads may have missed spiritually, by missionary remissness, appears to have been regarded as of no consequence, since thereby a political triumph was achieved over their Presbyterian rivals; wherein it is exultantly proclaimed, "The Mission of the American Board founded no communities. One of the most potential factors in the work of the Methodist Mission was its colonization feature. This was the determining element in the establishment of American institutions in Oregon."[13]

What solace for mission delinquency!

The dual reasoning of one of the Oregon missionaries is astounding. Although the supposed Methodist purpose was to spread the gospel light among the native population, one mission worker was able to write,

The Umpqua tribe, but a few years ago numbering several hundred, by disease and their family wars has been reduced to less than seventy-five souls. Under the impression that the doom of extinction is suspended over this wretched race, and that the hand of Providence is removing them to give place to a people more worthy of this beautiful and fertile country, we arrived at our place of encampment. . . .[14]

---

12 [See Brosnan, op. cit., pp. 291-315, for a survey of the McLoughlin-Waller land-claim controversy. Many of the crucial documents are published here. (Ed. note.)]

13 Atwood, op. cit., p. 236.

14 G. Hines, op. cit., p. 117-18.

What profound logic! Attributing the hand of Providence to the advent of syphilitic sailors and the spreading of the germs of deadly disease among the simple-minded, confiding Umpqua villagers! In the light of Hines' reasoning, surely, "He moves in a mysterious way, His wonders to perform."

The Presbyterian Missions

The two other members of the missionary trio, Dr. Marcus Whitman and Rev. Henry Harmon Spalding, Presbyterians, and their wives, were welcomed by Dr. McLoughlin at Vancouver early in September, 1836. In October Dr. Whitman and Narcissa, his wife, settled at Waiilatpu, among the Cayuses and near the Walla Wallas and Umatillas. Rev. Spalding and his wife, Eliza, headed for the Nez Perces, and reached the Clearwater, at the mouth of Lapwai Creek, November 29, 1836. They were housed for nearly a month in a large buffalo-hide tepee, supplied by the Indians until Spalding could build a house some two miles up the creek. This house was eighteen by forty-two feet, most of the logs being carried from the Clearwater by the Indians. In the summer of 1838, Spalding moved down on the bank of the Clearwater, built there a two-story house of smaller dimensions, bringing down timber from Lapwai.

Old Indians, among them Wottolen, who "remembered the coming of the Spaldings very well," contended that the Indians were compelled to carry the logs of the first house back to the Clearwater to be used in the more substantial building.[15] By this

---

15 Wottolen [Hair Combed Over Eyes], sometimes pronounced "Wot-tolee," remembered the Spaldings clearly. If his age is computed from known historical events, he was born in 1819, making him seventeen years old when the Spaldings came to the Clearwater. He died May 17, 1928.

time the domineering nature of the missionary was beginning to assert itself in the free use of both the scourge and his booted foot.[16] The older Nez Perces were emphatic in their statements that the lash and Spalding's boot were conspicuously evident in the transportation of the logs of the dismantled house. Rolling some of them, carrying others on their shoulders, the subservient workers submitted to the driving.[17] So declared not only Wottolen, but others of his contemporaries. There are stories told of one young Hercules among the Indians who always carried the heavy end of the log.

Rev. Spalding established his mission among the Nez Perces in the same year (1836) as did Dr. Whitman among the Cayuses. The following year (1837) he decided to send Mr. Gray to the United States with a band of horses to exchange for cattle. Three Indian chiefs started with Mr. Gray: Ellis; "Blue Cloak"; and "Hat."[18] When at the rendezvous

[16] Rev. Jason Lee, Methodist missionary stationed in the Willamette Valley, visiting the Whitman and Spalding missions in April, 1837, wrote his nephew Daniel Lee that Spalding ". . . has his troubles with them [the Indians] the truth is they are *Indians.* Both Mr. W. [Whitman] and Mr. S. [Spalding] use high handed measures with their people, and when they deserve it let them feel the lash." It would appear that the Methodist divine was far from disapproving, as we read, "Lee advised his co-workers along the Willamette to be firm. 'Let not the Indians trifle with you, let them know that you must be respected, and whenever they intentionally transgress bounds, make them feel the weight of your displeasure.' " (C. M. Drury, *Henry Harmon Spalding,* p. 180.)

[17] A remarkable story is told by General Scott of a Spanish priest among the Hopi Indians of Arizona who built a church of pine logs measuring twenty inches in diameter, which had been carried from the San Francisco Mountain near Flagstaff, Arizona, one hundred miles away. This was before the revolt of 1680, at which time the Spaniards were driven from (now) Arizona and New Mexico. After this purge the church was dismantled by the Hopis, and the logs used as rafters in the construction of their kiva, a sacred ceremonial underground chamber, where General Scott saw and measured the logs. The Hopis said that the priest was thrown from the rocks and of course killed. (H. L. Scott, *Memories of a Soldier,* (New York, 1928), pp. 476-77).

[18] [Drury concurs that the missionaries agreed Gray would return to the States. He adds however, that although Spalding favored Gray's proposal to take Indians with him, Whitman was opposed. See Drury, *H. H. Spalding,* p. 192. (Ed. note.)]

their horses' feet began to fail, and Ellis observed to his companions that they could not continue the journey, their horses being unable to stand the trip, and that they would die on the road. Then he and Blue Cloak returned, while Hat went on with Mr. Gray.

Ellis and Blue Cloak arrived in the fall at the mission of Rev. Spalding, who got very angry when he saw them back, and said that they had caused a great damage to the whole nation and that they deserved severe punishment. He then condemned each of them to receive fifty lashes, and to give him a good horse. He could not take Ellis, who had too strong a party, but Blue Cloak having come one evening with the others to prayer, Rev. Spalding saw him and commanded the Indians to take him; and as no one would move, the young chief, Nez Perce or Tonwitakis, arose with anger, took hold of the Indian and tied him up.

Then he said to Rev. Spalding, "Now, whip him." Rev. Spalding answered him, "No, I do not whip; I stand in the place of God, I command; God does not whip, he commands."

"You are a liar," said the Indian chief, "look at your image (pointing to an image hanging on the wall which Spalding had made for the instruction of the Indians); you have painted two men in it, and God behind them with a bundle of rods to whip them. Whip him, or if not, we will put you in his place and whip you." Rev. Spalding obeyed, whipped the Indian, and received from him the horse that he had exacted.[19]

---

[19] This story appeared in the testimony of John Toupin, as recorded by J. B. A. Brouillet. *(House Executive Document No. 38,* 35th Congress, 1st Session, pp. 18-19.) [It should be pointed out that Brouillet was hardly an unprejudiced reporter, as Spalding had recently been accusing the Catholics of playing an active role in fomenting the Whitman massacre. (Ed. note.)] In his summary of the causes of the Whitman massacre, Brouillet attributes the "whole

Gray returned the following year (1838), but Chief Hat was not with him. He had been killed by the Sioux or the Pawnees. Chief Ellis fiercely upbraided Spalding, "Hear me," he said. "The Hat who accompanied Mr. Gray has been killed; if we had gone with him we should have been killed too; and because we turned back, refusing to follow him, you wished us to be flogged; you intended then that we should be killed also."[20] Interpreter Toupin states that the Indians then met and kept all the whites living at the mission, "blockaded in their house for more than a month," and that he was sent by Mr. Pambrun at Walla Walla, where he had been employed as interpreter for seventeen years, to intercede for the prisoners, but not until the third trip could he "induce them [Nez Perces] to accept tobacco, sign of peace, and to retire."[21]

As shocking as was the seizing and administering of a fifty-lash flogging to Chief Blue Cloak when attending a mission prayer meeting and exacting a horse from him in the guise of a fine, there are numerous instances where this missionary's "message" and "song of praise" were quite in harmony with the cutting swish of the whip. Drury writes:

evil" to six outstanding wrongs that had been imposed on the Indians by the whites. Startling as it may seem, heading the list was Parker's unfulfilled promise to pay the Indians yearly rent for the lands on which the mission buildings were built. "Thence came the 'months of deep solicitude, occasioned by the increasing and menacing demands of the Indians' of which Mr. Spalding complains in his *History of the Massacre.*" (Brouillet, *op. cit.*, p. 27.) Second was the "Death of the Nez Perces chief, [Hat] killed on his way to the United States, when he was in company with Mr. Gray, and in his service." (*Ibid.*, p. 26.) It will be remembered that this death was laid at Rev. Spalding's door. It should be pointed out that the Nez Perce demand that they receive pay for water, wood, and air was not illogical to the Indian. As part of the earth proper, their inclusion should not be construed as a demand for rental over or apart from that expected or agreed on for the land. Spalding had the use of land, water, fuel and air. The rental covered all of these component parts.

20 *Ibid.*, p. 19.

21 Brouillet, *op. cit.*, p. 19.

One incident occurred in January (1838) following the protracted meetings, which should be mentioned because of the light it throws upon some of Spalding's methods. Two extracts from his Diary and a few sentences from a letter from Smith to Green tell the whole story. Spalding wrote,

"9 (Jan.) Williams wife left him last night. Joseph and others go after her.

"12. Williams wife is whipped 70 lashes. Indians come nigh whipping him."

Smith wrote, "He (Spalding) has been much in the habit of using the whip or causing it to be used upon the people. He has however failed not infrequently in getting individuals whipped when he has attempted. . . .

"In another instance after we arrived here, Mr. Spalding caused a woman to be whipped 70 lashes. He had married her to Williams, the Blacksmith. He abused her so she ran away. She was brought back and whipped. After she had been whipped the people were determined to whip Williams, and it was with great difficulty that Mr. Spalding could prevent it. He deserved it probably more than the woman and the Indians knew it."[22]

Seventy Gospel lashes for a heathen wife who dared flee from the abuse of a Christian husband, the mission blacksmith!

Spalding's journal also records an instance when he had three children whipped for stealing corn.[23] The desire for food is man's most basic impulse; yet here was a Christian whip for three children who plucked perhaps one each of August roasting ears. And this, too, after eighteen centuries of spreading the benevolent teachings of the world's greatest humanitarian and moralist who, when passing through someone else's field of corn with his disciples, not only permitted, but defended his hungry followers

---

[22] Drury, *Spalding*, p. 216.
[23] *Whitman College Quarterly*, Vol. III, No. 2, p. 4.

from their accusers, when they, with him, unlawfully plucked and ate the ears of grain.[24]

The Dreamer reaction to these dual influences brought by the advent of the missionary in the Indian country, is well expressed by the aged Wottolen.

I remember very well when the Spaldings came to the Clearwater. The missionaries brought with them a Good Book which told our people how to live and what to believe, that they might reach the land of a better life after death. A Book that told them what to believe so as to escape the Fire Land of the hereafter. A Book that told all this to the Nez Perces. Changing their lives to a better way of living; a better spirit life.

But the missionary had something behind him which came with him to the Nez Perces. Behind him was the whisky bottle along with his Good Book. We know what that bottle has done. It would have been better had the Good Book and the whisky bottle been kept from the Nez Perces.

Wottolen had lived to see civilization brought to his morally clean people, and with it profanity, drunkenness, smallpox, and wasting venereal disease. Is it any wonder that he deemed the cost far beyond any possible gain?

Christian Religion versus Dreamer Religion

Many of the "old-timers" regarded Rev. Henry H. Spalding as selfishly austere, a veritable tyrant who made slaves out of the Nez Perces who were willing to work for the Lord. Spalding's homestead of 640

---

[24] [In explanation of these harsh methods, Drury writes, "In a country where there were no jails or law-enforcing agencies, the white man adopted the lash as an effective way to punish wrongdoers and at the same time inculcate a little respect. Spalding in his diary makes reference to the use of the lash by the Indians themselves upon wrongdoers. It is doubtful that the missionaries ever used the lash, but may have requested its use from the chiefs." (Drury, *Marcus Whitman*, pp. 191-92.) (Ed. note.)]

acres, developed in later years, extended up the Lapwai, comprising, in great part, rich bottom land. However, in this Rev. Spalding was only yielding to the world-wide Caucasian tendency of acquisition, from which American missionaries in general were not immune, as is revealed in the title abstracts to choice land sites in the Hawaiian Islands. The Spalding claim was officially recognized despite the Nez Perce title guaranteed in the 1855 treaty, but the land was eventually restored to the Indians when the government paid Langford's heirs the Spalding claim of $20,000.

At the old mission site is a plat of ground encircled in part by a low ridge, which was formed with waterworn boulders cleared from the enclosed ground. This rude amphitheater was used for open-air religious services when the weather permitted. A handsome, elderly Nez Perce, wearing the unshorn braids of the Dreamer faith, in pointing out to me this historic spot, graphically portrayed his mind's picture of long-ago events in the following forceful manner.

"Injuns sittin' on rocks all around. Injuns sittin' on ground inside rock circle. Lots Injuns! Preacherman Spalding stand about here. Maybe on platform and talk. Spalding call to Injuns. Look Up. See Jesus. See Jesus up there!

"One hand pointin' Injuns to Jesus; other hand stealin' Injuns' land! That religion not good for Injun!"

The Indians also tell the story of Kosallihkin, a Nez Perce "dying," who came back to life the next day. He told of the wonderful sights he had seen in the spiritland, and foretold events to transpire. Rev. Spalding, hearing of this, went to the prophet and asked if he had seen Jesus in the better world.

Kosallihkin answered, "No, I saw only Indians up there." Spalding then warned him to keep quiet, to say nothing, or he would punish him in the presence of all the people. The oracle was revealed no further.

Dr. White and the Adoption of the Laws

Precursory of woe was the arrival of Dr. Elijah White among the Nez Perces, in 1843. White had served three years as the missionary doctor at the Methodist station in the Willamette Valley, and was dismissed by Jason Lee as morally unqualified for the position.[25] He returned to the States and soon appeared at the national capital, representing that he was there at the request of the Oregon missionaries who desired his appointment as Indian agent. Quite the opposite was the case for we read, ". . . the Methodist missionaries were rather dismayed to see one of their former numbers returned in a government capacity."[26] Dr. White's biographer, writes at some length in explaining how the appointment came to him unsolicited, and as a great surprise.[27] The preponderance of evidence however is against this claim that he was sought for, rather than went seeking, the post.

In any event he returned to Oregon in the autumn of 1842, bringing with him one hundred and twelve emigrants.[28] He claimed authority from the President of the United States to settle all troubles between the Hudson's Bay Company, the Indians and settlers, in short, "governing power of the United

[25] Wm. H. Gray, *History of Oregon*, (New York, 1870), p. 175.

[26] For an arraignment of Dr. White's unfitness for his official appointment, see Gray's *History of Oregon*, pp. 214-15; Drury, *Whitman*, p. 269.

[27] Allen, *Ten Years in Oregon*, pp. 138-39.

[28] *Ibid.*, p. 170; Drury, *Whitman*, p. 345.

States west of the Rocky Mountains."[29] Dr. White was the first Indian agent sent to Oregon by the Bureau of Indian Affairs which had been created in the War Department, March 11, 1824. His commission bears the date, January 24, 1842, and his report announcing his arrival in Oregon is dated April 1, 1842. His term of office was terminated April 14, 1846, by letter from the Commissioner of Indian Affairs. As the Department of the Interior was not set up until March 3, 1849, under which the Indian Bureau has since functioned, Agent White's incumbency was supervised by the War Department.

This pharisaical "wolf in sheep's clothing" was arrogantly narrow in his concept of justice and right dealing; coldly selfish and unsympathetic with all ideals not his own. The turmoil, confusion, and final frightful massacre which followed in the wake of his autocratic administration, typifies the wobbling, blundering miscarriages of a vacillating, political-machine-run Indian Department during more than a century's activities. As an adjunct to the missions, he contributed nothing constructive to their efforts.

Dr. White's first official visit to the Spalding Mission was December 3, 1843.[30] It had been hastened by report of open dissatisfaction among the Nez Perces. Perchance they were growing weary of the lash wielded by God's proxy, or fearful that God was too hard to placate. At any rate, the mission's followers had become defiant, and a spirit of rebellion was in evidence. Something had to be done to stay this dissatisfaction; a brace had to be provided for the crumpling mission powers, and to this end a Machiavelian code of laws was formulated.

At this mid-winter meeting with the Nez Perce

---

[29] Gray, *op. cit.*, p. 214.
[30] *Ibid.*, p. 181.

tribe, White, with oiled suavity, painted in glowing colors the "kind intentions" of the government towards them, and luridly portrayed the "sad consequences that would ensue to any white man from this time on who should invade their rights, by stealing, murder, selling of damaged articles for good, or alcohol." He dwelt on the efficiency of the work being accomplished by Rev. Spalding and Mrs. Spalding, the latter beloved, the former hated by the Nez Perces, and with what "pleasure the great chief [the President] had given them a passport" to come among them.[31]

Dr. White was followed by other speakers, first among whom was McKinley of the Walla Walla post of the Hudson's Bay Company, and White's interpreter, Rogers. But his trump card, in winning the recalcitrant tribesmen to the Caucasian way of civilization, was the oratorical skill of Thomas McKay, a half-blood in the Doctor's hire.

Then spoke Chief Pahkatos Qohqoh [Five Ravens] whose words were brief and solicitous, groping for something that was not. The aged Bloody Chief, more properly known as Many Wounds, of whom a brief sketch has been given in earlier pages of this volume, discoursed reminiscently and noncommittally.

Other chiefs spoke, and it all ended in the selection of a supreme, or high chief, with the remaining chiefs subordinate but with "equal power," and each of them to have five officers to help enforcement of "all their lawful demands." The code of laws referred to having been adopted, Ellis, the same whom Spalding was unable to lash because of his strong following, was selected as principal or high chief.[32] He was

---

[31] Gray, *op. cit.*, pp. 182-83.
[32] *Ibid.*, p. 186.

reputed to read and write English fairly well. A son of Red Bear, grandson of Many Wounds, his tribal name was Twvish Sisimnen [Sparkling Horn or Sparkling Light Horn]. Never regarded by the tribe as high chief, Sparkling Horn was foredoomed to repent the day of his tribal exaltation.

He and his people had been inveigled into adopting the following astounding code of laws.

Art. 1. Whoever wilfully takes life shall be hung.

Art. 2. Whoever burns a dwelling-house shall be hung.

Art. 3. Whoever burns an out-building shall be imprisoned six months, receive fifty lashes, and pay all damages.

Art. 4. Whoever carelessly burns a house, or any property, shall pay damages.

Art. 5. If anyone enter a dwelling, without permission of the occupant, the chiefs shall punish him as they think proper. Public rooms are excepted.

Art. 6. If anyone steal he shall pay back two-fold; and if it be the value of a beaver skin or less, he shall receive twenty-five lashes; and if the value is over a beaver skin he shall pay back two-fold and receive fifty lashes.

Art. 7. If anyone take a horse and ride it, without permission, or take any article, and use it, without liberty, he shall pay for the use of it, and receive from twenty to fifty lashes, as the chief shall direct.

Art. 8. If anyone enter a field, and injure the crops, or throw down the fence, so that cattle or horses go in and do damage, he shall pay all damages, and receive twenty-five lashes for every offense.

Art. 9. Those only may keep dogs who travel or live among the game; if a dog kill a lamb, calf or any domestic animal, the owner shall pay the damage, and kill the dog.

Art. 10. If an Indian raise a gun or other weapon against a white man, it shall be reported to the chiefs, and they shall be reported to Dr. White, and he shall redress it.

Art. 11. If an Indian break these laws, he shall be punished by his chief, if a white man break them, he shall be reported to the agent, and be punished at his instance.[33]

---

[33] Drury, *Spalding*, p. 296. For an amusing example of how the chiefs might administer the laws, see Appendix VIII, pp. 604-7, end of this volume.

This Christian code, enforced by the whip and the hangman's noose, was to supplant the simple and far more humane and effective oral mandates under which the "pagan" Dreamer Nez Perces had risen far above their social environment. These missionary mandates are stamped with a baroque narrowmindedness. Could there be a more ridiculous absurdity than Article Five, which suppressed a harmless, race-wide standard of social ethics going back unnumbered ages? The Indian's traditional admonition, "Lift the door-flap and enter," is only another form of, "The latchstring hangs outside."

Listed here were two capital offenses, four which entailed the degrading lash mandatorily, and three others enforceable at the discretion or whim of the chief in jurisdiction. With diplomatic adroitness Articles Ten and Eleven were so drawn that white violators were immune to Indian jurisdiction, which from all precedence implied exemption for such offenders from every form of code violations. These laws, as will be later shown, were destined to be taken advantage of by all classes of white interlopers, who used them to force lawless brutalities and trumped-up charges against the helpless tribesmen. These eleven articles which the Nez Perces had been inveigled into adopting as their own form of government, the peacefully inclined Nez Perces were doomed to endure through more than three decades. Excuses for extortions, whippings, and hangings were trumped up by every border poacher.

It has been a source of wonder that the proud, courageous, and dignified Nez Perces should have ever submitted to the lash. There can be but one solution. The code had been brought to them as emanating from God, as portrayed in the Book of Heaven, for which they once vainly sought. The missionary's God appeared greater, was richer than their own Hunyawat or Ahkinkenekii [Man Above, Above all, Deity] who had but two countries, Earth for this life, and *Ahkinkenekia* [Place of Happiness or Happy Hereafter]. Higher than all it is a fine country with nothing bad anywhere.[34]

But the missionary god had three countries. One above this, all sunny with great cities with gold-covered streets, where good people who believed certain things sit down with nothing to do but play a flute and sing. The other country owned by this missionary god was somewhere below. Deep down where all is night-darkness! Black darkness! It is a wide rimless fire-country. Nothing but fire! Leaping flames broader than all the prairies and without bottom. Hotter than any pitchwood fire! Into this awful region, after death, all who had not believed in the new god and his laws, who had never heard of his plans, were thrown to remain forever. No end to their burning. No yesterday, no today, no tomorrow! No wearing away or shortening of time. Always now! No sleep! No drinking cold water, no bathing in clear running streams. No rambling through shady glens and deep-forested solitudes of wild mountain fastness. Indescribable woe forever unbroken.

To the Nez Perces, this was the contrast between the two religions when the laws were brought to them. Devout, and seeking the better way to the spiritland, they had accepted the new faith in blissful ignorance of the multiple interpretations of its mystic symbolism. To avoid the dreaded, bottomless fireland which flanked the new-found "better way," this exacting Christian god must be placated. Their own simple religious faith gleaned from elemental

---

[34] See Chapter V, pp. 79-81 for a description of the Dreamer conception of the hereafter.

nature had held no constituent of fear or dread of death.[35]

The more reticent Cayuses, speaking the same language as the Nez Perces and intermarried with them, adopted the laws for their tribe largely because of Nez Perce influence. At the introduction of the laws to the Cayuses at the Whitman station, we read,

The laws were then read, first in English, and then in Nez Perce. Yellow Serpent then rose and said, "I have a message to you. Where are these laws from? Are they from God or from the earth? I would that you might say they were from God. But I think they are from the earth, because, from what I know of white men, they did not honor these laws." In answer to this, the people were informed that the laws were recognized by God, and imposed on men in all civilized countries. Yellow Serpent was pleased with the explanation, and said it was according to instructions he had received from others, and he was very glad to learn that it was so, because many of his people had been angry with him when he had whipped them for crime, and had told him that God would send him to hell for it, and he was glad to know that it was pleasing to God.[36]

In time the mission converts began to doubt that whipping was the passport to Heaven. Chief Sparkling Horn had wielded the lash with the greatest vigor.[37] But in so doing he lost the respect of his

---

[35] On this question, Rev. Samuel Parker says of the Nez Perces, "They have learned enough to fear the consequences of dying unforgiven, but not sufficient to embrace the hopes and consolations of the gospel." (Rev. Samuel Parker, *An Exploring Tour Beyond the Rocky Mountains* (N.Y., 1843), p. 283). Chief Luther Standing Bear, Ogalala Sioux author and lecturer, lamented to the writer, "Time was when the Sioux, a brave people, were not afraid to die. But the missionaries came among us with their story of the Christian endless hell, and now they are afraid to die."

[36] Hines, *History of the Oregon Missions*, p. 179. [In fairness to the missionaries it should be pointed out that Mrs. Whitman sincerely doubted the wisdom of having the Cayuses adopt the laws. She was much perturbed by this development which occurred during her husband's absence. (Drury, *Whitman*, p. 289.) (Ed. note.)]

[37] Hines, *op. cit.*, p. 143.

tribesmen and threw up his commission, a broken man. Ostracized, he went to the buffalo country (Montana), where he soon afterwards died of small-pox.[38] In time unable to determine just how they were being benefitted, the Nez Perces demanded pay, clothing and blankets in return for the concessions exacted from them.[39] One of the converts offered to pray an entire year for a coat and a shirt.[40]

All this appears diametrically opposite to Spalding's letter to Dr. White where he says, "The laws which you so happily prepared, and which were unanimously adopted by the people, I have printed in the form of a small school book. A great many of the school now read them fluently. . . ."[41] This code and the Bible were the paramount concepts taught in the mission school, and for a time the Nez Perces made an honest endeavor to adapt themselves to the new order of things brought to them from God, and showing a "better way to heaven."

As time passed, conditions at the Presbyterian missions grew more turbulent. This was more pronounced at the Whitman field. The Cayuses became convinced that their lands were being usurped through the machinations of Dr. Whitman himself. After adoption of the laws, they became greatly alarmed at the inroads of the "Bostons," as whites from the United States were called. In an earlier visit from Dr. White, they had gathered that their country was to be taken from them and they reduced to slavery.[42] Had Whitman not brought in hundreds

---

[38] McBeth, *The Nez Perces Since Lewis and Clark*, p. 52.

[39] Gray, *op. cit.*, p. 311; Hines, *op. cit.*, p. 157.

[40] Hines, *op. cit.*, p. 186.

[41] Allen, *op. cit.*, p. 205.

[42] G. Hines, *op. cit.*, p. 147. For testimonial complaint from the Cayuse Indians for the manner in which they had been deceived and defrauded by promises never kept by Whitman, who they declared

of emigrants, a thousand of them at one time, and settled them on the most choice lands without leave or least compensation to the rightful owners? Had he not raised fields of wheat, ground it into flour and sold it along with potatoes and other vegetables to the newcomers? Thus emulating Rev. Lee, Dr. Whitman became more interested in Oregon as a white settlement than in saving Indian souls.[43]

With pious presumption the mission head scorned and trampled inherent tribal concepts, which, for generations, had directed both the temporal and spiritual welfare of the race. As compensation for this ruthless abrogation of the simple and in many respects profound native religion, they were given a dogmatized treatise on which no two of the two hundred and fifty odd Christian denominations of the United States today can agree. There could be but one sequel. Within the shadow of all this can be discerned the latent but still ominous forces that hurled the fatal bolt of Waiilatpu, November 29, 1847.

The Cayuses were dying by scores, dying from an array of strange diseases brought to them by the

---

even threatened them with a greater influx of whites as punishment for their aggressiveness in demanding settlement of unfulfilled promises, see Ross Browne's report in *House Exec. Doc. No. 38*, 35th Cong., 1st Sess., pp. 18-29.

[43] [Aside from asking that a few "pious laymen" be sent to his station, Whitman took no active part in fostering immigration until his trip East in 1842-43. He returned in the fall of the latter year with the first of the great migrations of settlers to Oregon, although they would have come without him and encouraging immigration was not his primary reason for going East. According to Drury, "Whitman's letters after his return indicate his changing interests. Gradually he came to the conviction that the Indian could never keep control of the land. He felt that in the providence of God, Oregon was meant for the white man." (Drury, *Marcus Whitman*, p. 346). Spalding was never an active colonizer and retained a larger measure of his Indians' respect. He was anxious to "settle the Indians," convince them to give up their nomadic ways and turn farmer, but in this he undoubtedly felt sincerely that he was arguing for their own best interests. (Ed. note.)]

white stranger, brought to them as it had been to the Blackfeet.[44] The Indians began to look on Whitman as an evil "medicine man," the progenitor of all their woes. They knew of the meat he had poisoned for wolves.[45] The Cayuses thought they were being killed off that the whites might possess their country.[46] They would go, as had the Indians of the Willamette Valley, and the upper Missouri River! To save themselves, the evil "medicine man" must be killed! For two or more years before his death, Dr. Whitman was quoted as stating that he "had done nothing for the teaching of the Indians, because they would not listen to him."[47] The gathering storm was eventually to culminate in a dreadful holocaust of death, traceable to the usual broken faith on the part of the white man.

While Spalding had brought no emigrants to possess the Nez Perce lands, there were other grievances against him. His implacable temper and querulous belligerence often led to personal encounters and estranged his followers. Many of the converts began to feel that the laws "recognized by God" were entirely man-evolved—laws with which the Deity had naught to do. Spalding's famous two-trail ladder no longer meant any more to them than a picture.[48] They felt

---

[44] On the score of the Nez Perces and Cayuse Indians being cognizant of the manner in which the great smallpox scourge was brought to the Blackfeet, see Browne, *op. cit.*, p. 25. [However, virulent measles and dysentery were the epidemics wreaking havoc among the Cayuses and also Waiilatpu's white inhabitants in the fall of 1847, brought in by the immigrant train of that year. (Ed. note.)]

[45] Brouillet, *op. cit.*, pp. 21-22, 28.

[46] *Ibid.*, pp. 8-27.

[47] *Ibid.*, p. 16.

[48] See Browne, *op. cit.*, p. 31 and Drury's *Spalding*, p. 330. This "ladder" was of Catholic origin, a small, printed chart depicting Luther, the apostate, leaving the road to heaven and taking a byway leading to hell. Whitman smeared blood on one of these charts, denoting the Catholic persecution of the Protestants. To counteract the Catholic chart Spalding and his wife fashioned a huge drawing show-

they could no longer believe the missionary's words. As the swift and ghastly Waiilatpu tragedy is justly attributable to Dr. Whitman's injudicious management of the mission and his part in the colonization of Oregon, so can Rev. Spalding's sudden flight to the Willamette be ascribed to his vicious temper and unyielding dogmatism. His panicky flight may have attested a lack of faith in the protective powers of the God of which he preached, as well as in the friendship of his own converts. This was but natural although the Indians found in it a sign of cowardice. On this topic, Many Wounds expressed himself to the writer, "Spalding did not elevate himself heroically with the Nez Perces when he ran away. It was fifteen snows before he returned." But Spalding may have been right in deeming it wise to leave the Nez Perce country. Many of the Indians were smarting under the memory of lashings for no other offense than observance of old-time customs running back into snows long forgotten by the oldest of their tribe. Warriors who had resisted whippings "even to the

---

ing two roads, a narrow and a wide one. On the broad road the Pope was selling indulgences and forgiveness of sin, with Catholics passing and at the end of the highway plunging headfirst into hell. Luther was shown leaving this broad thoroughfare and was pursuing the correct path of righteousness. In his report, Browne comments on these ecclesiastical bickerings.

"In the autumn of 1847 Dr. Whitman and his family were murdered by the Indians. Mr. Spalding, another missionary, charges that it was done with the knowledge and connivance of the Catholic missionaries. I send enclosed the reply of Father Brouillet, which professed to refute this charge. A perusal of the pamphlet will abundantly show the bitterness of feeling existing between the different sects, and its evil effects upon the Indians. It will readily be seen that as little dependence can be placed upon the statements made by one side as by the other, and that instead of christianizing the Indians, these sects were engaged in quarrels with each other, thereby showing a very bad example to the races with whom they chose to reside.

"The fact is also shown, that as far back as 1835 the Indians west of the Rocky Mountains protested against the taking away of their lands by the white races, that this was one of the alleged causes of the murder of Dr. Whitman and family." (Ibid., p. 3.)

point of the knife," might well be regarded with apprehension.[49]

At the time of Lewis and Clark, the population of the Nez Perces had been estimated at six thousand souls.[50] Their population had probably not decreased markedly in forty-two years, and the fact that but fifty of the tribesmen composed the bodyguard for Spalding and his family in their ride to Fort Walla Walla, the first lap of their flight to the Willamette settlement, is worthy of note. It suggests that his adherents were comparatively few, but it also demonstrates that any danger of molestation from malcontents was negligible, thanks to the great esteem in which Mrs. Spalding was held by the Nez Perce people.

On the Spalding Mission site an imposing basaltic column, impressively plaqued, has been erected. It was brought from the neighboring hillside where, from time immemorial, it has been reverently regarded by the Nez Perces as an ancient landmark. To the Dreamers its removal was desecration, and Many Wounds lamented as he recounted its history:

That stone is Peli-Yivi, an old man who had control of this place. It is quite a story, but I will tell only a short part of it. In a great trouble with a great person he was changed into a stone. All the Indians knew and had great respect for Peli-Yivi. You see it now where the Christian white people have placed it.

In Deuteronomy XIX, 14; Proverbs XXII, 28, it is forbidden to remove landmarks set by them, of old time, and the fathers. The Bible also forbids setting up images to be worshipped. You see here what has been done. An ancient landmark of my people removed and made into an image with an ornamental plate of fine metal, just as worshipping Spalding.[51]

---

[49] G. Hines., *op. cit.*, p. 157.

[50] *Handbook of North American Indians*, II, 66.

[51] Later the full story of Peli-Yivi was obtained from Helping

Here was a Long Hair, a Dreamer, quoting Scripture. Astounded, I asked, "Where did you get all that?"

"I used to teach a Bible class in the Methodist church."

Many Wounds had "gone back to Egypt"!

Those who would scoff at the story of the stony termination of Peli-Yivi might well remember the salty fate of Lot's wife.[52]

Another, whose story of the Big Hole battle appears in McWhorter, L. V., *Yellow Wolf*, and who will be mentioned again in the course of this volume.

[52] See Appendix VII, pp. 598-603 for an account of Old Joseph and his relations with the Spalding Mission.

CHAPTER V

THE DREAMERS

AT THIS POINT A GLANCE AT THE SPIRITUAL CULT OF the semiprimitive Nez Perces would seem in order. Religion, in some form, has been inherent in all races of mankind. From whence Life, and whither Death —insoluble as the riddle of the Sphinx—have always lured man into seeking the first great cause. Each successive religion is necessarily a graft on a pre-existing form. The Dreamer cult which Lewis and Clark found with the Nez Perces, and which missionaries Whitman and Spalding opposed with such uncompromising vigor, was related to a former primitive worship.

The earliest mention in official documents of the religious culture of the Upper Columbia River Indians is by A. B. Meacham, superintendent of Indian affairs in Oregon. In his report of September, 1870, he complains: ". . . one serious drawback [to the adoption of white civilization] is the existence among the Indians of Oregon of a peculiar religion called Smokeller or Dreamers, the chief doctrine of which is that the red man is again to rule the country, and this sometimes leads to rebellion against lawful authority."[1]

He goes on to describe the Smokellers at Priest

---

[1] A. B. Meacham, as quoted, in James Mooney's treatise, "Ghost Dance Religion," *Fourteenth Annual Report of the Bureau of American Ethnology*, (Washington, 1896), Pt. 2, p. 711.

Rapids as the next-largest band of non-reservation
Indians, who "refused to obey my order to come
in. . . ."[2] This was the band of Smoholla, renowned
medicine man of the Wana Pums [River Dwellers or
River People, as they themselves interpret].[3] These
Indians are again mentioned by Commissioner
Meacham in 1872 as having:

> . . . a new and peculiar religion, by the doctrines of which
> they are taught that a new god is coming to their rescue;
> that all the Indians who have died heretofore, and who
> shall die hereafter are to be resurrected; that they will
> then be very numerous and powerful, they will be able to
> conquer the whites, recover their lands, and live as free
> and unrestrained as their fathers lived in olden times. Their
> model of man is an Indian. They aspire to be Indians and
> nothing else.[4]

General Howard dwelt, in his publications, on the
Dreamer religion as a factor in causing the war of
1877. This drew the attention of the American eth-
nologists, and in 1890-94, James Mooney included
along with his study of other kindred native tenets, a
resumé entitled *The Smoholla Religion of the Columbia Region.*[5] But Smoholla did not originate the
Dreamer religion, as credited by Meacham and General Howard, an idea later accepted by ethnologist
Mooney. However, Smoholla did graft thereon the
"Messiah" concept which carried with it the doctrine
of a material resurrection.[6]

---

[2] Mooney, *op. cit.*, p. 711.

[3] They are also wrongfully known as "Sokulks," an appelation of
which the remnant of the tribe, numbering but thirty-seven in 1939,
know nothing.

[4] Mooney, *op. cit.*, p. 711.

[5] *Ibid.*, Chapter VI.

[6] [It would seem that Spinden, in the one comprehensive anthropological study of the Nez Perces, tends to support McWhorter's
thesis that the Dreamer sect antedated Smoholla. He writes, "The
'Dreamer Religion,' which was built up by the great preacher Smoholla,
was a natural outgrowth of the primitive religious ideas of the

Smoholla was born late in the first quarter of the nineteenth century, but long before his time there arose a prophet named Swopscha or Schwapsch, of the Sohappy family of the Wana Pums, from which branch Smoholla was descended. Swopscha foretold the coming of a strange, white-skinned people, who would bring with them surprising customs and many new and wonderful objects, some of which would be useful to the Indians, while others would entail harmful and deadly dangers. The strangers at first would be kind and friendly, treating the Indians as brothers and sisters. Then the seer foretold wars and bloodshed. Dispossessed of their lands the tribes would become broken and scattered. There would be wasting sicknesses and diseases would be brought by the invaders with which the medicine men could not cope, sweeping away not only villages but entire tribes.[7] He visioned their nation's dead strewing the ground as driftwood along the Che Wana's stony shores.

From such foreboding prophecies Schwopscha evolved the Dreamer religion. His visions told him the dreaded scourge could be fought only through invocational channels, and hence the dance on bended knees, the suppliants' chanting of the prayer-songs that had "come down to the Prophet from above."

Indians of Shahaptian stock . . . The factors of Smoholla's doctrine which go back to the primitive faith are as follows: First, animistic conception of the world especially developed into the Earth mother aspect. Second, the importance of dreams as a method of holding communication with these forces or 'wills' of nature. The entire absence of agriculture before the coming of the whites, the presence of great natural supplies of camas and other roots, gave a practical basis for declaring against the operation of civilization . . . While it [Dreamer Sect] was developed after contact with the whites, its purpose was to maintain the ancient ideas and ancient forms of culture." (Herbert J. Spinden, "The Nez Perce Indians," in *Memoirs of the American Anthropological Association*, Vol. XI, Pt. 3 (November, 1908) p. 260). (Ed. note.)]

[7] For a startling revelation of the decimation of the Lower Columbia River Indians, see Parker, *op. cit.* pp. 191-92.

Born in the travail of gloomy forebodings, the ceremony was one of lamentation, a piteous supplication to the unseen, incomprehensible power. That Schwopscha's ghastly prophecy was frightfully fulfilled can be amply verified from our own annals, when the whites brought deadly epidemics to the Pacific Coast Indians.

Such was the origin of the Dreamer religion, a poetic belief in the creative perfection of all nature; how far it antedated the coming of Lewis and Clark is only conjecture. The cult spread rapidly throughout the great Columbia Basin, supplanting in some measure the tenets of the ancient medicine religion, but also absorbing to a great extent its original essence.[8]

In some of its forms the Dreamer religion was not unlike that of the Papists, and it was said by the Klikitats that when they first saw the Catholics in worship at Vancouver, they exclaimed, "Why their religion is the same as we have!" An aged Yakima of the Catholic faith informed me that the "Black Robes" prevailed on the Dreamers to discontinue their knee dancing and enact that form of the orison standing erect, to lessen the similarity between the two forms of worship. Study also shows that the Jewish Shekinah and the Dreamer reasoning of divine ruling, are not altogether unlike.

One of the greatest defects of the Dreamer faith proved to be the poetic sacredness with which the earth was guarded against the desecrating plow. The Dreamers believed that every need of the Indian in his primitive state had been provided for in the

---

[8] Chief Weyallup Wayacika, Yakima, who died December 16, 1915, was the last of his tribe to adhere strictly to the ancient medicine religion, as he declared to the writer shortly before his death. The recognition of a deity is the foundation of both of these religions. The writer attended the last medicine dance conducted by the chief.

earth's finished form as it was left by Hunyahwat [deity or creator] and any marring or changing by man was sacrilege. The earth is the mother of all life, both vegetable and animal, and in time all return to her bosom.[9] "When I die the earth will take care of my body!" reverently declared Chief Sluskin Weouikt, the Yakima, as we were riding across a desert waste. The Chieftaincy of the earth was to be kept inviolate.

The happy spirit abode in usually depicted as an ethereal one, but not always so. On this score an intelligent, primitive-minded Yakima huntsman explained as we exchanged ideas while lounging by a campfire in a deep mountain gorge, "Some Indians think when they die they go off to a fine place in some other country or somewhere. Maybe above! But not that way for me. I stay right here in this mountain. I like this mountain!" Thus it is seen that, while the Dreamer idea of a future state may be a kind of heaven, it must not be inferred that all severance with the mundane is implied. The author has pages of field-gathered data to the contrary.

With the Dreamer, the spiritual pervades all creation. To speak of the Indian paradise as the "Happy Hunting Ground" is a misnomer. Hunting, in the usual sense, implied death by killing; while the Dreamer conception of the hereafter rejects all idea of suffering and death. Should venison be craved, a deer would appear at the mere thought, and with a spirit knife the suppliant would sever whatever portion he would want, but with neither blemish or

---

[9] This sentiment was widely held by Indian peoples as witness both the speech and action of the great Shawnee Chief, Tecumseh, at the Vincennes council with Governor Harrison, 1810, where he refused a chair, preferring to repose on his "mother's bosom," the earth. (James R. Albach, *Annals of the West*, (Pittsburg, 1857), p. 832; Edward Eggleston and Lillian E. Seelye, *Tecumseh*, (New York, 1878), p. 182.

wound to the spirit animal. He pictures the next life conforming to nature's splendors as he observed and adored them in this life. For him, deep spirituality pervades all creation. Beauty everywhere! And, beyond the final sunset, he envisions not a city with pearly gates and golden streets, but splendidly towering mountains and deep forests, glens and glades with bubbling springs, cascading streams, lakes and rivers; boundless plains and silent desert expanses, all peopled with the wild life he loves so well.

The Dreamer transmission of the soul to the spiritland is beautiful in its poetic simplicity. The souls of children and of the more blameless adults are transported on the back of a small bird directly at death, while others, because of the bad life they have led, must take a more difficult course. They must travel afoot through a country that is poor and desolate, a dead country with no life of any kind. They must sit around and stay there a long time, until they clean themselves of whatever wrongs they committed in life. Not until they do this can they go on to the spiritland. It may be aeons of snows before they can pass on.

On this score, Sitting Rock, an aged shaman of the Wascos, answered my inquiries:

A man who has done more bad than good in this life dies and finds himself lost. He knows not where he is. It is desolate country. Nothing nice, nothing fine anywhere. He is lonely! Sees nobody anywhere! He is afoot; must travel afoot.

After a long, long time, maybe many snows, he finds himself. His mind, and his heart feel differently. By and by he thinks, "Where are my horses?"

Then he looks and finds tracks made by his horses. He follows after the tracks. By and by he finds his horses. He mounts his best horse and it takes him to the Good Land.

There he finds his friends! Everybody is friendly and nothing bad of any kind.

Schocishton [First Man, Deity] created everything just right! All good.

Some die, apparently, and get part way to the hereafter, but are stopped by a voice from an invisible source and turned back to make good some wrong they had done, and to warn their friends that they must live better lives before they can enter the Dreamer heaven. These returned persons always receive a song or chant to be used in worship with their revelation. Such songs are varied in nature but seldom consist of more than a very few short sentences.

The orthodox Christian teaching of the hereafter was at such variance with Dreamer concepts that many Indians wholly repudiated the strange new faith. They could not understand the god of the whites. He differed so drastically from their own deity, whose heart was kindly disposed toward all people. Benign and incapable of cruelty such as besets the minds of men, he offered an abode of perfect bliss. But not so with the new god. While the Indian sometimes burned his captured enemies alive, torturing them maybe for part of one sun, it was as revenge for a real or fancied wrong. The example set by the white man's god was entirely different. He burned people, many of them, in fire that was much hotter, burned them not just for one sun, but down through the unborn ages that never end. Surely he must do this for his own amusement, since there was no power so great as his own. No man, however vengeful, would like to see such suffering every sun, and for all time. There could be no good in the heart of such a god, and many rejected him. There was witchery in a fire that did not consume! But in time the endless punishment idea of the Christians, became a "graft" on the Dreamer philosophy and today is usually mistakenly regarded as an element of the original creed.

Fear is a recognized weakness, and it must be regarded as detrimental to the development of those positive attributes in the mental, moral and physical make-up of man; it is rather a negative quality to be combated and shunned. As bearing directly on this point, it is interesting to weigh the Christian religion as taught by the early missionaries, against the cosmic religion as then practiced by the tribes. Chief Standing Bear, Sioux author, when we talked on this subject, declared:

> The Sioux religious belief was, that the hereafter is a place of peace, and tranquility; where only good prevails, and therefore no Sioux was afraid of death. But white missionaries came, preaching two places in the hereafter. One of these in heaven; all light and happiness, where only good people measured by certain beliefs are permitted to go. The other is hell; a place of terrible fire, roaring flames and molten, glowing heat, yet black, eternal darkness. It is here that the bad people, those who do not believe certain teachings, are thrown forever. All this has made the once brave Sioux now afraid to die. Our God was one who took pity on His Children.

This same unspeakable terror is revealed as existing among some of the Nez Perces, back in the present century, who had heard the "message." Missionary Parker says ". . . They have learned enough to fear the consequences of dying unforgiven, but not sufficient to embrace the hopes and consolations of the gospel."[10]

Quite in contrast is the following comment on the pagan Indians of Oregon. "They are not ignorant of the immortality of their souls, and speak of a great country where departed spirits rest."[11]

---

[10] Parker, *op. cit.*, p. 283.
[11] Atwood, *op. cit.*, p. 24.

Under their primitive religion the Nez Perces reached a plane of moral integrity that elicited the admiration and praise of the early explorers. Were these outstanding tribal qualities improved, or even maintained under Christian contacts?

A factor in holding the Dreamer aloof from the Christian religion, was the prevalence of hypocrisy and double-dealing within the ranks of the latter sect. The late Yakima chieftain, Weyallup Wayacika, in an interview following the burial of his lamented wife, declared bitterly, "The white man's God must be bad, since his religion has not made the white man good." Surely it seems scarcely short of absurdity to speak of the Dreamer Indian as having no knowledge of the true God.[12] It does not seem possible that nature's god could be anything else than true.

The Nez Perces, like all the tribes, had their oracular forecasting of coming events. Many Wounds, who may be regarded as inheriting his father's mantle as tribal historian, gave me the following brief synopsis of an interesting branch of their occult:

Centuries before the advent of whites in our country, the Nez Perces had warnings of what was coming, revealed by their prophets, through Dream Songs. We still remember those songs, handed down through the generations.

[Here the narrator chanted a lament-like measure]. This Dream Song tells: "You do not know your name is picture painted. [Meaning that their names were to be recorded in some way, as, now, at Washington, D.C.]. Be a great change in life's living."

Another Dream Song revealed what might be termed political, or governmental troubles falling on the chiefs, headmen, and leaders.

"All you chiefs! You are confused and troubled! Vexed, dissatisfied and disagreeing, you find no resting place."

---

12 *Ibid.* p. 25.

[Pausing a moment in deep meditation, the dispenser of oracular lore chanted a sorrowful refrain, and continued]. That Dream Song gave warning: "All people, and animals! Creation as existing to be overthrown, destroyed! Buffaloes exterminated! Elk and deer fenced, confined. Eagles caged from flying! Indians confined to narrowed bodies of land. Liberty and happiness broken and shortened."

[Chanting a low, dirgelike measure, the interpretation was solemnly continued.]

That Dream Song was foretelling of the tearing of the Earth's surface. The ripping open of the Mother's bosom where life lies hidden.

[The chant was now more of a wail, as Many Wounds concluded].

Rough places, crooked places of Nature's beauty, some one will smooth and straighten. Flowers looking upward will no longer bloom. Forests will melt away, game disappearing. Rivers to be held back and lessened. Salmon no longer plentiful for the tribes. You ask why the Nez Perces did not tell this when the white man first came? It was then old. It was to be! The telling to the white man could not have stopped it.

The chanter ceased, and, turning away, stood gazing meditatively at a most gorgeous autumnal sunset. An endeavor to probe further into hidden tenets of the Dreamer faith brought the terse, though faintly smiling reply, "I think being honest is the best religion!"

The uncharitable branding of the Dreamer faith as "dirty heathenism,"[13] and the hypocrisy so manifest on the part of many of the Christians themselves, proved a bar to the more rapid absorption of Christianity by the Indians. Condemnation by the clergy, of Dreamer practices that were in line with Biblical records, often proved a thorn to the critic and proselyter. On this score, Many Wounds, proud of his an-

---

13 McBeth, *The Nez Perces Since Lewis and Clark*, p. 75.

cestral lineage, told the writer the following amusing incident. "Not long ago two preachers—I recognized their profession by their clothes and their speech— stepped up to me and one of them asked, not very politely, 'Is it true that your grandfather had eight wives?' 'Yes,' I answered, 'but King Solomon had seven hundred.' He shut his mouth."[14]

The Indian of today has also felt the impact of ecclesiastic intolerance under the garb of Christian civilization. They well remember the mandate of the twenties wherein the tribal or native dancing was to be discontinued on pain of drastic consequences. The writer recalls how the Yakimas came to him in their distress, when their ancient worship and pleasure dancing had been banned by bureau mandate. Being advised to disregard such absurdly unreasonable tyranny, they did so without serious consequences. Major Jay Lynch, head agent of the Yakima agency, had departmental orders to cut the hair of the Dreamer element, but he discarded the tyrannical edict. One of the agency's officials declared to me: "It is the object of the Indian Department to break the Indians away from the tribal customs of every kind and nature, including root digging and their so-called native arts. Their religious views and ceremonies tend to keep them from taking up the white man's customs."

A paramount characteristic of the Dreamer religion is the devout care bestowed on the hair, which is not to be profaned by cropping other than to shape a foretop pompadour. Spirit visions are invariably depicted with a superabundance of wondrous flowing hair, often of a golden-yellowish tinge. The treat-

---

[14] Many Wounds had an expressive way of demonstrating the "mouth shutting" feature when narrating such stories, by covering his own lips with his finger tips.

ment accorded the hair in this life affects the life beyond the grave. The missionaries and their successors insisted that converts undergo a hair-clipping as an essential adjunct to their acceptance of the new faith. Discussing this obtuse requirement with a half-blood Nez Perce, he solemnly declared, "If hair keeps people out of heaven, God would have created man baldheaded!"

It does not do credit to our country's honor that more than one and a half centuries elapsed before there was any recognition of the Indian right to worship God after the dictates of his own conscience, as constitutionally guaranteed. Finally the Indian's rights were recognized during the administration of Indian Commissioner John Collier, who writes:

The date of my "manifest recognition" of the native Indian religions would be I suppose, about 1922, when we commenced the struggle for religious and cultural freedom. The battle went on until I became Commissioner and at that time I formulated the orders, endorsed by Secretary Ickes, establishing complete liberty of native religion. I should be glad to know more about the harassment of the Nez Perce and about their "dreamer" doctrine.[15]

---

[15] Letter, John Collier to L. V. McWhorter, June 1, 1942.

CHAPTER VI

THE WAR-CREATING COUNCIL OF 1855

AT A JOINT COUNCIL HELD AT WALLA WALLA, JUNE 1855, three major Indian reservations were created. Named in the order of their founding, they were the Umatilla, the Yakima and the Nez Perce. The government was represented by Isaac I. Stevens, governor and Indian superintendent of Washington Territory, and General Joel Palmer, Indian superintendent of Oregon Territory.

In his speech formally opening the council, Governor Stevens elaborated on the benevolence of the government in its dealings with the Indians. He dwelt on the tender solicitude of the "Great Father" for the welfare and happiness of his "Red Children." He told how the tribes beyond the mountains had made treaties and that the name of the "Great Father" at the time was Andrew Jackson who said: "I will take the red man across a great river into a fine country where I can take care of them."[1]

Had this sanguine treaty-maker combed the annals he could not have unearthed for a model a greater travesty on just and honorable dealing. The Governor drew a thrilling picture of how these Indians, the Cherokees, by then established in their new country for twenty years had their "own government,

---

[1] "Proceedings at the Council held at Camp Stevens, Walla Walla Valley, May 30, 1855." Typescript copy in McW NP 48, p. 16, referred to hereafter as "Proceedings."

their own schools, their own laws." He told what a smart man was "their chief John Ross," comparing him intellectually with himself and General Palmer. He explained that Ross was a Cherokee Indian,[2] a lawyer, and how, when he goes to Washington "to see the Great Father, the President, he sits with him at table as you sit with us at table. . . ." He told how John Ross and his people were given "a tract of land into which no white man could go without their consent. . . I repeat again, no white man can go there unless the red man consents to it."[3] A flowery picture was painted of the "Great Father's tender solicitude for his red children, the Cherokees, how he had removed them, so as to protect them always from bad white men."[4]

Charity would suggest that Governor Stevens was sincerely honest in his depiction of the Cherokee removal under the New Echots Treaty, signed in Georgia, December 29, 1835, but reason is against such a deduction. The Governor could hardly be guilty of such ignorance. President Jackson was a national figure, indeed international, and his venomous hatred for the Indians was both open and viciously indulged. Our southern-border annals are full of accounts of oppressions with which he had to do.[5] Suffice it to say that the coveted Cherokee do-

---

[2] John Ross, chief of the Cherokees, was born in Rossville, Georgia, October 3, 1790. He died in Washington, August 1, 1866. His father was a Scotch immigrant, his mother a quarter-blood Cherokee. (Hodge, *Handbook of American Indians*, Pt. II, p. 396.) He was not made chief of the Cherokees until after that nation's removal to Indian Territory. His name does not appear as a signer of the Treaty of New Echots, December 29, 1835.

[3] The above summary is from the "Proceedings," May 30, 1855, p. 16.

[4] *Ibid.*, p. 17.

[5] Consult Thomas L. McKenney, *Memoirs Official and Personal*, (New York, 1846) I; Joshua Giddings, *Exiles of Florida*, (Columbus, Ohio, 1858); Helen Hunt Jackson, *A Century of Dishonor*, (Boston, 1887).

main, exceeding in size Connecticut, Rhode Island, and Massachusetts, was pirated from them under the mandate of the originator, in the United States, of the system of, "To the victor belongs the spoils."

Governor Stevens could also have informed the Walla Walla assembly of President Jackson's solicitous care of the hapless Shawnees. These Indians had a reservation in Allen County, Ohio, improved with comfortable homes and a gristmill, the latter built by Quaker missionaries. The whites coveted this reservation, so a special commissioner was appointed, in the person of James B. Gardener, an unscrupulous, drunken reprobate, who with John McElvain, Indian agent for the Indians resident in Ohio (consisting of Wyandots, Senecas, and Shawnees), was to conclude a treaty with the Shawnees. Gardener drank a special brand of whisky, was a long-winded speaker, and a most proficient prevaricator. This emissary of evil succeeded in obtaining signatures of the Shawnee chiefs and headmen to a treaty of fourteen articles, without its being read and explained to them. This shameful document was concluded at Wapakoneta, August 8, 1831, and proclaimed eight months later.

Afterwards a delegation of the Shawnee chiefs and headmen, accompanied by their missionary, Henry Harvey, went to Washington, petitioning that the Gardener Treaty be set aside and a new one drawn up, but to no purpose. President Jackson refused to see the delegation, "declaring that the Shawnees should fare no better than the Cherokees did."[6] With drunken, dishonest officials supporting the padded claims of thieving traders against the Shawnees for trumped-up indebtedness (deducted from the money received for their improvements), they landed in the

---

[6] Henry Harvey, *History of the Shawnee Indians*, (Cincinnati, 1855, p. 189).

West impoverished and with many broken in health.

In Article X of the Wapakoneta Treaty we read: ". . . and the United States guaranteed that the said lands shall never be within the bounds of any State or territory, not subject to the laws thereof. . . ."[7]

Where are the Shawnees today?

Judging from Governor Stevens' war-kindling treaties, and his subsequent declaration of relentless extermination for the patriotic tribesmen of Puget Sound who dared lift the hatchet against the usurpers of their homes, he knew well that he was following the model of President Andrew Jackson.[8]

Even a casual study of the various treaties conducted by Governor Stevens with the Pacific Northwest tribes discloses the same covert methods employed so frequently in the Indian treaty-making history of the United States. Deception and chicanery appear to be the accepted procedure. The Indian had no voice in treaty formation. "Made in Washington," the same edition answered for widely separated tribes and linguistic families with names and locations to be written in. No changes were made in the format. No leeway was given the Indian. At the command of the masters, he made his mark on the dotted line, or if he refused, it was done for him.[9]

---

[7] Charles Kappler, *Indian Affairs: Laws and Treaties*, (Washington, 1904), II, 885.

[8] In Ezra Meeker's memoirs we read, "In the Journal of the House of Representatives of the Territorial Legislature for the session 1855-56 is published a message signed 'Isaac I. Stevens, Governor and Supt. Ind. Affs. Wash. Ty.' in which the following remarkable sentence is found (p. 155) 'I am opposed to any treaties, I shall oppose any treaty with these hostile bands. I will protest against any and all treaties made with them;—nothing but death is a mete punishment for their perfidy—their lives should pay the forfeit.' "

". . . The reservation set aside for these Indians was less than four acres a head; land so heavily timbered that there was no room for pitching a lodge, land if cleared, unfit for cultivation." (Meeker, *Pioneer Reminiscences of Puget Sound*, (Seattle, 1905), p. 342, p. 268.)

[9] The name Leschi, a later-day martyr, appears third in the list of Indian signers to the Medicine Creek treaty, while Meeker shows con-

Ratified by Congress, the treaty became law. Law recreant to its every trust! Law complacent to violation by its own minions! Law that laughed at justice! Law ruled by souless, mammonized greed! Law that was lawless!

In all Governor Stevens' treaty councils, the Indians claim that there were promises and assurances made that do not appear in the body of the official treaty. The late Rev. Stwire G. Waters, chief of the Yakimas, declared to the writer:

clusively that Leschi in a rage, tore up his commission as chief which the Governor had given him, did this in the Governor's presence, and left the council grounds a day before the treaty was signed. (Meeker, *op. cit.*, p. 236, p. 242, p. 255.) Another writer says, "Leschi's name was forged into this important document. Other names to other treaties were forged. Boys ten and twelve years of age, acted as witnesses to the treaties." ("Building a State" (Washington State Historical Society, Tacoma, 1941), p. 493.) The name of Governor Stevens' son, Hazard, a lad of twelve years, appears as a witness to the Medicine Creek Treaty.

Chief Kamiakun, named "Head Chief" of the Yakimas by Governor Stevens, always claimed that he was deeply wronged in the Walla Walla Treaty, declaring that he had signed no papers for Governor Stevens. Neither had his brother, Skloom, nor his brother-in-law, Chief Owhi, who with him made up the first three in the list of fourteen. This trio of prominent leaders held out to the very last against signing the treaty, but finally, so the story goes, in a *pledge of friendship only*, as they understood, each in turn "touched" a little stick as it made a little mark. Kamiakun was named as "Head Chief" of the Yakimas, by Governor Stevens. Thus were the signatures of the three leading Yakima chiefs affixed to a treaty to which they had never agreed. Moreover, the journal of the council proceedings for June 9, ends with this telltale entry, "Kamiakun was present at the General Council during the day but did not speak; and in the evening immediately after the adjournment of the Council he called upon Governor Stevens for the Treaty and signed it. Owhi and Skloom did the same, as also the Palouse Chief Kahlatoose, and all the Chiefs present, named by Kamiakun as being under his jurisdiction. Several of the bands at Dalles and above, who were in attendance during the first days of the Council, had returned home to catch their usual supply of Salmon, these, Kamiakun said, as also all that he had named would sign the Treaty whenever it was presented to them if Governor Stevens thought it necessary." Comment seems futile, but since there is no record or even a tradition that the treaty was ever presented to the several absentee chiefs, and yet their names are found duly attached to the treaty, what can one infer but that they were written-in without their knowledge? Fifteen years later (1870) the government attempted to deliver six hundred blankets to Chief Kamiakun, as annuities due the head chief of the Yakimas. Although in penury and rags, he proudly disdained acceptance of the goods, declaring, "I never signed that treaty!"

At a treaty on the west side of the Cascade Mountains, [Medicine Creek] I saw Governor Stevens stand with hand uplifted just like a preacher and tell the Indians, "So long as Mount Rainier stands! So long as water runs down to the ocean! So long as the sun travels across the sky shall this reservation belong to the Indians, and no white man shall be allowed on it."[10]

The Yakimas contended that they were given this same extravagant assurance at the Walla Walla Treaty, and the Nez Perces affirmed that they were promised "a wagon load of gold as much as six mules could pull over level ground," if only they would sign the treaty. Unscrupulous promises destined to cost the Indians dearly were handed out in profusion.

LOOKING GLASS [the Nez Perce chief] : I want to know if an Agent will stay up in my country?

GOVERNOR STEVENS: As long as there are people.

LOOKING GLASS: Will the Agent be there that long to keep the whites from pushing into our country?

GENERAL PALMER: None will be permitted to go there but the Agent and the persons employed, without your consent.[11]

Both Governor Stevens and General Palmer must have known, from the scrapping of more than a hundred prior treaties, that their promises were not to be kept or honored by the government. The Indians had just cause for mistrusting the sincerity

---

[10] At the Medicine Creek Treaty with the Nesqualli, Puyallup and kindred tribes, signed December 28, 1854, the council's oral proceedings were not rendered into any of the Indian tongues. The uncouth and elastic Chinook jargon, consisting of not more than three hundred words, formed the sole medium of communication. When the treaty copy was handed Colonel B. F. Shaw, interpreter with the query, could he get the Indians to sign it, he replied, "Yes, I can get the Indians to sign their death warrant." (Meeker, *op. cit.*, pp. 250-51.)

After the Indian wars of 1855-56, which were traceable indirectly if not directly to Governor Stevens' treaty-making trip, the jargon-negotiated treaty of Medicine Creek was discarded, and the Indians given lands adapted to home building.

[11] "Proceedings," June 8, 1855, p. 48.

of the white man's pretensions. On this score Eagle From the Light had previously spoken at some length, saying among other things,

"A preacher came to us, Mr. Spalding. He talked to us to learn, and from that he turned to be a trader, as though there were two in one, one a preacher and the other a trader. He made a farm and raised grain and bought our stock, as though there were two in one; one a preacher the other a trader.

And now from the East has spoken and I have heard it. I do not wish another preacher to come and be both trader and preacher in one. A piece of ground for a preacher, big enough for his own use, is all that is necessary for him."[12]

The urge was to get the Indians to accede to the reservations as laid out, and Governor Stevens, following Chief Eagle From the Light, said, in part:

"Though near the great roads, you are a little off from them, and you will not be liable to be troubled by travellers passing through.

"We can better protect you from bad white men there. We can better prevent the trader and the preacher all in one man going there. We can better prevent bad men telling you to dance, and cheating you with lies. We can better stop the thief who comes to steal your horses. Your horses will be saved to you and there will be no thieves to throw in to the hell-fire."[13]

Chief Looking Glass was the leading opponent of the reservation boundary as agreed to by Lawyer before the former chief's return from the buffalo country. Looking Glass arrived at Walla Walla June 9, ten days after the treaty council had convened and when negotiations were almost completed.[14] Look-

---

[12] *Ibid.*, June 4, 1855, p. 30.

[13] *Ibid.*, June 4, 1855, p. 31.

[14] Of the belated arrival of Chief Looking Glass's contingent on the council ground, Camille Williams writes, "These people came over the [later] Mullan's Road, the only pass then open. Among

ing Glass was of the Dreamer faction, believing that
the earth was only loaned, was to dwell upon during
life, and should not be profaned by barter. On the
other hand Chief Lawyer and his followers were
Christians and strongly pro-white. As recently as
the day before the convening of the council, the
Lawyer faction had refused to join the Cayuse and
the Walla Walla chief, Peopeo Moxmox[15] and Chief
Kamiakun of the Yakimas in a general council.[16]

This rebuff was naturally resented by the tribes re-
questing the council, as the sequel disclosed. Governor Stevens makes no mention of the story which
tells how Chief Lawyer in the darkness of the following night moved his lodge and family well within the
bounds of the white camp. In later years this secret
shift of campsite by the leading Nez Perce chief has
been classed as a piece of great heroism. He is pictured as seeking the Governor after nightfall and
apprising him of the discovery of a Cayuse plot to
fall upon and massacre the Governor's entire company. Lawyer is quoted as saying,

---

them were three elderly men of moment. Chief Cloud Piler and his
scout, Wetyetmas Ilppilp, Apis Wahykt [Flint Necklace], and Kolkol
Nenne. These two chiefs signed the treaty, the last name appearing as
Koolkool Tilki of the Clearwater band. Flint Necklace, while not identified on the published list, signed as head of the Asotin band. He was the
father of the later Looking Glass of history.

"When Flint Necklace saw Governor Stevens, noting his diminutive
size, he became furiously mad. Riding so far to see and listen to his
talk or lies! He proceeded to relieve his mind to the Governor in a
manner not at all complimentary to that dignitary's individuality,
which, however, was not understood, or adroitly concealed by the
diplomatic interpreter.

"Chief Cloud Piler was of the Pekonan, or Snake River band, to
which later the renowned Chief Toohoolhoolzote of history became
the head. Piling Clouds refused to sign away his domain, nor did his
scout, Red Swan, cast a vote."

[15] Peopeo Moxmox, "Yellow Bird," wrongfully interpreted "Yellow
Serpent," noted chief of the Walla Wallas, was foully murdered by
troops while being held an unarmed hostage.

[16] "Proceedings," May 28, 1855, p. 11.

"I will come with my family and pitch my lodge in the midst of your camp that those Cayuses may see that you and your party are under the protection of the head chief of the Nez Perces." He did so immediately, although it was now after midnight, and without awakening the suspicions of anyone, he caused it to be reported among the other Indians that the commissioners were under the protection of the Nez Perces.[17]

This course of action reputed to one of Chief Lawyer's standing casts a cloud of doubt over the story. Warrior that he was, had such an attack been indicated, all known facts of Indian behavior would suggest that shifting his family to the very point of intended attack would have been most foreign to his mind. Reputable Nez Perces scoffed at this claim of intended violence on the part of the accused tribes. One of these, a Carlisle graduate, declared to the writer, "Lawyer moved into the white camp to save his own hide. No such plotting existed among the tribes so accused. Lawyer became scared." That Governor Stevens makes no mention of so momentous an event in his account of the council proceedings, certainly throws considerable doubt on the authenticity of the tale.

While it is true that the three tribes in question, along with the Salmon River Nez Perces, refused to accept tobacco and provisions at the opening of the council,[18] this must be viewed solely as a precautionary measure on their part, rather than any declaration of hostility. It was wise not to embarrass themselves with hasty or premature pledges of friendship before they knew the direction of the proposed trail.

---

[17] Hazard Stevens, *The Life of Isaac Ingalls Stevens*, (New York, 1901), II, 47. Quotation by permission of the Houghton Mifflin Co. The author seemingly overlooked the fact that Lawyer had not yet been proclaimed head chief when this occurred.

[18] Letter, Isaac Stevens and Joel Palmer to George W. Manypenny, June 13, 1855, typescript copy, McW NP 48, p. 6.

But that the blunt refusal of the Nez Perce leader to join the other tribes in council, induced friction is amply implied in the curt speech of Five Crows of the Cayuses on the eighth day of the council. This young leader rose and challenged pointedly. "Listen to me you chiefs! We have been as one people with the Nez Perces heretofore; this day we are divided. We, the Cayuses, Walla Wallas, and Kam-a-ah-kans people and others will think over the matter tonight and give you an answer tomorrow."[19]

This speech alone should halt for all time the claim of near massacre and martyrdom which now hallows the memory of the Walla Walla treaty commission, and which historians have been quick to accept at face value.[20] The Yakimas hold not so much as a tradition of any such plot.

The journal for the last day of the Nez Perce council, June 1, contains the following entry,

TINTINMEETSEE: (speaking) "I understand you well. We are never the beginners in doing wrong to the whites. All Indians here understand well what has been said. When your white children come into this country they do things at random. (To the Indians) You have heard all that has been said and now let us go home and do right."[21]

---

[19] "Proceedings," June 7, 1855, p. 42.

[20] For example, George W. Fuller suggests that Lawyer, in moving his tepee, placed himself where he would be killed in a fight; and the plotters dared not act, fearing the Nez Perces would turn on them should Lawyer be killed. (Fuller, *History of the Pacific Northwest*, (New York, 1931) v. 2, p. 47, p. 48, p. 60.)

[21] "Proceedings," June 11, 1855, p. 54. Interpreter Williams [War Singer] says of this orator, "Tintin Mechez is Selish, a Flathead name and he was a quarter-blood of that tribe. A stockman he had cattle and horses, and settled on the Umatilla Reservation where he later died. He was not a chief." For a geographic distribution of the Nez Perce chiefs at the time of the 1855 Treaty as defined by the older members of the tribe, see Appendix IX, pp. 608-10.

CHAPTER VII

THE CRIME OF 1863

THE TREATIES OF WALLA WALLA USHERED IN A PERIOD fraught with developments culminating in an unhallowed war and the ultimate undoing of the Dreamer Nez Perces. The document presented to the Indians in June of 1855, was finally ratified March 8, 1859, and proclaimed the following April 29. But the order thus established was not to last for long. Just ahead were momentous events, precursory to woe, looming on the Dreamer horizon.

Gold is Discovered

In August, 1860, Captain Elias D. Pierce, experienced in both British and California mining, with a small company of prospectors, attempted an invasion of the upper Clearwater region in quest of rumored placer gold. They were twice turned back by the vigilant Nez Perce vedette, or mounted-scout patrol, enforcing their tribe's treaty rights. After being sternly warned that drastic measures would be taken if he was again caught trespassing, Captain Pierce, under cover of nightfall, sought the aid of the friendly Christian, Chief Timothy.[1]

Captain Pierce explained where he wished to go and why. He asked if there was not another route by

---

[1] Byron Defenbach, *Red Heroines of the Northwest*, (Caldwell, 1929), p. 259.

which the region might be reached, one free of Indian guards. Yes, the Chief knew of such a way but it was far and circuitous, and in places the trail was so dim and intricate that only with the best of guides could the journey be accomplished. In any case, a guide could not be considered, so watchful were the Indians. But this dilemma was solved by Timothy's eighteen-year-old daughter, Jane, who volunteered to pilot the interlopers to their coveted goal, a betrayal to be many times repeated in the difficult days of 1877. The trip was accomplished and free gold was discovered on a tributary of the Clearwater, later mapped as "Oro Fino Creek."[2] Here was the beacon destined to bring gold-mad prospectors swarming into the Nez Perce Reservation.

Pierce hurried to Walla Walla. A company of thirty-three armed men were organized for the purpose of returning and establishing a mining camp at the new gold site. Notwithstanding the solemn treaty pledges to enforce the reservation boundaries, this move was unopposed by the military. On this score Bancroft says, "The party was followed as far as the Snake River by a detachment of dragoons whose duty it was to prevent their entrance on the reservation, but who failed to execute it."[3]

Pierce had hardly reached his camp on the Clearwater "before he received a visit from A. J. Cain, the Nez Perce Indian agent, who did not find it necessary to interfere with the party, but on the contrary expressed himself as pleased with their behavior...."[4]

Following these indictments, Bancroft gives a de-

---

2 *Ibid.*, pp. 259-63.

3 Bancroft's *History of Washington, Idaho, and Montana* (San Francisco, 1890), XXXI, 235.

4 Bancroft, *op. cit.*, pp. 235-36.

piction of how Superintendent of Indian Affairs E. R. Geary, conferring with Colonel Wright "in reference to the threatened complications in Indian matters," consequent on continued invasion of the reservation the following spring by ever-increasing parties of miners ". . . repaired to the upper country, held a council, and made a treaty with the Indians to meet the exigencies of the coming mining excitement, promising them military protection, and the enforcement of the United States laws—a compact of necessity rather than a choice of the natives."[5]

Of this consequence of the 1860 gold discovery, we also read that the Nez Perce Reservation was

> . . . soon overrun with settlers rushing to the mines, and to avoid a conflict between them and the Indians an agreement was entered into but not confirmed by Congress, on the 19th of April, 1861, between Superintendent Geary and Agent Cain on the one part, and Chief Lawyer and forty-seven chiefs, head men, and delegates on the other part, whereby that portion of the reserve lying north of the Snake and Clearwater Rivers, the South Fork of the Clearwater, and the trail from the said South Fork by the "Weipo root ground" across the Bitter Root Mountains, was open to the whites in common with the Indians for mining purposes. . . In defiance of law and despite the protestations of the Indian Agent, a town-site was laid off in October, 1861, on the reservation, and Lewiston, with a population of twelve hundred, sprang into existence. . . To this and other grievances was added, in the distribution of annuities, articles being supplied in inadequate quantities. In 1862, only 247 blankets were furnished the tribe, or one blanket to six Indians, and 4,396 yards of calico, which was less than two yards to each Indian . . . yet this was all that could be distributed owing to the meagre appropriations allowed.[6]

---

[5] *Ibid.*, p. 238.

[6] *Report of the Commissioner of Indian Affairs*, 1877, pp. 9-10.

As to the laying-out of the Lewiston townsite, Bancroft states that not only was it done with the consent of Lawyer and his headmen, but that they received some compensation for their reasonable attitude.[7] Judging from the craven welcome Agent Cain gave to Captain Pierce and his interlopers at the Oro Fino placers and his part in formulating an agreement with Chief Lawyer and associates whereby a vast gold-bearing domain of the reservation was thrown open to the whites in common with the Indians for mining purposes, it is easy to imagine what the nature of his protests against laying out a townsite must have been. Ugly rumors were rife without contradiction and logical deduction points an accusing finger.

It is surely significant that nowhere is there found any provision for royalties, or a percentage of the gold mined, to be awarded to the Nez Perces. This together with the "compensation" previously alluded to in connection with Chief Lawyer and other headmen in the laying-out of the Lewiston townsite, makes the following story which was rife, with not a syllable of repudiation, apropos.

The legend says that Paukalah, returning from Alpowa late at night and reaching the mouth of Lapwai Creek, caught a glint of light at the window of the Indian agency office and dismounted to see what it meant. The door was not locked, and entering he saw that the windows were covered with blankets, and at a table, on which was a pile of gold coin, sat the agent and interpreter with Chief Lawyer and a few other headmen. Lawyer immediately handed him a twenty-dollar gold piece with the admonition, "Take this one piece and go about your business!

---

[7] Bancroft, *op. cit.*, p. 238.

Original Lapwai Indian agency, which has now been transferred to Spalding, Idaho

Courtesy Camille Williams

INDIANS WHO NEGOTIATED THE TREATY OF 1868

Seated, Timothy, Lawyer, and Jason. The standing white men are unidentified. These Nez Perces, together with Utsinmalikhin, who died under mysterious circumstances in Washington, D.C. before this picture was taken, there negotiated the treaty of 1868 which was now engrossed

Indian Agent J. B. Monteith standing; seated, left to right: James Reuben, Archie Lawyer, and Mark Billy, young Nez Prece Christian converts educated at the Spalding Mission. Archie Lawyer was later sent to Indian Territory by the government, where he served as minister to the Nez Perces held there in captivity.

Speak no word of what you see here!"[8] Paukalah, deeming it safer to do as told, hurried away, and aside from confiding to his wife how he came by the money, kept silent. But in time the transaction became known to others. Paukalah was reputed a truthful man, and later became an ardent member of the Presbyterian Church.

Naturally the Dreamer Nez Perces associated this midnight conclave around the gold-laden table with the spoils of the treaty, but they believed that the bribe money was furnished by miners and other interests rather than the government, although with the full knowledge and connivance of its officials.

In later years other stories were afloat disparaging to Chief Lawyer's honor as a leader. There were open rumors of clandestine visits to the agency warehouse with favored individuals who were secretly supplied with clothing and blankets. In the ring were Felix Corbit, as he himself admitted, and Joe Craig, half-blood son of William Craig, confidential interpreter working with Lawyer who had once declared, "The Indians are ignorant and easily cheated!"[9] In after years a metal vessel, or pot containing a goodly sum of greenbacks and gold coin was ploughed up on

---

[8] The venerable John Allen, Nez Perce, renowned for his accuracy as a tribal genealogist said that Chief Lawyer was not a full-blood Nez Perce, that his father, Sahayah, was born and grew up in Montana, and was of the Selish or Flathead tribe. This belief was echoed by Toolitlo and others of the older tribesmen. However, there are those who contend that Sahayah was only half Selish. He was known as Black Bear, so dubbed from his wearing a black-bear skin as a blanket in lieu of a buffalo robe. Of the tragic death of Lawyer's father, Interpreter Williams [War Singer] writes: "Old Man Sahayah, the name appears Siouan, was drowned along with his daughter and niece in the Selway River when their raft was carried over the Selway Falls. The bodies of the two girls were never recovered, but that of Sahayah was found between Kamiah and Kooskia. He was a large, fleshy man and was dragged a short way from the river and buried. When the railroad was being constructed, his skeleton was unearthed by the workmen."

[9] Craig's boast was overheard by Henry Powakee, who, in 1928, was still living at Lapwai.

Lapwai Creek a short distance above the mouth of Bell Creek by a white laborer. Some thought it had been buried by the interpreter, Reboin, and accumulated during his incumbency. He lived some distance down the creek from where the trove was unearthed. Of it Interpreter Williams writes: "Many believed that the find belonged to an old man who had lived on the grounds and admitted that he saved money for his grandson. But the boy died and the grandfather never told anyone where it was buried, and the secret went with him to the grave."

Before the close of 1862, where the city of Lewiston now stands at the junction of the Clearwater and the Snake, a steamboat landing had been built and a tented population of twelve hundred adventurers had gathered. Armed bands of prospectors roamed at will. The amount of gold taken from Indian lands can never be accurately computed.[10]

Protests against this intolerable situation were made by the Nez Perces to their agency. The response was the construction of Fort Lapwai and the stationing there of a garrison of United States troops, ostensibly to keep law and order; but as events proved, with the actual function of intimidation, and suppression of any attempt by the Nez Perces at defense of their justly claimed domain. In other words the United States soldiers were brought to protect trespassing miners in their lawless looting. A weak people, the spiked heel of oppression on their neck, felt the mailed hand of despotism smothering their cry for justice. Surely the assurances Governor Stevens and General Palmer had given them seven years before, and Agent Geary's later promise of "military pro-

---

[10] By one estimate, the value of this gold was about $57,000,000. (*Geology and Gold*, Bulletin No. 7, University of Idaho School of Mines, p. 13).

tection and the enforcement of the United States laws," were meeting with a reception which the trio well knew to be inevitable.[11] Witness the treatment of every treaty the United States had ever made with the native Americans.

Almost simultaneously with the gold-seeker's rush into the mountainous regions of the Nez Perce reservation, white settlers invaded the beautiful Wallowa Valley, long a Nez Perce habitat and conceded as part of the domain of Old Chief Joseph in the treaty. All pleas for justice proved unavailing.

No attempt was made to clear the Indian domain of white interlopers. To do so would entail great cost to the government and the loss of prestige and votes to state and territorial politicians. There was an easier, more effective way of clarifying the situation. Following long-established precedent, a *new treaty* would be inaugurated. True, objections by the rightful owners could be expected. But the way was clear for a successful, if not altogether legitimate, transfer of title. The Nez Perce lands now coveted, both mineral and agricultural, belonged in large measure to the "long hairs" or Dreamers, already separated from their Christian tribesmen by a deep element of discord. The Christians constituted a strong majority, estimated at two-thirds of the entire tribe, which fact was all the more favorable to the baneful plan of the despoilers. No one would mind rebuking the sinful Dreamers.

At this point it seems appropriate to look briefly at the Nez Perce leaders who aided the whites during these difficult days. What of Captain Pierce's right-hand aid in his historic gold discovery, Chief Timothy, at whose fireside was molded the wedge destined to cleave not only the Nez Perce reservation but the

---

[11] Bancroft, *op. cit.*, p. 236.

called the treaty legal. These districts were considered same as counties of today, as each county has no jurisdiction over the other, that was the reason each district had its own chief.

This was legal to the Indians. Even today, pleas of justice are denied from Commissioner of Washington, D.C. They make no attempt to investigate the agency office, when informed of graft by government employees. Just as 1863 treaty, the reservation boundary lines were surveyed by soldiers, that same year. So gold was stolen from the Indian for about three years.

The Treaty of 1863

As touched upon previously, the great Nez Perce tribe, when first contacted by the whites, consisted of numerous bands each with its own chief and counselors. War parties and hunting expeditions were headed by chiefs or leaders chosen for the occasion. While the chieftancy was hereditary, subject to a recognized standard of qualifications, this honor was also attained through prowess and daring in forays and battle. There were no clans, no fraternities. Although they would amalgamate for mutual protection or common cause against an enemy tribe, these several bands recognized no supreme or central head, no one-man ruler. Their form of government, simple throughout, was adequate for their needs, and seemed to have been predicted on the rudiments of "states rights," which was also true of kindred tribes. This system was not interfered with by Hudson's Bay Company's post governors.

The Nez Perces were inveigled into adopting a centralized government by Dr. Elijah White, whose outstanding contribution was the adoption of the principle of the head chief. Here was the beginning of disintegration, but the second, and more decisive, bolt was driven on June 11, 1855, when Governor

this instrument was the
H. Spalding, who had bu
Willamette where he fled
disaster. He could not r
and thigh" the hated Dre
chiefs and "head men" w
longed to the Christian e
two, who had been trapp
sionary contingent the D
conpensated for the loss
and spiritual benefits to
tact with Christian eleme

The antipathy betwee
Perces which the treaty
abated. The Dreamers,
homes, may well be rec
for umbrage; but not so
party to the crime. Bu
heavily on this unclerical
cessantly underlined by
has been a factor in keep
social hatred engendere
last as long as there rem
Unfortunately the new
one another," has found
sionary's teaching.

As the grisly Waiilatp
to Doctor Whitman's c
and disregard of the C
which had probably bee

17 See McWhorter, *Yellow Wol*
H. Clay Wood's *Supplementary*
of Young Joseph and his Band o
p. 6, Hohots Stortee, there sp
the 1863 treaty, where "chiefs
but he himself was opposed to
ceived into permitting the use
forgery.

Stevens steered and secured the appointment or election of the famous orator and Christian, Lawyer, to succeed the spirit-broken and diseased head chief, Ellis, of mission fame. These were the two wedges destined to completely divide a people who, for centuries, had flourished as one people, amid the onslaughts of bordering warlike tribes. The culminating blow was the treaty of 1863, the nucleus about which the storm gathered for a sanguinary explosion fourteen years later, almost to the day.

In territorial Idaho, but newly born, chaos was in the saddle and stabilization was destined to be attained largely through intrigue and force. The gold-sprinkled mountains, the grass-carpeted valleys, birthright of the Dreamer Nez Perces, duly confirmed by solemn treaty compact, were now to be had for the taking, with legalization assured through governmental chicanery.

The plot to dispossess the Dreamers of their homes and holdings was rapidly taking form. A new treaty, a piece of hijacking almost unequalled in a century of Indian treaty-making, was being hatched. Of the need for the negotiation of this treaty, E. A. Hayt, Commissioner of Indian Affairs at the time of the war, writes:

By the spring of 1863 it was very evident that, from the change of circumstances and contact with the whites, a new treaty was required to properly define, and, if possible, curtail the limits of the reserve. Accordingly, on the 9th of June, 1863, Calvin H. Hale, Charles Hutchins, and S. D. How, Commissioners on the part of the United States, and Chief Lawyer, whose opinion Governor Stevens held in higher esteem than of any other Indian in the Territory, with fifty other chiefs and head men (twenty of whom were parties to the treaty of 1855) on the part of the Nez Perces, made a new treaty, whereby the reserve was reduced to its present limits, excluding the Wallowa, Salmon River. After

the conclusions
divided into tw
and the non-tr
Joseph, Lookin
Light.[14] Chief
treaty of 1863
where they wer
until the encro
ernment to take
non-treaty Nez

We shall no
treaty, a trave
that for the n
wrested from
prominent in
homes were n

___

[14] Neither Looki
at the time of thi
fell upon the two s

[15] *Report of the*

[16] [The Nez Per
title by the Nez I
included within th
required to move
date of ratificatio
any lands they t
forced to vacate
could be sold to a
tillable acreage on
residue of the lan
allotment. The tr
claims, over half
to the reservation,
annual installmen
to be paid them i
Other monies were
hospital, blacksmit
of which appropri
of the Treaty of
vation for the use
rights were secur
mitted the United
Affairs: Laws an
It is obvious th
buildings, salaries,
whose lands were
Therein lay the sw

ding's hot-tempered arrogance against the Dreamer element can be credited with sowing the seeds of hatred within the Nez Perce tribe. This was taken advantage of by the gold-and-land pirates of 1863, when they were able to align the Christian Nez Perces as allies in one of the most stupendous of governmental plunderings since the case of the hapless Cherokees. The spiritual ardor that had prompted the coming of the divines to the far Oregon country had waned, swept aside by the desire for colonization and the temptations of personal mercenary aggrandizement. Within a twelvemonth of the gold find on the Clearwater tributary by Pierce and associates, we find Rev. Spalding organizing a select party of three to join the rush to the diggings.[18] A year later (1863) this missionary and two of his friends located land claims on the lower Clearwater within the reservation, and the post commander at Fort Lapwai had the houses dismantled and the logs thrown into the river.[19]

Chief Lawyer, pride bloated by his recognition as head of the Nez Perce nation, seconded by Timothy and others of the Christian faith, lent himself unreservedly to the conspiracy.[20] It should be remembered that Rev. Spalding was appointed government teacher, or superintendent of education on the Nez Perce reservation, in the spring of 1862. Some place his appointment in the fall of that year, and yet because of his bickerings with the Catholics, he was expelled from the reservation,[21] to be reinstated the following

___

[18] Drury, *Henry Harmon Spalding*, p. 374. [About this incident Drury adds, "Nothing has been found to show whether or not these plans materialized. The assumption is they did not." (Ed. note.)]

[19] *Ibid.*, p. 379.

[20] Lawyer was never recognized as head chief by much more than half the tribe.

[21] That peace and harmony might be instilled in the Indian missionary field throughout the United States, President Grant in 1870,

and thereon hangs a bit of h
story of his fate is brief bu
cations:

Those chiefs were not sent
treaty. We had the Treaty of
all had agreed. Then came the
by the Lower Nez Perces only
lands of the Upper Nez Perc
lawfully. It was because of t
Nez Perces through miners an
and overrunning our reservati
all of them signers of the 1863
ton. They were Lawyer, Timot
who traveled around Cape Ho
chiefs very well. Chief Utsinn
warrior.

Nathaniel Taylor or his ager
Jason whisky. Utsinmalihkin
speaker, he refused to sign
against some of its wording
from a high window and kille
when he returned home. White

With a tingle of resentme
concluded,

The government made stron
to the Nez Perces, but its own
lips of our tribe's delegates th;
to a treaty which the people l
worded solely by the white m
murdered because he would no
to be a good man.[27]

The specific provision c
the proposed treaty, where

spring, holding office during the critical treaty period
of 1863. During this time he has been credited with
leading the Nez Perces in spiritual things.[22]

The payment of the purchase money of the 1863
treaty covered a period of sixteen years. The expendi-
ture was "to enable the Indians to remove and locate
upon the reservation, in the ploughing of land, and
the fencing of the several lots" [of twenty acres each]
intended for homes.[23] The trail of official and civilian
swindlers who followed in the wake of this distribution of spoils is indeed murky. A single example will
suffice to show the pattern. James O'Neill, agent
at Lapwai from 1864-68, was able to abscond with
$10,000. No inconsiderable amount of this was
ledgered as salaries for teachers, when there were no
schools.[24]

The Amendments of 1868

A little-known sequel to the treaty of 1863 was the
document, which followed five years later, amending
the former agreement. Divided as the tribe was by
the treaty of June 9, 1863, the breach was further
widened by the amendment treaty of August 13,
1868. It was a treaty of concessions on the part of

---

27 [The editor has searched three
on this story. No mention is made
of the story lies not so much in w
fact that the Upper Nez Perces
undermining their scanty hopes th
by the whites. (Ed. note.)]

by virtue of an act of Congress passed the previous year, parcelled
the Indian r rvations out among the various church denominations,
with exclusive rights thereon. In a few instances two denominations
were permitted on the same reservation, with no trespassing strictly
enforced. This was found necessary to minimize the quarreling
among the different sects, especially between the Catholic and Protestant clergy. So repugnant was this to the Dreamers, that Chief
Joseph scathingly expressed himself as against a religion where
there was "quarreling about God."

22 McBeth, *The Nez Perces Since Lewis and Clark*, p. 65.

23 Kappler, *Laws and Treaties*, II, 845. For exposure of a fence-
building swindle under Nez Perce Agent D. M. Sells, see *Report of
the Commissioner of Indian Affairs*, 1873, p. 159.

24 *House Exec. Document, No. 198*, 42nd Cong. 2nd Session, p. 3.
Agent O'Neill acknowledged his fraudulent activities when investi-
gated.

the Nez Perce d
from the master
a travesty on tl
dealings betweeι

Whereas certai
Perce tribe of Ind
ninth day of June,
are willing to ass
agreed by and bet
on the part of the
and Jason, chiefs ο

The scene of ʈ
It is indeed puz
if any, the Nez
1863 treaty thr
prising the full ʈ
Lawyer, Timotl
member to the Ι

_____

25 Kappler, Laws aι

26 [The three articl
within the boundary
not occupied by the
by the agency, and sο
male over 21] to th
decided by the agent
that if there was iní
residing on the rese
occupied and improv
that the Indians shal
tect the timber on th
of the head chief; aι
1864 and not used ʈ
appropriation and t
of the teachers. (Ka
surely be argued th
government rather t
that no mention haο
States' intention to
boundaries all land
agency buildings anc
1868 agreement, the
But the farcical aspε
concluded with those
the five nontreaty baι

ing outside the reservation as defined in Article Two of the 1863 treaty, "shall be removed to and located on allotments within the reservation," appears to have been the stumbling block that plunged the lofty-minded Utsinmalihkin to his death. It is not certain that Wottolen's story is true, but true it is that the chief faithful to his convictions never returned to his people. Of the same tragedy, Interpreter Williams writes:

All I know of Utsinmalihkin, he was seen lying near a gutter one morning dead. He laid there part of a day when a Women's Club took care of the body and buried him. This is what a Miss Fletcher told when here allotting Indian lands, 1888-93. She was eight years old at the time and her mother belonged to the Women's Club. So, today no one knows whether he was killed or probably fell from the window. I never heard that the three returned chiefs ever admitted how their partner died.

Chief Utsinmalihkin was a signer of the two prior treaties between the Nez Perces and the United States. On that of Walla Walla, June 11, 1855, his name is seventh in line, spelled "U-ute-sin-male-cun." In the Lapwai treaty of 1863, he is second, spelled, "Ute-sin-male-e-cum." The names of all three of his companion delegates appear in both of these treaties, Lawyer as head chief. On the "Treaty of Peace and Friendship between the United States and the Nez Perce Tribe," made at Colonel George Wright's camp, Walla Walla, 1858, the second in the Nez Perce list is Hatesemalikin, still another version of Utsinmalihkin.[28]

_____

28 [At the Battle of Four Lakes in Colonel G. Wright's campaign of 1858 Utsinmalihkin was cited for special bravery by Lt. Mullan who commanded the Nez Perce scouts. (Col. G. Wright to Maj. W. W. Mackall, September 2, 1858, Report of the Secretary of War, House Executive Document No. 2, 25th Cong., 2nd Sess., p. 389. (Ed. note.)]

Aftermath of Timothy's Trip to Washington

Chief Timothy, whose loyalty to the whites is amply shown in the timely services he rendered the hard-pressed Colonel Steptoe expedition in 1858, was averred by the older Nez Perces to be in later years a "tipper" or moderate drinker. The Indians tell how, upon the return of the delegates from the national capital, Timothy addressed his people when assembled for the midwinter festivities, and bringing forth a supply of whisky said, "My children, while I was in Washington the Indian Commissioner gave me whisky. Now we will all take a drink, men, women, so we can dance strong."

Some of them, both men and women, refused to drink, even though threatened with punishment for disobeying their chief. Before his trip to Washington Timothy had never used intoxicants of any kind. That the delegates were plied with whisky can hardly be gainsaid, but it is improbable that the Indian Commissioner did the treating.

Chief Timothy, although steadfastly in league with the whites, was considered by the Upper Nez Perces to be honest and truthful. His son, young Timothy, heads the list of fifty-three Nez Perce scouts, couriers, and messengers, named in Article Ten, Nez Perce agreement with General O. O. Howard, 1877.

CHAPTER VIII

THE CRIMSON TRAIL—A STORY OF WHITE ATROCITIES

THE PERIOD OF DISASTER, WHICH DAWNED FOR THE Dreamer Nez Perces with the discovery of gold in their mountain realm, was in no manner allayed by the treaty of 1863. On the contrary it was augmented. The solemn fact that no treaty could be enforced until after senatorial approval, which in this instance was delayed until April 17, 1867, was spurned and ignored by the outlaws and state and national governments alike. The white man's account of this period is rosy with acclaim of progress attained in the march of Western empire-building. But the Dreamer Nez Perces' oral history reveals a lurid period, full of ghastly unprintable disclosures.

The Indians were wholly unprotected. The unnumbered outlaws, dominant among the three thousand interloping gold seekers, were unbridled in their drunken bestiality and held an unrestrained orgy of crime. Tepee homes were darkened by the vulture wing of moral debauchery; camp and village were overshadowed by the stalking specter of rape and murder.

This chapter will treat first the period of Colonel George Wright's conquest of the Coeur d'Alenes, Paloos and Spokane Indians in 1858. Despite the fact that many Nez Perces acted as scouts or were otherwise useful in the military under Colonel Wright, rendering signal and telling service as allies, the Colonel's proneness to hang Indians "on suspicion," found victims even among his own Nez Perce allies.[1] One of these, Heyoom Tookaitat, or Tookihtat, was hanged at [now] Lewiston in 1859. During the war, Heyoom Tookaitat had been engaged as a supply packer from the boat landing at the mouth of the Clearwater on the Snake, to the troops in the field. He lost a bag of meal or flour and was hanged "on suspicion" by order of Colonel Wright, the morning after his return to the landing. A cottonwood tree stood about one mile up the Clearwater, on the south side of that stream. It was standing only a few years ago [1926]. This tree was the gallows. Red Duck, an old man who witnessed the execution, said that a wagon was used as a platform or scaffold. It was driven from under the condemned, leaving him swinging from a limb. During this same period, by order of Colonel Wright, Waykat, who was in the service, was hanged on suspicion at Walla Walla. Citizens aided the soldiers in this execution. Waykat was generally known to be honest and of good reputation.[2] Whatever the grounds for the death penalty of these two Nez Perce auxiliaries, Colonel Wright's

---

[1] See B. F. Manring, *Conquest of the Coeur d'Alenes, Spokanes, and Palouses* (Spokane, 1912), for an account of Nez Perce assistance to both Colonel Wright and Colonel Steptoe.

[2] [Colonel Wright reported neither of the executions in his dispatches, but there is no reason to believe they did not occur. His policy toward Indians was brutally ruthless, and his dispatches are full of accounts of summary executions. For example, he writes, "I have this moment finished with the Palouses. . . I demanded the murderers of two miners April last. One man was brought out and hung forthwith. Two of the men who stole the cattle from Walla Walla valley were hung at my camp on the Ned-whauld. . . I then brought out my Indian prisoners and found three of them were either Walla Wallas or Yakimas. They were hung on the spot. One of the murderers of the miners had been hung on the Spokane." (Wright to W. W. Mackall, September 30, 1858, "Report of the Secretary of War," in *House Exec. Document No. 2*, 35th Congress, 2nd Session, p. 402). (Ed. note.)]

mania for stringing up redskins was savage.[3]

A NARRATIVE OF EARLY WRONGS

When the author decided to attempt making a summary of the Nez Perces murdered by the whites from the time of the gold rush to the outbreak of open hostilities in 1877, an appeal was made to the blind centenarian and tribal historian, Wottolen, as the most likely reliable source of information. There were the usual moments of silent meditation, then came the response.[4]

It is bitter, this recalling sorrowful memories of the past. Memories my heart would like to forget. But it will be good to let the world know the wrongs that we, a weak people, were made to suffer because of a great nation. I am willing to speak.

Whites invading our country killed Indians both secretly and in the open. In no case was a white man ever punished for his crime. As one of the oldest of my tribe, I will give the names of several of the killed, and the places and circumstances.

Tennawnahsut, and Hemese Wahiat, were both shot to death at Lahkoahko [small forest of young trees], between now Pendleton, and Wallowa. These men followed the old Indian religion, worshipping with dancing, singing the pompom drum. The government had a ruling, or law, against war-dancing and Chief Lawyer, Christian, had soldiers kill the

---

[3] The older Yakimas have given me a list of victims "strung up" or shot during the brief period of Colonel right's participation in the Yakima War, 1855-6. These executions were summary, usually without hearing or trial. Some of the victims, reputedly nonhostile and of Catholic faith, were in one instance dragged from their morning devotions to the nearest tree. Others, found beyond timberline, were made to face the rifle. Those so executed, including warriors who had already surrendered, exceeded by far the number slain in actual conflict.

[4] The list of victims by Wottolen was not proofed for chronological order. By far the worst period was ushered in by Captain Pierce's gold strike of '61 to flourish with but little abatement until the bursting of the storm in the early summer of '77.

two pompom dancers. Maybe the soldiers did not know the different dances, but Lawyer did.[5]

Three miles below the mouth of Alpowa Creek, north side of Snake River, an old man was killed by whites. He was a peaceable man, doing harm to no one. His son, Illikookt, died a few years ago. Konish Autassin [Wounded Buzzard] was shot by a white man named Amos and killed on Alpowa Creek, about one mile from its mouth. Wounded Buzzard was riding with a young Indian, Husis Capsis [Bad Head], going up the stream when some white man came meeting them. A half-breed had stolen a horse from these men, which neither of the boys knew anything about. The whites were looking for this horse, and Amos killed Wounded Vulture. Husis Capsis was permitted to go free. He is still living at Spalding, Idaho. (1926)

Itsyiyi Opsun [Coyote Flint] was killed up Slate Creek. The last seen of him he was going with two white men. The next day Coyote Flint was found dead, his neck broken by twisting. He had been struck on back of head and forehead with some weapon. He was a middle-aged man.

Where Cottonwood town now stands, a white man found the dead body of Hias Moolmool, which is a Flathead name, but he was a Nez Perce. Moolmool, had been alone with white men, and the man who found his body said they had killed him. He had a fine horse which was missing.

Yelmahhootsoot was killed on Sweet Water Ridge in the timber above the old stage station, Foundling.

---

[5] The Yakimas tell how, in compliance with some such departmental rulings, their agent, Rev. James H. Wilber, forbade the continuance of the Dreamer worship at their *pompom*, or long house, as was their wont each *Sapalwit*, or Sunday. A delegation of the Long Hairs waited on the Methodist divine with a request that he attend one of their meetings, and learn for himself the true nature of their performance. This he did, and never again officially interfered with such gatherings.

He was riding a sorrel horse which a white man wanted to buy. Yelmah did not want to sell, and the white man killed him with a club and took the horse. Joe Broncheau, a half-blood French Nez Perce, saw the killing. A few days later the wife of the murdered Indian recognized her husband's horse this side of West Lake, and took it. The murderer was there in camp with several white men, traveling toward the old Spalding Mission. Nothing was done about this killing.

Koosouyeen was killed about 1870 at a place [now] called Wawawai, on the Snake River about thirty miles below Lewiston. Wahleilah had stabbed and killed Tahmalum. When Missionary Spalding heard of this, he sent his son to have Wahleilah hanged. Young Spalding tried to act as officer, but was not an officer that the Indians knew of. He arrived at the village, and the stabber was found, but his cousin, Koosouyeen, a headman, decided strongly against the authority of Spalding. Young Spalding shot and killed him in the presence of many witnesses; and among the village tepees. Rev. Spalding determined against Koosouyeen, upholding his son's action.[6] This son was staying at now Almota, on the Snake. A brother of Koosouyeen was Tsatsikath, who died some years afterwards.

A young man named Motsqueh [Chipmunk] was killed at the mouth of White Bird River by Sam Benedict. Motsqueh was said to have been taking a pint bottle of whisky at the time.

---

[6] The date of this occurrence is uncertain. It appears that Henry H. Spalding, Jr. settled at Almota in 1872. (Eliza Spalding Warren, *Memoirs of the West*, Portland, 1916, p. 36.) At that time the code introduced by Dr. Elijah White was being most efficiently enforced by the lawless gold-seeking rabble overrunning the reservation. It would also appear that at the time mentioned, the senior Spalding was touring in the East, returning in the autumn of 1871. *(Whitman College Quarterly*, Vol. III, No. 3, p. 10.)

At Pierce City, one of the first mining camps, the wife of Jack Eemonwahtoe [Garter] was killed in 1872 or 1873. Some of the Indians raised small patches of wheat and vegetables and the old couple had brought some to exchange for gold dust or money, and they camped near the mines. The miners were drinking heavily and attacked Eemonwahtoe. His wife came to his rescue, not thinking that the miners would harm a woman, but one of them drove a miner's pick entirely through her body, striking her in the back. She was killed instantly. No account was taken of this deed. Eemonwahtoe told about it when he reached home, but no authority listened to him. There was no law against killing Indians. The agent said that he had no control over outside affairs.[7]

Heyoom Totskin was killed on horseback in streets of Lewiston by the marshal or police. No bad charges against this man. The officer knew him well; knew where he lived on Hatwai Creek.

A Nez Perce woman known as Mrs. Jim, was found dead one morning somewhere around White Bird. Three known white men had done this, murdering her in a very brutal manner not printable. Nobody was punished for this crime.

Koopnee [Broke] had an irrigation ditch on Salmon River, above White Bird. He was killed by a white man for his own water, for the ditch made by himself. This was some of the foundation for the war in the White Bird Country.[8]

Dacoopin [Wounded or Broken Leg] was killed by a settler or stockman in the Imnaha Valley. She was removing a horse belonging to the white man, from her garden patch. No punishment meted out to the murderer.[9]

---

[7] Confirmed by John Allen, aged tribal historian.

[8] Confirmed by Peopeo Tholekt.

[9] See McWhorter, *Yellow Wolf*, p. 46.

Chief Tipyahlanah Siskan [Eagle Blanket, or, Eagle Robe] the father of Wahlitits was killed on Salmon River, by Rolleot [Larry Ott], a white man. The chief owned land where he gardened every year. This white man came and settled near by on land owned by the Nez Perces. He said that he would not bother Eagle Robe's land, but only after a few snows he was fencing on the chief's garden spot. The chief went to him and said, "Hold on! You fence my land!"

Other words were spoken, and the white man, wearing a six-shooter, shot the chief who died a few hours later. This was between the mouths of White Bird and Slate Creek, opposite side of river. Wahlitits was not quite full grown and his father said to him, "Do nothing to the white man for what he has done to me. Let him live his life!"

Wahlitits grew to a young man, and, the war trouble coming on, he went with two kinsmen to kill the white murderer of his father, but did not find him. Knowing of danger he hid himself away. He would have been the first white man known to be killed by Nez Perces had Wahlitits found him.[10] He had fled to the Florence mines.

Kitstsui Shamkin [Metal Shirt] was killed in the

---

[10] It has been universally conceded that the Nez Perces shed no Caucasian blood until the outbreak of hostilities on the Salmon River in June, 1877. This may not be strictly true. It is possible that the three fur traders, Rezner, Le Clerc and Pierre Dorion (this last a half-blood French and Indian) were killed on the Snake River about 1810-15 by bands of roving Nez Perces in retaliation for one of their number who was brutally hanged by John Clark of the American Fur Company. (See Washington Irving, *Astoria*, (New York, 1836), pp. 339-48). However, the older Nez Perces always declared that the first white man killed among them was by a half-blood known as Finlay. His grandfather was hanged for his supposed part in the Whitman massacre, and Finlay was often heard telling how he longed to "cut up" some white man in revenge. The Indians would twit him, that he had not the nerve, the courage to kill anybody. This was kept up until the 1877 break was apparent when Finlay did get his man. [This man, a half-blood, was considered a Nez Perce and should not be confused with A. B. Findley who killed Wilhautyah in 1876. (Ed. note.)]

Mount Idaho country some years before the war. Nobody knew only that white men did it. Maybe it was for his horse and saddle. A young man, no one assumed that name following his death.

Wilhautyah was killed on the Wallowa River not long before the war broke out. I know not particulars of this murder, which was never punished.[11]

§

To this imposing list of Wottolen's, Raven Spy, warrior, added the following, in November, 1926.

When trying to get the Nez Perce prisoners released from bondage, James Reuben saw all the old people, and obtained correctly the names of every Nez Perce known to have been killed. This record must be somewhere in Washington, D.C. It was left with a department where judges pass on cases to be decided.

I know some of the people killed, but not all of them. Ittahsahnah was a humpback who always associated with the whites. He discovered gold in the mountain, and went to show some miners where it was. He never returned. He was murdered by the miners after guiding them to the gold.

A few white people went up the Clearwater to cut timber, and raft it down to Lewiston. They had one Indian with them, hired. At the mouth of Big Canyon they tied the Nez Perce's hands and feet and threw him in the river. Helpless, of course he drowned. This was done to avoid paying him for his work.

I think you have from Wottolen the other killings that I know about. The names of some of the Indians killed are lost to our memories.

Still another incident was related by Yellow Wolf:

Five Nez Perces, hunting the Wallowa Mountains, killed a deer and hung it in a tree from the wolves. Two evenings later they stopped to camp there, and Welotyen [Hallooing while Running] climbed up to loosen the ropes that secure the deer, while his companions gathered night-wood and

---

[11] See below, pp. 124.

started a fire. Three white men riding by fired a volley into Welotyen, who fell to the ground dead. The Indians had un-saddled their horses and set aside their guns and the marauders, riding hard, easily escaped. I know the place in the timbered mountains where Welotyen was killed, but I do not know how to tell you to find it. This was some time before the war. Those white men went free.

The murder destined for the most far-reaching historic import—that of Wilhautyah [Wind Blowing]—Peopeo Tholekt, of the Looking Glass band, discribed as follows:[12]

Wilhautyah was killed by two white men in the Wallowa country, who accused him of stealing their horses. Blowing Wind was an honest man and the horses being found proved him innocent. That almost started war.

Before this trouble, Motsqueh [Chipmunk] was found killed near the mouth of White Bird Creek, where a mean white man kept a saloon store. Chipmunk was not reckoned a bad Indian and I do not know for what reason he was killed. He would not have done anything for which he should be shot to death. This saloon man was always robbing Indians by keeping change money coming to them when buying anything from him. He never gave back their change no difference if cents or dollars. Chipmunk's body was found some distance from the saloon-store.

Near the breaking out of hostilities, Koopnee [Broken] and a partner, Mokouse, both elderly, had a field fenced and under cultivation on the Salmon river. A white man named Rob Raleigh settled lower down that river but near their improvement. He proceeded to usurp their cultivated field. Koopnee attempted to stop him from hauling rails along their own fence when Raleigh shot and killed him while alone. Leaving his horse still harnessed and chained to its load of rails, the murderer ran to a Chinese mining camp where he remained dressed as a Chinaman until the breaking out of the war when he was enlisted as a scout for General Howard. He was never punished for his crime.

---

[12] This is the same occurrence spoken of previously by Wottolen. See above, p. 123.

In addition to the other murders he recorded, Wottolen told of two cases of hangings by cattlemen acting "on suspicion." Two boys were hanged for stealing a cow. Later developments proved they were innocent. A man was hanged by cattlemen, accused of stealing a cow or heifer, which was afterwards found with other cattle. Thus, irrespective of the two earlier hangings by Colonel Wright, we have recorded the names of twenty-eight, of the list of thirty-two victims, compiled by James Reuben in the days following the war.[13] Thirty-two Nez Perces murdered by government-protected outlaws!

Of the twenty-eight Nez Perces, victims of unrestrained outlawry listed in this chapter, investigation shows that all were of the native Dreamer faith. It was those whom the whites labelled, "Heathens!" "Pagans!" "Savages!" "Renegades!" who had suf-

[13] Himslehkin [Raw], a Nez Perce, was hanged at what is now Elk City, Idaho. His offense was the reclaiming of a gift horse. In tribal custom it would appear that under certain circumstances a gift was recognized as subject to recall at the donor's election. Looked upon as more of a loan, having cost the recipient nothing, its title was still vested in the original owner, who might, on occasion of need or even of caprice, reclaim the object, even years later. On this question of tribal laws governing gifts, Many Wounds, who was a recognized authority, said:

"The hanging of Himslehkin was not in accordance with the old tribal Nez Perce laws. It was, and still is, if you go by the ancient law, that when you give anything to your friend as a real gift you never take it back. Also, if you promise anything to your friend, that promise you must accomplish, or make good. Whatever the gift—horse or anything—you give best in your possession. Only when somebody steal your property could you take it back."

The evidence was that Himslehkin's horse was taken in a wrong way, and not by friendship, and hanging was through ignorance of the chief, Tuinyanin, in mixing with the white man's laws. Himslehkin had done nothing to forfeit his life. Hanging him was murder.

Since no such tribal law was in vogue in pre-white days, it must be inferred that the "law" which hanged Himslehkin was fashioned after Dr. White's sanguinary code. About this incident Williams wrote: "The story of the hanging of Himslehkin is true, and it was Chief Tamyanin [Tuinyanin] who passed sentence upon him. The man to whom he had given the horse started with a party of Nez Perce for Montana, and Himslehkin followed and overtook them at now Elk City. The man gave up the horse, but some one told him to see the chief, as there was a law concerning such things. The man did so and the Indian was tried and hung."

fered. And yet not a solitary charge of reprisal can be laid at their relative's doors.

Alongside this is the fact that not until 1873 was a white man sentenced to death in Idaho for killing an Indian. June 7, 1873, the Nez Perce agent, John B. Monteith, wrote:

> Last week the trial of James Picket, the man who killed an Indian woman and attempted to kill her husband last September as reported at that time, was concluded and the same was found guilty and sentenced to be hung at Boise City, July 25, 1873. This is the first instance where a white man has been brought to justice for the murder of an Indian in this territory.[14]

The victim was a Nez Perce woman, killed in Shoshone County, Idaho Territory. The judgment of the lower court was affirmed by the Supreme Court of the Territory, January term, 1874, but the court records do not show that the sentence was ever carried out.[15]

Major Wood's Investigation of Nez Perce Grievances

Owing to the confusion attendant to the title of ownership to the Wallowa-Imnaha domain, augmented by the shifty rulings of President Grant,[16] Major H. Clay Wood, assistant adjutant general of the Mili-

---

[14] See *Report of Sec. of Interior*, 1873, p. 526, for mention of this incident.

[15] ["James Picket was indicted, tried and convicted at the May term, 1873 of the District Court of the 1st Judicial District of the territory held in Nez Perce county, for the murder of an Indian woman of the Nez Perce tribe, committed in Shoshone County, and upon conviction was sentenced to suffer the extreme penalty of the law." (James Picket v. United States, 1 *Idaho*, 523). "This judgment was affirmed by the Supreme Court of the Idaho Territory in the January term, 1874. But the court records do not show the judgment was ever carried out." (Letter Ora B. Hawkins, State Historian of Idaho to L. V. McWhorter, May 21, 1941). (Ed. note.)]

[16] See below, p. 135.

tary Department of the Columbia, made an exhaustive study of the situation, publishing his findings in pamphlet form.[17] Stirred by the brutal aggressive killing of Wilhautyah, June 23, 1876,[18] Joseph and Ollokot and other members of the Wallowa band met with Major Wood in council at the Nez Perce Indian Agency, July 22, the proceedings being published as a supplementary to Wood's first report. Here we read:

Joseph began his speech with the customary formal and complimentary phrases, addressed himself to Major Wood, as "My friend," said that he had heard he was coming; that he had waited several days for his coming, but that he was now glad to see him; that it was true one of his brothers had been killed by whites in Wallowa Valley; that the Indian who was killed was much respected by the tribe, and was always considered a quiet, peaceable, well-disposed man; that the whites who killed him were bad, quarrelsome men, and the aggressive party; that the whites in the valley were instigated by those in authority, and others in Grande Ronde valley, to assault and injure the Indians while fishing and hunting in that section of country; that he wished the white who killed the Indian to be brought to the agency, to be there confronted with his accusers. Joseph said that among the Indians the chiefs controlled the members of their bands, and had power to prevent bad Indians from doing wicked things and in case of their so doing to punish them; and if the chiefs did not restrain or punish bad Indians, they themselves were responsible for their bad acts; and he reasoned that those in authority over the whites had or should have, the same control over their men; and hence the white authorities in the vicinity of Wallowa Valley and elsewhere were directly responsible for the killing of his brother; that his brother's life was of great value; that it

---

[17] Major H. Clay Wood, *The Status of Young Joseph and his Band of Nez Perce Indians*, (Assistant Adjutant General's Office, Portland, 1876).

[18] See Wottolen's story above, p. 123. The date of this crime is given variously, but in Major Wood's report, and that of the *Report of the Secretary of War*, 1876, p. 7, it is the same as here given.

was worth more than the Wallowa valley; that it was worth more than all this country; that it was worth more than all the world; that the value of his life could not be estimated; nevertheless, that now, since the murder had been done; since his brother's[19] life had been taken in Wallowa valley, his body buried there, and the earth there had drunk up his blood, the valley was more sacred to him than ever before, and he would and did claim it now as recompense for the life taken; that he should hold it for himself and his people from this time forward forever, and that all the whites must be removed from the valley."

Young Joseph [Ollokot] spoke almost to the same purpose as his brother, except that he did not want the whites, Findley and McNall tried and punished for their crime, but wished them to leave that section of country that he might never see them more, and in that the whites in the Wallowa Valley were furnished arms and ammunition by one "Smith," a bad white man, for the purpose of assaulting the Indians

---

[19] Chief Joseph was speaking metaphorically. Writers have since spoken of the Indian killed as Joseph's own brother, but they were not related. A brother of Joseph was killed, but in another way. An older brother of Joseph, Sousouquee [Brown], was shot from his horse by Wayouh Yuch [Blue Leg], the arrow piercing his leg. Yellow Wolf said of this tragedy:

"Chief Joseph's brother was killed on the Wallowa River by Blue Leg, about twelve snows before the war. They were drinking at the time. Whisky made bad blood among our people. It brought death to Chief Koolkool Lesahcosmin of White Bird Creek."

Of this fatality Wottolen added, "This older son of Chief Wellamotkin was a man of some age, but not too old. Just a little past middle age. Good-looking and about the right size. He was not an outlaw, nor was he killed by whites. It was on the Wallowa, where some young men were drinking. Otskai, one of the drinkers killed him. Sousouquee was supposed drinking, but he was not a hard drinker. A man that everybody liked."

And War Singer writes:

"Blue Leg killed Joseph's brother in self-defence. Sousouquee was drunk at the time. Blue Leg's horse was exhausted and thinking he would be killed by Sousouquee, he drew his bow and sent an arrow into his leg at which he aimed. They were both drunk. Sousouquee must have bled to death.

"Blue Leg fled to the Spokane reservation, from which in time he returned. Chief Joseph shot at him one night, the bullet passing through the shoulder.

"Later Joseph would have killed Blue Leg, only that Wottolen knocked aside his rifle. In after years the two men became close friends, going through the war together. Blue Leg was not considered a first class fighter, but he escaped to Sitting Bull and finally died at Stites, Idaho."

while hunting and fishing in their own country. He wished
the white settlers to remove from the valley and to give up
the land to the Indians.[20]

No Indian witnessed account of the slaying was, it
would seem, ever recorded. Those who saw it were,
a year later, swallowed up in the great retreat to
Montana, never to return. They fell in battle or were
victims of the deadly malaria of the Leavenworth
swamps, or the sweltering climate of Eeikish Pah
[Hot Place] to which they were exiled. The following
version of the tragedy was given the writer more
than a quarter of a century ago by James Edward
Cashcash, a lineal grandson of the victim, Wilhautyah.

Wells McNall was a settler on the Wallowa River, at the
mouth of Whiskey Creek. Of a quarrelsome, trouble-making
disposition, the Nez Perces regarded him as an avowed
enemy. It was claimed that he peddled intoxicants among
the drinking Indians. He forebade them catching and curing
salmon at their accustomed place near his residence. So disliked he made himself that Chief Ollokot and interpreter
Smith[21] whom all the tribesmen liked, waited on him with
the warning, "You better be moving from here at once! This
is Indian country, and not your land!"

This warning did not tend in any manner to an abatement
of the growing trouble between this bullying land thief and
the suffering Nez Perces. The date was about June 16,
1876. Eight Indians were camped on the Wallowa, estimated
as about six miles above where McNall lived. Four of the
number were, Melmelstalikaiya [Selish name], Peter Pli-
ater, Waptas Wahhaikt [Eagle or Feather Necklace], and
Wilhautyah. The names of the others are lost. None of the

---

[20] H. Clay Wood, *Supplementary* to *Status of Chief Joseph*, pp. 2-4.

[21] See Wood, *op. cit.*, pp. 2-4. Evidently there were two Smiths that
figured in the early history of the Wallowa, both of them dealing with
Ollokot. First we have Smith, a bad white man, evidently in the
role of trader, who furnished ammunition to the whites. Then we have
Interpreter Smith whom the tribesmen all liked. Other traces of
these characters are to be found in connection with the Wallowa
troubles.

eight Indians were armed. Hunters in camp, their rifles were stacked.

When the campers saw McNall and Findley riding toward them in a manner appearing unfriendly, and knowing their dispositions, all but Wilhautyah, mounted their horses and started away. Two shots were fired at them, McNall jumped to the ground and grabbed hold of Wilhautyah. There was a scuffle fight. McNall, finding himself worsted, called to Findley to shoot the Indian. This Findley did, killing him.

The other Nez Perces were eyewitnesses to this murder from where they sat their horses a short distance away.

It developed that the white men were looking for some missing horses, and suspected the Indians of having "rustled" them. McNall cried, when he realized that an entirely innocent man had been killed.

None of those seven witnesses to this murder are now living. They joined in the war, and none of them ever returned. Neither Findley nor McNall were punished for their crime. Interpreter Williams writes: "Eskawus, was also present when Wilhautyah was killed. Eskawus was supposed to be one of Chief Joseph's bravest warriors. He was tall and raw boned the same as Jackson Sundown whom you knew. They were both brothers."

Findley's son-in-law wrote the following account of the tragedy for the author:

Findley and McNall were out looking for some strayed horses and rode into the Indian camp. It seems that Findley and McNall both had guns. They accused the Indians of running off the horses and McNall and the Indian got into a fight over possession of McNall's gun, and in the fight the gun was fired, and McNall thinking that the Indian was getting the better of him yelled to Findley to shoot the Indian and Findley did so. As soon as he shot the Indian they both got away from the Indian camp.

I think that was the first of the war of 1877. The Indians moved across the Snake River to White Bird in Idaho and commenced killing white men and women. The Indians did not kill anyone in the Wallowa Valley that I know of.

CHAPTER IX

WAR CLOUDS AND OFFICIAL BLUNDERING

AGENT MONTEITH'S NARRATIVE

BY THE SUMMER OF 1872 FRICTION IN THE WALLOWA COUNTRY between the encroaching settlers and Chief Joseph's band had grown so acute that Agent Monteith decided to investigate personally. In response to a message from the settlers, who had gone so far as to send out for arms and ammunition, he hastened to the Wallowa, accompanied by two Indian guides and an employee, riding the distance of "about 105 miles . . . over a bad trail across the mountains," in the space of two days.[1] In his first interview with Monteith, Joseph explained "that his father had never traded off that country [Wallowa] and on his dying bed, about a year ago,[2] bequeathed the whole country to him for his band." Joseph desired the presence of the settlers at the conference, and the following morning, August 23, about thirty settlers and eighty Indians, the latter with faces painted, assembled in a lodge they had especially provided. Monteith continues.

. . . Joseph opened the council by saying—his father planted a stick on the mountains between the Grand Ronde Valley and the Wallowa, that now that stick had grown to a large tree, that the whites were trying to get on their side and drive them away from their food, that his father bequeathed to him that

---

[1] Report of John B. Monteith to F. H. Walker, Commissioner of Indian Affairs, August 27, 1872, typescript copy of dispatch in Old Lapwai Agency copybook, McW NP 51, p. 3, cited hereafter as "Monteith's Report, 1872."

[2] Most writers have accepted the date of elder Chief Joseph's death as 1872, but the circumstance under which this instance of 1871 is of record renders it invulnerable to successful contradiction. Major H. Clay Wood also gives the date as 1871. (Status of Young Joseph, p. 45.)

Findley went out to the Grand Ronde Valley and gave himself up but they would not do anything with him and after the war O. O. Howard had him brought to trial but the Indians would not appear against him saying that McNall was to blame for the shooting.[22] I have seen the widow of the Indian that Findley killed. She used to come down here sometimes and would come to Findley's for dinner. They were on friendly terms, but I think if the Indians could have got hold of McNall they would have killed him.[23]

---

[22] See Appendix X, pp. 611-20, for an account of the affair by H. K. Findley, son of A. B. Findley. The arrest of Findley by General Howard after the war, if his prosecution depended on the testimony of the Indians, would prove a farce. Killed or prisoners of war, there were no eyewitnesses to the murder to appear against him. The wife of Wilhautyah was not at the camp when invaded by the two armed white men who had nothing to fear from the unarmed Indians.

[23] Letter, Jack Johnson to L. V. McWhorter, December 22, 1926.

country for subsistence of himself and band and wanted all the whites to leave the valley.

I told him that the treaty of 1855 gave them the right to hunt and fish on their old grounds and herd their stock on unoccupied land, that his father signed said Treaty. Also again in 1863 there was another Treaty made which sold still more of their lands, that the Government had acted in good faith to them and expected the same on their part and would hold to the contract. The settlers were willing that they should hunt and fish in the valley and would not disturb or molest them in any way, and that I had come to them as their friend to keep them out of trouble and hoped they would take my advice, which was not to interfere with anyone, but attend to their hunting and fishing and when done, return home.

Joseph said as to his father signing the Treaty, "It was a lie, that his father never traded off that country and never received anything for it, that his father had been taught to read but when he found out the whites were trying to get the Wallowa Valley he tore up the treaty and testament and joined his people. All he wanted was for me to order the whites out of the Valley."

I answered, "As far as I know from laws and Treaties, the Country was sold to the Government, that it had been surveyed and brought into the market and the Government would protect the settlers, that they must not interfere with anyone, must not set out any fires to burn any improvements of the whites or the hay they were putting up, that I had no authority to remove the settlers and it could not be done, that if they committed any depredations against the whites, it would be my duty to go there with force enough to bring the Indians on the Reservation where I could take care of them.

Joseph answered—"I know you are my friend and you are a good agent, and I do not like to talk to you so, but these people you see here are the cause of the trouble, all I want is for them to go away and leave us our country."

I told him it was useless to talk about sending the whites away, that they were there by higher authority than I and I could not remove them, that it was to their interests to keep the friendship of the whites, and the Government would protect them in all their rights. To be careful and not let any of his young men do any rash act, but when they got ready to come home, come as they went, "at peace with all."

Joseph said he would not let any of his men do anything that would cause trouble, but would have the matter settled peaceably.

We then broke camp and after counseling the settlers to keep away from the Indians and not interfere with their hunting and fishing, left bidding all a good-bye.

... It is a great pity that the valley was ever opened for settlement. . . One man told me that the wheat was frozen while it was in the milk. It is a fine grass country, and raising stock is all that can be done to any advantage. It is the only fishery the Nez Perces have and they go there from all directions. . .

The Indians who caused the trouble live on the outside of the reserve on Snake River and some of them told the whites they would fight before they would ever go on the reservation. If there is any way by which the Wallowa Valley could be kept for the Indians, I would recommend that it be done. There is not one house in the valley as far as I could ascertain, but some will be built this fall.

The question will have to be settled soon in regard to those Indians living on the outside of the Reservation as you will see by the enclosed extract cut from the "Idaho Statesman." The settlers are getting in earnest.

An Agent can not have control of Indians when they are allowed to live off the Reserve from 50 to 100 miles from the Agency.[3]

It is well to note that in the foregoing, Agent Monteith advocated setting aside the Wallowa Valley for the Indians, taking note of the fact that as yet no settler dwellings had been constructed. To what extent Monteith's recommendations were considered in Washington may be conjectural, but in any case, acting promptly upon the request of Edwin P. Smith, Commissioner of Indian Affairs, and the recommendation of Secretary of the Interior Delano, President Grant, on June 16, 1873, set aside the greater portion of the Wallowa Valley "as a reservation for the roaming Nez Perce Indians."[4] Unfortunately this official sense of justice proved short lived. A letter of bitter protest from Leonard P. Grover, governor of Oregon, giving a false picture of the situation, induced the then Commissioner of Indian Affairs, Edwin P. Smith, to advise the return of the newly created reservation to the public domain, which the President did June 10, 1875, again opening the valley to settlers. Meanwhile Chief Joseph and his followers remained passively on their old domain, with never a breach of Joseph's pledge to Agent Monteith of amenity and consonance on the part of his people. Soon, however, the situation was to be further confused by the killing of Wilhautyah, and the subsequent negotiations between Joseph and Major Wood, the account of which was published in his *Supplementary* to *The Status of Young Joseph.*[5] Wood's interference (at Howard's request) in the Nez Perce affairs rankled Monteith, as is clearly evident in the following:

I respectfully report the following in regard to Joseph's band of Nez Perce Indians. Some four weeks

---

[3] "Monteith's Report, 1872," McW NP 51, pp. 4-5.
[4] The text of this order is found in Major H. Clay Wood's *Status of Young Joseph*, p. 33.
[5] See Chapter VIII, pp. 127-29.

ago, while a party of four of said band were hunting in the Wallowa Valley they met two white men and got into a dispute about something. The white men proceeded to take the firearms from the Indians.

During the scuffle to get possession of the guns, one of the Indians proved to be too much for the white man whereupon the other white shot the Indian dead.

As soon as I heard of the affair, I sent for Joseph, who in due time came to my office, I talked with him and advised him to let civil authorities deal with the murder in accordance with our laws and told him I thought justice would prevail. I told him to keep his people quiet and that all would end well. . .

Joseph seemed to care but little for the man killed and seemed satisfied with the state of affairs until about one week ago when Col. [Major] Wood, Adj't Gen'l of General Howard's came to Fort Lapwai and desired to hold a council with Joseph and his brother, which he did at this Agency at which I was present. . . During the talk but little was said of any consequence except that Joseph demanded the Wallowa Valley be cleared of all whites and turned over to him in payment for the man killed.

On the evening of the 23rd inst. Col. Wood held another council with said Indians and this time at Fort Lapwai. I was not present and can report only what I have heard. I learned that Joseph exhibited much bad feeling and said he would make trouble unless the matter was settled satisfactorily. Colonel Wood said that General Howard had recommended that a commission of five men be appointed to come here and treat with Joseph and settle all difficulties.

I have given the above statement of facts and desire to submit my view in regard to the matter.[6]

---

[6] Monteith to J. Q. Smith, Commissioner of Indian Affairs, July 31, 1876, typescript copy of report in Old Lapwai Agency Copy Book, McW NP 51, p. 6, hereafter referred to as "Monteith's Report, 1876."

July 3rd, I addressed General Howard a letter (copy herewith which speaks for itself). To this communication I have received no reply. After my letter had time to reach General Howard, he (the general) telegraphed the commanding officer at Fort Lapwai to see Joseph and try and pacify him, etc.

Later up comes the General's Adj't and holds a council with Joseph, all this I consider very unwise, as I had attended to the matter, had pacified Joseph and seemingly he was satisfied, at least he neither made or showed any disposition to make threats or trouble and in my opinion never would, had he not been made acquainted with the fact that Col. Wood came all this way from Portland to hear what Joseph had to say. Holding councils with him and informing him as to General Howard's recommendation in regard to five commissioners being sent. All this made Joseph think that it must be a matter of great importance, more so than he had thought it to be and that the whites must really be afraid of him and his band and that it was an opportunity to push his claim and show more interest and feeling in the matter. Again it creates dissatisfaction among the treaty Indians who see so much consideration shown to the "non-treaties" and makes them feel as though they were being imposed upon in as much as they are kept on the reserve while the "non-treaties" are allowed to go where they please.[7]

[Agent Monteith continues at length, opposing all councils or settlements of any difficulties among Indians except by authorized agent, bitterly decrying the military stepping in without being requested by the agent as being destructive to the agent's influence. With apparent perturbation the writer continues,]

---

[7] "Monteith's Report, 1876," McW NP 51, pp. 6-7.

If it is necessary to take part . . . let it be by request of the Agent and let it always be understood—by the Indians—that the agent is their authority and that no person can deal with them except through their Agent. . .[8]

I have communicated the above that the department may act understandingly in case different report is made by anyone else. I would add that the murderer in question has been arrested and will in due time have his trial.[9]

Of the board of commissioners that had been proposed by General Howard to pass upon the legality of the 1863 Treaty, Agent Monteith elucidates:

. . .In regard to the Commissioners, I learn my name was of those sent on, instead of five, I recommend that only three be appointed and instead of those recommended by General Howard, I would suggest that Rev. E. R. Geary, D.D.[10] of Eugene City, Oregon, and Hon. Joel Palmer, whose address I am not acquainted with be appointed. Both of these gentlemen have been Superintendents of Indian Affairs in Oregon, have made treaties with these Indians, are acquainted with them and their country and take an interest in the elevation of the Indians.

I cannot help but feel that the recommendation is an interference. If exigency of the service demanded such a move, I think, I ought to be the party who would know it, and potent to say: had my plans been

---

[8] Under the old regime, the U.S. Indian agent was vested with the power of a major of the regular army, activities confined of course to the bounds of his particular Indian reservation. Infringement by the military could be excusable only, perhaps, through the direst of emergency.

[9] "Monteith's Report, 1876," McW NP 51, pp. 7-8.

[10] Geary secured Monteith's appointment to the Nez Perce Indian Agency. (See Drury's *Spalding*, pp. 392-401). Geary was a Presbyterian minister.

left alone and carried out no prominence could have been given the affair and Joseph would have had no opportunity to create any uneasiness in the minds of anyone and the great expense incident to a commission being appointed would not be incurred.[11]

It was inevitable that Agent Monteith's complaints would carry little weight against the ponderous political and military juggernaut that was steam-rolling, not only the Wallowa, but also the gold-gemmed waters of the Salmon. Perhaps his letter was a "feeler," a sportsman's sifting of the traditional tobacco crumbs to determine the course of the air. Be this as it may, from this time on he is found, not only in cordial step with the spoils procession, but quite often well in its lead. It would have redounded to his honor had he stood by his initial gestures of condolence and justice toward these mistreated contingents of the once great Nez Perce nation. General Howard from the very first showed not the remotest compassion for the maligned and mistreated nontreaties. They were Dreamers!

§

The Five Commissioners—A Travesty on Justice

General Howard urged Washington to action, to "save money and further complications and promote the welfare of both whites and Indians."[12] He stressed the fact that the government had opened the Wallowa Valley to settlement, and that Joseph still claimed that this valley belonged to him and his band, that Young Joseph had no exclusive claim as against any Nez Perce Indians, but had his right in common with that part of the nation not a party to the treaty of 1863, and that the extinguishment of the Indian title was imperfect and incomplete.[13]

---

11 "Monteith's Report, 1876," McW NP 51, pp. 7-8.
12 *Report of the Secretary of War*, 1876, I, 91.
13 *Loc. cit.*

General Howard then quotes at length a letter from Rev. A. L. Lindsley, a Presbyterian minister, advocating a plan which would "bring a pacific settlement and ultimate satisfaction to all parties, or justify harsher measures." Lindsley suggested:

> Let a commission of well-qualified men be appointed by the Government to negotiate with the Indians (not the chiefs alone) for the relinquishment of all their land-claims by fair purchase; pursuade them to enter within the reservation in a reasonable time; with permission to hunt; as heretofore, beyond the lines; provide for their children additional schools, the existing provision being inadequate for the present demands; protect them in the enjoyment of rights equal to those of other Nez Perces not on the reservation.[14]

After this quotation, General Howard continued in his own strain:

> This recommendation does not conflict with the conclusions of Major Wood's report—(see pages 41-45 inclusive).
>
> I concur in the recommendations, and hope the conclusions of the report will be carefully considered by the Department of the Interior and the law-officers concerned.
>
> Major Wood, using all the means of knowledge within his reach has spent considerable time and taken great pains to put into succinct and comprehensive form everything of importance bearing upon the relations of the Government to these Indians, and he has succeeded in making the subject clear and the difficulties easy of solution. Our Government will be derelict and responsible for the consequences, if a permanent and just settlement with these Indians is not speedily effected.
>
> I recommend that the commission suggested consist of five members: Judge M. P. Deady, U.S. District Court; Hon. T. B. Odineal, R. R. Thompson, esq., Gen. Joel Palmer, Hon. J. W. Newmith. Any of them would be just and fit men for the work, and they are familiar with Indian subjects. The department commander (O. O. Howard) and the

---

[14] *Ibid.*, p. 92.

Nez Perce Indian Agent (J. B. Monteith) should in my judgment, constitute two members of the commission.

I send also herewith Dr. Lindsley's letter . . . and renew my recommendation of a commission to hear and settle the whole matter before war is even thought of. The Nez Perces have never been up to the present time, hostile to our people.[15]

On September 1st, General Howard writing of conditions at Fort Lapwai, says:

Since my visit, (spring) there has been some little trouble between a branch of the Nez Perce, Joseph's band situated in the Wallowa Valley, and some white men of the neighborhood. An Indian was killed by a white man in a dispute concerning some stock. Captain David Perry was directed to see the chief Joseph, and do what was necessary to preserve the peace. Maj. H. Clay Wood, my adjutant-general, afterward visited Lapwai and made a report dated August 1, 1876. I attach a copy for the information of the War Department. It gives the view this non-treaty band take of their difficulties and suggests a good solution. Probably I cannot do better in this annual report than attach also Major Wood's report on *The Status of Young Joseph*, and his Band of Nez Perce Indians. The subject matter of this tribe and its trouble with citizens and government, with the suggested remedies, are here fully set forth. I call especial attention to my endorsement thereon.[16]

It seems significant that, aside from General Howard himself none of the men suggested by Agent Monteith and General O. O. Howard are found on the commission board appointed in October 1876, by the Secretary of the Interior. Instead were the following, David H. Jerome, Saginaw, Michigan; A. C. Barstow, Providence, Rhode Island; William Stickney, Washington, D.C.; Major H. Clay Wood, Military Department of the Columbia, Portland, Oregon. Mr.

[15] *Loc. cit.*
[16] *Op. cit.*, p. 91.

Jerome was made chairman of the Committee and Mr. Stickney, secretary.[17]

It would be difficult to conceive of a more brazen travesty on justice than this politically picked commission which was to sit in judgment on the non-treaty Nez Perce land frauds. The crime of June 9, 1863 had been consummated not only with the connivance but with the consent and guidance of governmental officials. Now a government-selected commission was to pass judgment on the validity of that government's action. The language of General Howard's letter quoted above betrays his mind was already made up as to the proper procedure.

The commission arrived at the Nez Perce agency, November 7, 1876. Agent Monteith had instructions to "lose no time in sending for the non-treaty Nez Perce Indians, and especially for Joseph and his band, to be there at that time."[18] The effort to get the Indians to hurry was futile. It was on this occasion that Chief Joseph made his mark in history as a man of leisure. With a considerable following he had come by easy stages and pitched camp on the evening of the eleventh, within a few miles of the agency. A call upon him by Chairman Jerome, Agent Monteith, and the interpreter, James Reuben, only resulted in their learning that, "his business, even now, did not demand haste."[19] Not until noon of the thirteenth was a meeting finally arranged to be held in the church. Joseph's well-mounted column soon appeared and "with military precision and order massed itself in front of, but at considerable distance from the church."[20]

---

[17] *Report of the Secretary of the Interior*, 1876, I, 394.

[18] "Report of the Commission to the Nez Perce Indians," in the *Report of the Secretary of the Interior*, 1877, I, 607.

[19] *Loc. cit.*

[20] *Loc. cit.*

The council was held in the church at Lapwai, and the commission's report of the opening scene reads: "From the first it was apparent that Joseph was in no haste. Never was the policy of masterly inactivity more fully inaugurated. He answered every salutation, compliment, and expression of good will in kind, and duplicated the quantity. An alertness and dexterity in intellectual fencing was exhibited by him that was quite remarkable."[21]

The commission early explained that the President claimed to have extinguished the Indian title to the Wallowa, in the Treaty of 1863, "which bore the signatures of a majority of their chiefs and head men, but in a spirit of generosity he was disposed, rather than press his right to issue, to treat for an adjustment of present difficulties."[22] The coldness of the climate and the presence of settlers who had already invaded the region, which was within the limits of the state of Oregon, were specifically held up as deterring Indian occupancy.

The philosophy of the Earth Mother and Chieftaincy of the earth, together with the cosmic laws by which these Indians were governed, whose *shamans* found no marks or lines left by the creative power that might authorize a division of the earth's surface, proved most irksome to the impatient, hard-headed commissioners. In their findings they held to the legality of the 1863 treaty because it had been accepted by a majority, and blamed the Dreamer priests for the recalcitrance of Joseph, Ollokot, and their followers in removing to the Idaho reservation. On this score we quote.

The dreamers, among other pernicious doctrines, teach that the earth being created by God complete, should not

---

[21] *Loc. cit.*
[22] *Ibid.*, p. 608.

be disturbed by man, and that any cultivation of the soil or other improvements to interfere with its natural productions, any voluntary submission to the control of the government, any improvement in the way of schools, churches, etc., are crimes from which they shrink. This fanaticism is kept alive by the superstition of these "dreamers" who industriously teach that if they continue steadfast in their present belief, a leader will be raised up in the East who will restore all dead Indians to life, who will unite with them in expelling the whites from their country, when they will again enter upon and repossess the lands of their ancestors.

Influenced by such belief, Joseph and his band firmly declined to enter into any negotiations or make any arrangements that looked to a final settlement of the questions pending between him and the government. . . . We therefore recommend,

First. That the leaders and teachers of what is known as the "dreamer" belief be required to return to the agencies where they belong forthwith, and in case of refusal that they be removed from further contact with the roaming Indians by immediate transportation to the Indian Territory.

There is at least one such "dreamer" with Joseph's band, to whom reference has been previously made in this report.

Second. With this pregnant cause of trouble removed, so long as Joseph and his band remain in the Im-na-ha Valley and visit the Wallowa Valley for hunting, fishing, and grazing for only a short time in each year, we recommend a speedy military occupancy of the valley by an adequate force to prevent a recurrence of past difficulties between the whites and the Indians. Meanwhile the agent of the Nez Perces should continue his efforts to settle these Indians in severalty upon the lands of the reservation that are still vacant.

Third. Unless they should conclude to settle quietly as above indicated, within a reasonable time, in the judgment of the department, they should then be placed by force upon the Nez Perce reservation, and in satisfaction of any possible rights of occupancy which they may have, the same aid and allotments of land granted to the treaty Nez Perces should be extended to them on the reservation.

Fourth. If these Indians overrun land belonging to the whites and commit depredations upon their property, disturb the peace by threats or otherwise, or commit any other overt act of hostility, we recommend the employment of sufficient force to bring them into subjection, and to place them upon the Nez Perce Reservation.

The Indian Agent at Lapwai should be fully instructed to carry into execution these suggestions, relying at all times upon the department commander (General O. O. Howard) for aid when necessary.[23]

In this suggested solution no restrictions or penalties are recommended for whites who might infringe on the Indians' possessions or personal rights; and this in the face of a recent invasion of an Indian camp by two white men, who, according to their own story, in the temporary absence of the occupants, took possession of their unguarded arms, and when the owners returned, provoked a quarrel in which one of the unarmed Indians was killed. In reality the Indian was murdered, the crime going unpunished as usual.[24]

In the bitter stress the commission placed on the Dreamer religious cult, the hand of General Howard is plainly discernible. Of the commission's personnel, General Howard avers, "No better men could have been selected for that purpose. They tried their best to get the consent of Joseph, Ollikut, and the other non-treaty Indians to a settlement of all their troubles..."[25]

Of the particular drawn-out night session mentioned in the commission's report, the late Mrs. Frances Monteith wrote the author:

---

[23] *Ibid.*, pp. 609-10. The Nez Perce Dreamers did not subscribe to the belief, current among some Dreamer groups, of a resurrection of the dead to drive out the whites as claimed in the commissioner's report. See Chapter IX, p. 147.

[24] See Chapter VIII, p. 124.

[25] General O. O. Howard, *My Life and Experiences Among our Hostile Indians*, (Hartford, Conn., 1907), p. 243.

My father, Perrin B. Whitman, was oftimes interpreter at Indian councils of which I attended many; one when but ten years old. As a young woman I was present at the commissioner's night session of which you speak.

The commission was sent to influence the Joseph and other Indians to come to the Nez Perce Reservation. That night session was long, drawn out, and the Indians were outspoken in their objections to leaving their old homes. It became so emphatic that Chairman Jerome suddenly adjourned the meeting.

Reaching home we all felt greatly relieved. Chairman Jerome declared: "I deemed it better to adjourn than to have a massacre!" on which all agreed had been imminent. The Indians were all wearing heavy blankets which were suspected of concealed weapons.[26] Of course Mr. Jerome had not witnessed as many such cases as I had, but his judgment was good. It was the general opinion of the commission that the young Indian men led by Chief Joseph's brother "Ollocut," whispered, and made signs, some even laughing. After that the Chairman read his instructions, ending with . . . "you must come on the reservation, and Agent Monteith's instructions you have just listened to say the same thing. We work together."

At the time General Howard held these councils with Chief Joseph and his band relative to coming on the reduced reservation, I was twenty-two and a half years old, and had been married three years. Therefore I was of mature and sober mind, with no prejudices, but with a clear, persistent observance of every event.

At this November 1876, council—the war following the next June—the five commissioners were our guests. They

---

[26] To a later query as to whether the weather were chilly or rainy, came a reply from Mrs. Monteith which certainly would justify the wearing of heavy blankets. "The entire day of the council had been dark, and threatening. With the evening came not only a mist, but showers. Before the Indians assembled, and while we sat expectantly awaiting their arrival, an ominous shower began pelting the shingled roof of the low, frame building. When the first Indian slowly came in and others following, emulating his example, disdained the seats provided, pulled their heavy blankets closely about them, casting implacable glances at the commissioners. My father, who was the official interpreter, made no remark nor sign until later and after the last Indian had left the room when he said: 'If there had been one word contrary to their wishes, and any argument whatever, the consequences would have been disastrous,' and as Mr. Jerome expressed later, and as I have said elsewhere, a 'massacre.'"

had been appointed by the President with instructions to "make it final!" Knowing the attitude of Joseph and his young men, the Modoc War of 1873 did not seem so far away. After the council adjourned and we returned home, all were rejoiced to know that a tragedy had been averted by a Higher Power, through a wise man (Chairman Jerome) who said: "I thought that a report would be better than a massacre." Then he immediately added: "Major Monteith, will you get me a perfectly trustworthy Indian to carry a dispatch to Walla Walla for the Secretary and Commissioner of Indian Affairs?"

Of the commission's findings, War Singer [Camille Williams] commented:

These men seemed to go against Chief Joseph and his following because of their religion. The Dreamer belief is about the same as that of other denominations, that God created the earth. Their faith is that "Honesty is the best religion." They have always, from the very first, had respect for the Seventh Day. No hunting or any kind of work on that day.

They did not teach that a "Leader" would come from the east; that all dead Indians would come to life when a horn or trumpet was blowed. A dead body becomes earth after a time.

Chief Joseph and brother and all others were not influenced by such things. Their belief was, "Never relinquish the claim to the land. No band had any right to sell land belonging to another band. Their different tracts were like counties making up a state, but a state cannot sell its counties."

Major H. Clay Wood's signature does not appear with the others of the commission on the report of their findings. There has been no explanation of its omission[27] but perhaps the answer can be found in his

---

[27] [Apparently Major Wood made a minority report, not printed with the "Report of the Commissioner of Indian Affairs," which recognized Joseph's band might eventually have to be moved, but recommended that "until Joseph commits some overt act of hostility, force should not be used to put him on the reservation." (see J. P. Dunn, *Massacres of the Mountains*, N.Y., 1886, p. 646). (Ed. note.)]

opinions as expressed in his publication of the previous year, where he said:

In my opinion, the non-treaty Nez Perces cannot in law be regarded as bound by the treaty of 1863, and insofar as it attempts to deprive them of a right to occupancy of any land, its provisions are null and void. The extinguishment of their title of occupancy contemplated by this treaty is imperfect and incomplete. This, however, is a question which demands and should receive the earnest and careful consideration of the Government through the Department of Justice and the Judiciary.

It remains for the commissioner of Indian Affairs to solve the problem of a politic and just disposition of the non-treaty Nez Perces. Except that I suggest a departure from the temporizing policy, and a conciliatory and just, yet speedy solution of the problem, I have no matured sentiments to present.

I cannot refrain from adding a word to express my convictions of the real cause of the dissatisfaction existing among the Nez Perces with the treaty of '63. Nature has implanted in the human heart a strong and undying love of home—the home, with its scenes and attachments, of childhood. This sentiment pervades the heart of the child of the forest and plain—the rude child of nature—no less, perhaps with a more fervent glow, than the breast of the native of the city, the pampered child of enlightened and luxurious civilization. The birth-place of Lawyer, the homes of his followers, the parties to the treaty, were included within the limits of the established reservation; while its contracted area excluded the homes of Joseph and all the prominent non-treaty chiefs and their bands, and ceded their venerated penates to the United States. To the parties to the treaty, it brought no loss, no change; to the non-treaties it revealed new homes, new scenes; it left behind deserted firesides; homes abandoned and desolate; casting a shadow upon their wounded and sorrowing hearts to darken and embitter their future existence. In this God-given sentiment—the love of home—is to be found the true cause of the Nez Perce division."[28]

---

[28] Major H. Clay Wood, *The Status of Young Joseph*, p. 41.

CHAPTER X

STORMY COUNCILS—PRELUDE TO WAR

THE NEZ PERCE COMMISSION'S REPORT DULY MADE, events moved rapidly toward a climax for the Dreamer Nez Perces. Joseph was given to understand, while winter yet lingered in 1877, that he and his band were to move within the bounds of the Nez Perce reservation.[1] February 9, 1877, Agent Monteith wrote J. Q. Smith, Commissioner of Indian Affairs:

I have given Joseph until April 1, 1877, to come on the reserve peaceably. They can come one time just as well as another, having nothing to hinder them in moving.

If the department intends to compel Joseph to comply with its wishes, I would recommend that the officer in command of the troops who are to occupy Wallowa Valley, in the interest of peace, be instructed to call on Joseph and inform him that unless he goes on the Nez Perce reserve on or before April 1, 1877, he will be forced to do so by the soldiers, and also inform him that he must remain on the reserve, not leaving it without a pass from the agent at Lapwai. This would have a tendency to hurry him up and show him that the department is in earnest. If he is allowed to have his own way this time, it will only make him more stubborn in the future.[2]

---

[1] [January 8, 1877, the Commissioner of Indian Affairs authorized "the Indian Agent at Lapwai . . . to take preliminary steps to carry into effect the several recommendations of the commission for the adjustment of difficulties existing between these Indians and white settlers in that valley and adjacent country, and if found to be necessary, will be instructed to call for military aid to enforce a settlement of this question." *(Rep. of Sec. of War, 1877, I, 586).* Apparently Monteith saw in this sufficient authority to demand the removal. (Ed. note.)]

[2] *Ibid.,* p. 116.

That Agent Monteith, knowing the climatic conditions of the region as well as he did, should urge the removal of the Indians and their stock at that season of the year, is appalling. And apparently Monteith did not inform General Howard of the time limit he had set, for on March 12, the General wrote Monteith: "I do not understand that we can take the offensive at all until further instructions from Washington. I am glad, indeed, you did not fix any time for the ultimatum of Joseph's coming."[3]

Size of Joseph's Following

There is a bit of interesting history connected with Chief Joseph's band that is not of record. Quite a contingent of his membership had been with him less than a score of years when the 1877 trouble came upon him and his following. Camille Williams tells me that in former years there was a group known as the Canyon Band, whose domain embraced half of Wallowa Lake. Lahpeealoot [Three Flocks Alighting on Water] was of this group, and said that in about 1859 their chief, Toaktamalweyun, was killed in a fight with the Snake Indians, and that his followers never elected a successor, but in time joined Old Joseph's band. Usually they wintered apart from the main group.

In a letter to Commissioner Smith, dated February 9, 1877, Monteith gives the number of Joseph's band as follows, "There were present in the lodge where the council was held about forty Indians, and fifteen on the outside, which is the strength of the band who claim Joseph as their chief."[4] The special commission

---

[3] *Ibid.*, p. 587.
[4] *Ibid.*, p. 115.

appointed to pass on the legality of the 1863 treaty, says of the numerical strength of Joseph's following as assembled for the council November 13, 1876, "Joseph and his band, sixty or seventy in number (including malcontents)."[5] From these indications it would appear that the Wallowa band could not have exceeded fifty-five or sixty males, young and old from which a fighting force of twenty-five, at most, could be mustered, since none under the age of seventeen took any part in the fighting, according to every warrior consulted. Besides there were slackers in the Indian camps, as among the white ranks.

The Umatilla Council

As winter drew to a close, both the civilian and military authorities prepared to coerce the nontreaties into removing to the shrunken Nez Perce reserve. Councils were held, and the first of these proved to be fraught with fire.

A little-known incident is that the Joseph contingent sponsored a plea that all of the nontreaties be permitted to go to the Umatilla reservation instead of the Nez Perce preserve. There were obvious grounds for such a petition. The Dreamer Nez Perces were blanket Indians as were the Umatillas. The two groups subscribed to the same primitive religious tenets, and, through intermarriage, blood ties were strong. They recalled that they had always been friendly toward the whites, even to joining them in war against their own race in 1855-58, and that their hands had ever been free from the stain of white blood.

---

[5] "Report of the Commission to the Nez Perces," in *Rep. of Sec. of Interior*, 1877, I, 607.

No record, as such, of this proposal appears in published government documents, but there is some evidence to support it in General Howard's supplementary report of the Nez Perce campaign, wherein he says:

When at Walla Walla in March, I met there Mr. Cornoyer, the Umatilla Indian agent, who informed me in substance, as follows: Joseph and his people, or some of them, are wishing to cross the Blue Ridge and visit the Umatilla Indians, particularly to see me (Cornoyer) and learn what the government proposes, claiming that the interpreter at Lapwai, in the fall, had not altogether spoken the "truth." I replied that he had better encourage these Indians to make their proposed visit. Mr. Cornoyer subsequently visited me in Portland, and told me these Indians were coming, and that he should meet them upon his return to the agency. Therefore I sent my aid-de-camp, Lieut. William H. Boyle to be present at the Agency interview. This took place April 1.

Joseph's younger brother, whose name is Ollicut (sometimes called "Young Joseph"), and Old Too-at or Dreamer, and a few others of Joseph's Indians were there. After the talk Ollicut expressed a desire to see me, and wished me to appoint the time and place. Lieut. Boyle telegraphed me accordingly as soon as he reached Walla Walla. Taking Ollicut for Joseph, I replied (April 11), that I would meet him at Fort Walla Walla April 19.[6]

A full account of what occurred at this interview at the Umatilla Agency has been told by Captain W. C. Painter of Walla Walla,[7] to his son Harry

---

[6] *Rep. of Sec. of War*, 1877, I, 590.

[7] W. Charles Painter was captain of the Walla Walla Volunteers, Bannock war of 1878, and saw service on the famous gunboat of the Columbia River. Governor Ferry commissioned Painter a lieutenant colonel of volunteers, and Governor Chadwick of Oregon, gave him authority to take command of all Oregon companies and groups of Oregon volunteers during the campaign. He refused to command the Walla Walla Volunteers in the conquest of the Nez Perces, the previous year. His sympathies were all with the nontreaties, believing that they were in the right and were being woefully defrauded of their lands. He preferred the jeers of his countrymen to an accusing conscience.

Painter. The elder Painter and Agent Cornoyer had been volunteer associates in the Indian war of 1855-58. This, and his open sympathetic friendship for the nontreaty Nez Perces, assured him a welcome place at the interview.

Lieutenant Boyle opened the meeting, with a request that the Indians speak what was on their minds. In the absence of Chief Joseph, Ollokot arose in an unmistakably happy frame of mind. He expressed for himself and his people their warm gratitude to General Howard for his promise that they could come to the Umatilla instead of the Nez Perce reservation, as better suited for their living. The Umatillas, like themselves, still wore the blanket, and were of the same religion and manner of living; as hunters, fishermen, gleaners of wild berries and herbs; and above all they were closely allied through intermarriage.

He spoke, through the interpreter, of the Nez Perce friendship for the whites in the past: in résumé, of their befriending Lewis and Clark, the explorers, when they came among them weak and ill from hunger. How they helped them in their continued traveling to the Big Water; how they had brought missionaries Walker and Eells safely through the after days of the Whitman massacre; how they had saved Spalding and helped him to reach shelter in the Willamette Valley; how they had always kept the treaty brought to them by Governor Stevens in 1855; how they aided Colonel Steptoe in the 1858 war; for all of which they looked back with glad hearts. Never had a white man's blood been shed by a Nez Perce; and now they felt repaid by General Howard's permitting them to come and live with their good friends and brothers, the Umatillas.

Chief Ollokot sat down amid the sanctioning, "Ahs! Ahs!" of his people. Lieutenant Boyle arose and spoke abruptly, "You are not coming to the Umatilla reservation! General Howard orders that you move to the Nez Perce reservation! That you get ready to move at once!"

There was no explanation. No attempt at softening the blow. It seemed incredible, and for a full moment the Indians sat in silence as if stunned. Then Ollokot was on his feet, and stepping forward with outstretched arm, first and index finger spread, (indicative of a serpent's tongue) pointing at the officer, he addressed him with scathing bitterness.

"*Nesammemiek* [liar or liars], who are you? Where General Howard? He promised to come to this council. I came, a chief to talk to a chief! General Howard sends one of his boys to give orders to the Nez Perces! I did not send one of my young men to talk to a chief! I am a chief and I came! Where is General Howard? General Howard talks with a forked tongue! He has lied to the Nez Perces! Was he ashamed to meet men to whom he talked two ways? Is he—a commander of soldiers—afraid? He has insulted me! Made me ashamed before my people! I am done!"

Major Cornoyer [his nominal military rank] and Captain Painter often discussed this Umatilla meeting afterwards and decided that General Howard had promised the Nez Perces they could remove to the Umatilla reservation, and that he had done so in good faith. Being officially rebuffed for this solution from Washington, he could not bring himself to break the ugly news to the Nez Perces, and so sent his young aid-de-camp for that purpose. He doubtless knew of the blind rejection his pacifying proposal had met when he conversed with Agent Cornoyer about the proposed meeting.[8]

---

[8] The above paragraphs are summarized from several letters written by Harry Painter to the author. (McW NP 35, pp. 1-33.)
In his report of December, 1877, Howard speaks of a wire from

If the story of Painter is accepted, this blindly arrogant act of Indian Bureau officialdom, three thousand miles from the scene of operation and therefore utterly incapable of judicious action, may be blamed for the wholly unnecessary and terribly unjust conflict of 1877.

The Walla Walla Council

Another council, the one requested by Ollokot at his meeting with Boyle, followed, April 20, at Walla Walla. Howard was present and says of the meeting:

On the 19th, in the afternoon, Ollicut, with several other Indians, makes his appearance at Fort Walla Walla, and excuses his delay, and explains that his brother (Joseph) is not coming, but that he himself wishes to have a talk with me in presence of several of his people. Colonel Grover has a barrack room prepared, where the interview took place, commencing at 10 o'clock A.M. on the 20th.

There were present Ollicut, Young Chief of the Umatillas, the Dreamer before mentioned, and several other non-treaty Nez Perces. Besides my aids, several officers of the fort and some citizens were present. The Indian agent Cornoyer and his interpreter, McBain, participated.

I explained the requirement of the government; that the

Lieutenant Boyle at Walla Walla, in which he mistook Ollokot for Joseph, *(Rep. of Sec. of War,* 1877, I, 590), but in his *Nez Perce Joseph,* p. 36, he reverses the mistake as having been made by the Lieutenant, which is evidently an error, since the wire was sent at Ollokot's request subsequent to the Umatilla council.

[Some doubt as to the credibility of the Painter-Cornoyer conclusions is suggested by the report of the five-man commission to the Nez Perce, in the fall of 1876, of which Howard was a member. Their recommendations suggested the abandonment of the Umatilla reservation, because of the extreme attractiveness of the area for white settlement, and the removal of the Umatillas to the Nez Perce preserve. (See *Rep. of Sec. of Int.,* 1877, I, 611-12). Why should Howard, who had apparently concurred in this recommendation, himself suggest the nontreaties join the Umatillas on a preserve there was considerable likelihood would soon be abandoned? It would seem more likely that the nontreaties themselves had initiated this solution, perhaps receiving some official encouragement which they interpreted as acceptance of the plan. (Ed. note.)]

Indians would be required to go on the reservation—some reservation; that the government had consented to allow Joseph and his people a yearly visit to the Imnaha Valley for hunting and fishing, but always with a pass from the agent.

The Indians seemed at first to wish to join the Umatillas, then it appears there was a project (probably originating with white men) to combine the reservation Indians of Umatilla with the non-treaty Nez Perces, and ask for them thus joined the Wallowa and Imnaha country giving up the Umatilla reserve. But I replied that the instructions are definite; that I should send troops very soon to occupy the Wallowa, and proceed to Lapwai as soon as possible in execution of my instructions.

Ollicut, who manifested a good disposition, was evidently afraid to promise anything, and I was aware that some representative of the Indian Bureau should take the initiative in dealing with these Indians, so that I was glad to have him ask to gather the Indians, all the non-treaties, to meet me at Fort Lapwai during my coming visit.[9]

While General Howard merely mentions in his official report the presence of Young Chief, of the Umatillas, at the Walla Walla council, later he wrote, ". . . Young Chief, the Umatilla friend and advocate, wishes some new lands in Wallowa that will hold them all (Cayuses, Walla-Walla, Umatillas, and non-treaty Nez Perces) in fellowship. Really matters did not look much like war. . . ."[10] It is indeed unfortunate that Howard did not make a more precise account of these developments.

Ollokot's Maps

Considerable has been written relative to a map (or maps) used at these councils that had been drawn

---

[9] *Rep. of Sec. of War*, 1877, I, 590.
[10] Howard, *Nez Perce Joseph*, p. 43.

by Ollokot, setting forth the Nez Perce claims. This map is first mentioned by Major Wood in his supplementary report, where he speaks of it as a,

> . . . crude but quite accurate sketch, drawn on paper with pencil . . . embracing the Grande Ronde, Wallowa rivers and Imnaha Rivers . . . all of which was claimed by the brothers. The area indicated on this map is much larger than that of the reservation as established by the Executive Order June 1873, which contained 912,000 acres. This sketch (and another also by Young Joseph) was covered with the usual Indian pictures representing whites, Indians, and Indian women, animals, guns, etc., intended to depict the scene and actors in the killing of the Indian . . . a kind of historical painting of that event [McNall-Findley crime].[11]

Lieutenant W. R. Parnell, acting recorder for Major Wood, later gave an interesting description from memory of this remarkable pictograph-map. He speaks of it as drawn in ink, on a peculiar yellowish paper. He gives the size as about sixteen or eighteen inches square.[12] Mr. A. C. Smith, whose friendliness for the Nez Perces had tarnished his reputation among the Indian-hating settlers, declared that Chief Joseph told him that General Howard drew a map of the Nez Perce reservation leaving out the Imnaha and Wallowa country. Joseph refused to recognize this map and drew one himself which included those valleys. The General agreed to endorse this map and took it, and also retained the one drawn by himself. The Joseph map was never afterwards heard of. General Howard turned in his own map as having been accepted by the chief.

Possibly there is something to this story from Mr. Smith. Andrew Whitman, Nez Perce, claims to have seen the map, or maps in question, along with one

---

[11] Wood's *Supplementary* to *The Status of Young Joseph*, p. 5.
[12] W. R. Parnell, "The Battle of White Bird Canyon," in Brady, *Northwestern Indian Fights and Fighters*, (N.Y., 1923), pp. 96-7.

drawn of the White Bird country in the archives of the Indian Office, Washington, D.C. He examined also, he declared, a map of an earlier date, possibly 1848, delineating the Nez Perce domain in its original entirety.

Diligent inquiry among the survivors of the Nez Perce war failed to disclose the remotest trace of this sample of Indian pictography. If Ollokot was the sole custodian of the map, and if it was not lost or destroyed during the long, weary retreat, it may have been interred with his body at the battle of Bear Paw Mountain or burned in accordance with an ancient racial custom. But with these latter suppositions, Wottolen disagreed. He was of the opinion that all papers or drawings would have been taken over by Chief Joseph as of great importance. However this may be, unless it comes to light some day in the files of the Indian Office or elsewhere in the national archives, this relic of unsurpassed interest has been irretrievably lost. On this score, the following comment by War Singer is appropriate,

I am told by an old Indian [Paul Slickpoo] that was present at the time Ollokot tore up the map [that Major Clay Wood drew] in the presence of all government officials at Lapwai Agency, telling this Major that the map was drawn by guess. All the faces of the officers turned red but none of them said a word when the torn map was thrown on the floor. Maybe after that Ollokot may had [have] drawn the map of the area that they owned. They owned Grand Ronde of Wallewa [the Indian name] on north and east sides, as some of his band used to live twelve miles north of the mouth of the Grand Ronde River. They owned largest district in Nez Perce tribe. If Ollokot kept the map, Joseph must have got it, and if he had it, it must be in his grave today. I was once asked if I could help in getting out some important papers that was thrown into Joseph's coffin at the time he was reburied in Nespelem.[13]

---

13 This reburial just referred to by War Singer was at the placing

The Lapwai Council

We have noted how General Howard, at the ineffectual Walla Walla council, welcomed a prospective meeting with all the nontreaties at Fort Lapwai on the Nez Perce reservation. Accordingly the council convened May 3, 1877, with only Joseph, Ollokot and about fifty Dreamers present, the council being opened with a prayer by Father Cataldo from the near-by Catholic mission.[14] Because of mountain snowdrifts and slippery trails, Chief White Bird and others of the Salmon River bands failed to reach the grounds until the next day. To Joseph's suggestion, "You must not be in a hurry to go till all can get in to have a talk," General Howard reluctantly agreed, adding significantly, "Instructions to him [White Bird] are the same as to you. He can take his turn."[15]

General Howard had no patience with the Dreamer desire for time to talk "many days about the earth, about our land," and informed them that no matter how long they talked, in the end they must obey the orders of the government. To this Agent Monteith added, "Now you must come, and there is no getting out of it. Your Indians and White Bird's can pick up your horses and cattle, and come on the reservation."[16] At that time, the herds of the Dreamers were scattered over a vast territory, a fact of which Monteith could not have been ignorant.

General Howard speaks of his threat to arrest and punish two old Dreamers for being saucy and quarrelsome in their manner. Obviously aware that

---

of the Chief Joseph monument in 1905. The Nez Perces tell that, at the request of Professor Edmund Meany, the body was exhumed and exposed to view; for what reason is not known, unless for positive identification.

[14] Howard, *Nez Perce Joseph*, pp. 51-3.

[15] *Ibid.*, pp. 53-4.

[16] Howard, *Nez Perce Joseph*, pp. 54-5; *Rep. Sec. War*, 1877, I, 593.

establishing such a precedent was a flagrant breech of ethics in a council where free exchange of ideas was supposed to operate, the General apologizes, "Severity of manner in dealing with savages is believed by many of the Indian's friends to be always uncalled for and decidedly wrong. It may be so, but the manner of dealing must depend upon the peculiarities of the people with whom you have to deal."[17]

That day's council closed with nothing accomplished, and convened the next day, the fourth, with White Bird and Toohoolhoolzote both present. Alpowa Jim, a treaty Christian Nez Perce, offered up a prayer in his native tongue at General Howard's request.[18] Nothing was accomplished at this meeting except an increase in tension to which sparring between General Howard and the Nez Perce spokesman, Chief Toohoolhoolzote, contributed. General Howard betrayed his hostility to Toohoolhoolzote in his description of him as a "large, thick-necked, ugly savage of the worst type."[19] His domain was a wild, rugged country lying between the Salmon and Snake rivers, and his following was not large. Again General Howard says of him, "The Chief of this band, since my acquaintance with it, was Too-hul-hul-sote. He was a cross-grained growler, a sort of sub-chief to White Bird, and a 'Dreamer drummer,' called by the Indians too-at."[20] Actually Toohoolhoolzote was under no other chief. He had his own distinct following and his own recognized domain. At the winter councils the Nez Perces had chosen him to talk for them all

---

[17] Howard, *Ibid.*, pp. 55-6.

[18] *Rep. of the Sec. of War*, 1877, I, 593.

[19] *Loc. cit.*

[20] Howard, *op. cit.*, p. 18. "Tewat" is the proper spelling of the term for medicine man or medicine woman. Toohoolhoolzote was not in any manner a medicine man.

at the spring meetings they knew to be inevitable. He was not a medicine man as Howard insisted.

It is regrettable that the General's depiction of the Lapwai councils are so tinged with self-heroics. First, Joseph and Ollokot are branded with the unpardonable sin of having inherited from their mother the blood of the "fierce and treacherous Cayuses."[21] Their mother was a full Nez Perce, and their father was half Nez Perce and half Cayuse.[22] And as for Ollokot's unqualified stand for war,[23] according to every warrior talked with, not one of the chiefs favored an appeal to arms.[24]

Perturbed by the unlooked-for turn of events at this assembly, General Howard welcomed a three-day delay in the council proceedings, hoping for time to bring troops from Walla Walla and other points as a precautionary [intimidating?] measure against any possible emergency when the council should reconvene the following Monday, May 7th.[25] At least soldiers would serve as a nerve-bracer for fear-racked officialdom. The specter of the Modoc massacre seemed ever present.[26]

The council convened the morning of the seventh, with many additions to the Indian aggregation. As the sequel well proves, General Howard held no hope for a favorable termination. In granting the request for a council Howard, in reality, recognized the Nez Perce right to air their grievances, but his subsequent mandatory procedure reveals that was not his inten-

---

[21] *Ibid.*, p. 2.

[22] See Appendix VII, "Old Joseph," p. 598.

[23] Howard, *Nez Perce Joseph*, p. 25; *My Life and Experiences*, p. 255.

[24] See McWhorter, *Yellow Wolf*, p. 42.

[25] *Rep. of the Sec. of War*, 1877, I, 594; *Nez Perce Joseph*, pp. 59-60; *My Life and Experiences*, pp. 252-53.

[26] *Nez Perce Joseph*, p. 23, 67.

tion. One might almost say his paramount object was to strike at the Dreamer cult, to strike and if possible break the power of that "Too-schul-hul-sote, by name, a large thick-necked, ugly, obstinate savage of the worst type."[27] Despite Toohoolhoolzote's assertion that he was not a medicine man, and was not so regarded by his followers, General Howard seemed to insist that he was such and so accosted him.[28] Had the General been better acquainted with Indian life, he would have known that the insignia of the medicine man was the wing of an eagle, which on state occasions such as this assemblage, was gracefully poised against the tip of the nose. Chief White Bird was a medicine man and so displayed his emblem, only to have General Howard interpret it as face-hiding.[29]

It would seem appropriate at this point to explain just how Chief Toohoolhoolzote came to pose as spokesman for the Nez Perces at the Lapwai councils. Red Elk, who was well informed on the oral history of his tribe, gave the following interesting account of the chief's elevation to the position of leadership on this occasion.

After the killing of Wil Hutyo, [Wilhautyah], in the Wallowa, great excitement prevailed and fighting came nearly taking place. That fall—1876—the bands of Chiefs White Bird, Joseph, Looking Glass and Toohoolhoolzote, gathered in council about ten miles above the mouth of the White Bird, on the Salmon.

At this winter council the chiefs appointed Toohoolhoolzote, head speaker for all the bands. So, in May, when meeting General Howard in council, Toohoolhoolzote had power to reply to any request or demand coming from the

---

[27] *Rep. of the Sec. of War*, 1877, v. 1, p. 593.

[28] *Nez Perce Joseph*, p. 66; *My Life and Experiences*, p. 255.

[29] *Nez Perce Joseph*, pp. 58-65; *My Life and Experiences*, p. 255; Howard, *Famous Indian Chiefs I Have Known*, p. 192.

General of whatsoever nature. He could agree or refuse as seemed best. One of the great stumbles was the thirty days set by General Howard for removal to the smaller reservation. The chiefs all thought that a year was short time enough; or until autumn at the least.

At the winter council Toohoolhoolzote had compared the status of the two races, to the planting of two trees in close proximity. The trees would grow as they have room. Suns, moons, and snows, go by. They grow! Taller their tops, wider their branches. Their limbs come together, twining and twisting about each other. Their growth is not equal. The larger, the stronger tree holds the smaller, the weaker tree down. The one grows stronger, the other becomes weaker.

That is the way of the two races. In future snows they will be mixed. The whites many, the Nez Perces few. They, the smaller will be smothered by the larger tree, the whites.

Wottolen quoted the following speech of Toohoolhoolzote at the winter council on the Salmon, prior to the Lapwai Council:

Who is it that lives above? Is it the First Man, or is it the Second man? You are second man, I am second man. We are but children. I am a child. He who lives above, set me down where the rivers flow, where the mountains stand. I must not make him angry by going elsewhere. I have no willing mind to listen to anyone telling me to move to a different place.

Toohoolhoolzote could not be scared. He said, "When I was born, when I came from my mother into life, I was a baby. I grew to be a boy. I learned to use the arrow and bow. I hunted the birds and the rabbit. When I shot any kind of bird, when I killed, I saw that its life went out with its blood. This taught me for what purpose I am here. I came into this world to die. My body is only to hold a spirit life. Should my blood be sprinkled, I want no wounds from behind. Death must come fronting me."

Toohoolhoolzote and General Howard

Perhaps never in the history of councils convened between the Caucasian and the American Indian were the opposing interests headed by leaders so divergent in their thinking, and yet so similar in temperament. Both deeply religious, and equally devoted and sincere in their convictions, each was impious in the sight of the other. Chief Toohoolhoolzote, whose domain lay on the upper Snake River, was dominant over the nontreaty or Upper Nez Perces. He proudly traced his lineage through a line of noted warriors, to Hime Payex, a legendary hero. Primitive-minded, an integral part of the wilderness life in which he had been reared, profoundly imbued with the Dreamer philosophy, Toohoolhoolzote was the chosen spokesman of all the bands. He believed that the creator [the First Man, the Flying Person] had, in his superior wisdom, left the earth in finished condition, to remain thus undisturbed; that he had geographically distributed or parcelled his domain among the various tribes and nations as he intended they should thereafter abide. Here was a deistic Dreamer, profoundly reverent of the spiritual in nature, holding fast to his ancestral traditions against any apocryphal, alien cosmogony.

There was, in the mind of this primitive priest, no animosity toward Christianity or other alien religions, as such. But an infallible judge of human nature, he instantly saw in General Howard an implacable enemy, and in his own way he met the challenge. General Howard's obtuse and arrogant enforcement of official decree wrecked an already weakened friendship, and as the sequel reveals, he reckoned without his host. In depicting the council scene, Howard says in part:

Too-hul-hul-sote, the cross-grained growler, was again designated as the speaker, and he took up his parable. He was, if possible, crosser and more impudent in his abruptness of manner than before. He had the usual long preliminary discussion about the earth being his mother, that she should not be disturbed by hoe or plow, that men should subsist on what grows of itself, etc. He repeated his ideas concerning "chieftainship," chieftainship of the earth. Chieftainship cannot be sold, cannot be given away. Mr. Monteith and General Howard, he said, must speak the truth about the chieftainship of the earth.

He was answered, "We do not want to interfere with your religion, but you must talk about practicable things. Twenty times over you repeat that the earth is your mother, and about chieftainship of the earth. Let us hear it no more, but come to the business at once."[30]

Although scholarly and learned, the General was also a pedant, and, in addition, inclined to underestimate the ability of a numerically weak, though highly patriotic and resourceful antagonist. Proudly arrogant in his ideas of race supremacy, sedulously pious and austere in his religious views, the "Bible General" was intolerant of all heathenish proclivities. His imperious garroting of justice where the tribesmen had been invited to speak and show their minds was destined to cost staggeringly in life and treasure, leaving a murky tinge athwart the halo of our exalted national escutcheon.

According to the few remaining warriors who were at the council, the crisis came when General Howard demanded of Chief Toohoolhoolzote, "Do you intend coming on the reservation peaceably, or shall I put you there with my soldiers?"

The Chief answered, "You have brought a rifle to a peace council. If you mean but thirty suns for gathering of our stock, yes. We will have to fight."

---

[30] *Nez Perce Joseph*, p. 64.

Chief Toohoolhoolzote was arrested and imprisoned, not for any crime, not for any treason against a government which he could not understand. General Howard's excuse that the seizure of the Nez Perce spokesman was necessary to carry out department orders will not hold under scrutiny. Violence should have been the last resort, and certainly could not have been legally executed until the expiration of the time limit for removal to the reservation. The time allowed for this removal was to be the pitiful span of thirty days. Seven hundred and twenty hours, three hundred and sixty daylight hours, in which to bring together thousands of horses and cattle scattered over hundreds of miles of valley and rugged mountain region seamed by swift, flood-swollen streams. A glaringly preposterous order!

At various times, in various ways, the General has mentioned that he ordered the arrest of Toohoolhoolzote because he saw evidence of armed resistance among the Nez Perces assembled. In 1881 he said, "I noticed some of them had weapons."[31] Again, in 1907, ". . . for every Indian appeared to have just at that time, some weapon ready at hand for use . . .

"At that instant some of the Indians were on the point of plunging their knives into my breast, but Joseph and White Bird both counciled delay."[32] But the most blood-curdling portrayal is the following from a still later publication:

Joseph said: "Too-hul-hul-sote will speak."
The old man was very angry and said, "What person pretends to divide the land and put me on it?" I answered: "I am that man."
Then among the Indians all about me signs of anger began to appear. Looking Glass dropped his gentle style and

---

[31] *Ibid.*, p. 65.
[32] *My Life and Experiences*, p. 254, 256.

made rough answers. White Bird, hiding his face behind that eagle wing, said he had not been brought up to be governed by white men, and Joseph began to finger his tomahawk and his eyes flashed. Too-hul-hul-sote said fiercely:

"The Indians may do as they like, I am not going on that land."[33]

It is rather significant that these depictions of knives and Joseph's tomahawk, do not appear in the General's first publication, *Nez Perce Joseph*, off the press in 1881, four years after the war, although therein are found many uncomplimentary comments on this chief and his philosophy.

As to the Nez Perces being armed at this council, the late Peopeo Tholekt of the Looking Glass band, who was present, mildly but emphatically declared:

Not so! There was no talk of making a fight. Only Peopeo Moxmox had a side knife, and there were no guns of any kind among them whatever. Peopeo Moxmox, Sr., was killed some time before the war, and the son did not join in the war which followed the arrest of Chief Toohoolhoolzote.

There was a feeling that the Dreamers should settle on the North Clearwater, and the Christians remain in the Lapwai country. None of the chiefs wanted war. They knew they could never win.

Of what immediately followed on the arrest of their speaker, Wottolen, White Bird's faithful adherent and councilor declared, "I was not there when our chosen speaker was arrested. I came into the council place a few minutes later and when told what had been done, I asked, 'Why submit to this wrong?

---

[33] *Famous Indian Chiefs I Have Known*, p. 192. [In his official report of the council, written May 22, Howard mentions no show of force on the part of the Indians at all, and indicates his only aim was to teach the chief a lesson. (*Rep. Sec. War*, 1877, I, 595). (Ed. note.)]

Why not make resistance?'" When Wottolen was informed of General Howard's claim that the Indians were armed, that his life was in danger, the blind old warrior replied in his usual even tone:

It is a lie! General Howard saw restlessness, but no weapons. Had there been arms among the Indians, our head speaker would not have been jailed. I know the Nez Perces were not armed, but I saw soldiers on both sides of the council gathering, with guns in their hands.

Had General Howard created Toohoolhoolzote, the chief would have minded his orders and moved to the reservation. But it was otherwise and he had to remain where placed from his birth. The Flying Person was greater than General Howard, who might kill by gun and sword and destroy with fire, but that was all. The chief had to observe the rules and laws first given by the true Creator of all life. He was not to be scared at threats against his own body. He was not to tremble at death of any form. He was not to be scared at death of any form. He did not want war and had General Howard been more kind there would have been no war.

All the Indians will tell you that had he allowed more time for gathering up our stock and moving to the reservation, there would have been no war. Why such hurry at that time of year? Time was not quitting, was not stopping! The big, swift rivers in full flood, much stock was sure to be lost in the crossing. We all believed Monteith wanted war, and that General Howard thought he would just have a walkaway.

Of the arrest, the Indians avowed, "It was a soldier, a tall fellow who first took hold of Chief Toohoolhoolzote." General Howard's depiction of the scene runs, "I called for the messenger, but he being away, Colonel [then captain] Perry and I led Too-hul-hul-zote out of the council."[34]

---

[34] *Nez Perce Joseph*, pp. 66-67; McWhorter, *Yellow Wolf*, p. 40; *Rep. of the Sec. of War*, 1877, I, 595.

Was the Arrest of Toohoolhoolzote Necessary?

Mrs. Frances Monteith, who as a young woman was present at the Lapwai council, made this reply to the author's inquiry in 1933 as to whether there was necessity and justice in the arrest of Toohoolhoolzote in the midst of a peace council,

You ask if I was present at those Lapwai councils. Yes, and my eyes and ears are my undeniable proof. My father (Perrin Whitman) was the Official Interpreter, my husband, Charles Monteith, was the Secretary, my brother-in-law, John B. Monteith, the Indian Agent. If we were to be massacred we would all go together, and it looked as though we might, more times than once. The scare is something to look back upon as a thrilling experience but the reality at the time was nothing pleasant.

I note you say: "I have thought that Gen. Howard was unduly alarmed." I am personally able to most emphatically contradict that! The records are true. The Too-hool-sote's arrest no doubt in the minds of Agency men, and everyone present, prevented then and there an armed resistance. His fiery and threatening speech was noticeably inflammatory. When the Sergeant of the Guard who was nearby was called to take him to the Guard House, the rebellious attitude from Joseph and his brother instantly became the attitude of acquiescence, and when the council closed that afternoon it was with the agreement that Joseph and his aides would choose their homes which, as you will read, they did.[35]

The Dreamers were agitators, violently opposed to any sort of governmental control, and naturally had many followers, and his arrest at that particular time was necessary. The whispering and under blanket attitude ceased peaceably.

Personally, I could see nothing but trouble long drawn out, probably, but there was a very definite state of reversion by the Tewats, "Dreamer Medicine men." The arrest was the only way to convince and compel authority, and it was effectual at the time. In the united opinion of the army officers at Fort Lapwai it was necessary. General Howard then and there became the master of the situation.

---

[35] John P. Schorr, who was present at the council as a sergeant under Lieutenant Wm. R. Parnell, wrote in reply to an inquiry, "If the Indians were armed, it was not noticeable."

CHAPTER XI

THE ALIGNMENT OF FORCES

IT HAS BEEN NOTED WITH WHAT UNTIMELY HASTE Agent Monteith pressed the removal of the nontreaty Nez Perces from their ancient habitat and rightful homes. General Howard could not legally proceed to use force to transfer them until formally requested by the Indian Bureau through the local agent. Such notice was not delayed as the following, written May 3, 1877, attests, "I would respectfully request that you assist me in the removal of Joseph's and other roving bands of Nez Perce Indians to and locate them upon proper lands within the boundaries of the Nez Perce reservation by the use of such troops as you may deem necessary."[1] Thus it will be noticed, Agent Monteith's call for military interference bears the date of the first day of the peace council, and the two days that followed under the guise of attempted conciliation can be stamped as supreme mockery.

But with Chief Toohoolhoolzote imprisoned and the mailed hand at their throats, the remaining chiefs accompanied General Howard and Agent Monteith for the purpose of selecting lands for their future homes. Thirty days, from May 14, was the time limit for gathering their widely scattered stock and moving within the smaller reservation. "Protection papers" were given the four Nez Perce chiefs proper,

---

[1] "Letter, Monteith to Howard, May 3, 1877," *Rep. of Sec. of War,* 1877, I, 117.

and thirty days granted them for getting themselves and stock within the limits of the smaller reservation. Owing to the greater distance to be traversed, the Paloos contingent was favored with an extra time limit, minus "protection," of which General Howard explains, ". . . Hush-hush-cute [Husishusis Kute] was given thirty-five days. He was the only Indian who at this time, betrayed any symptoms of treachery. His protection papers were withheld on account of it, and given to the agent, to be presented to him when the agent should be satisfied of his good intentions."[2]

As to the symptoms of treachery the General observed in this young Dreamer, every tenet of the Dreamer philosophy was traitorous in the zealot eyes of Howard. There is however, a Nez Perce version of the withholding of the protection papers, fraught with amusing irony. The proud Paloos orator, incensed at the penury of the time for their removal, is supposed to have refused the paper with the bland retort, "I do not want it. I might get the *temis* [paper] dirty!"

Contrary to Howard's statement, Husishusis Kute was not chief of the small Paloos band. A priest or religious man, he was renowned for his eloquence of speech and for this reason he was selected to second Chief Toohoolhoolzote as a pleader for their cause. But he was accorded no opportunity to talk, hence his sarcasm relative to his protection paper.

According to Camille Williams, Husishusis Kute was a sort of sub-leader-chief of that section of the Paloos band whose habitat was at Wawawai. This group and the Paloos proper (who lived at the confluence of the Snake and the Palouse) spoke the same

---

2 Howard, *Nez Perce Joseph*, p. 72.

language and were in reality the same tribe. Husis-husis Kute was the chosen spokesman for both groups at the Lapwai council, where they constituted the smallest nontreaty aggregation. He had inherited both the name and mantle of his elder brother who was an outstanding Dreamer prophet, and a general favorite with all the people.[3]

Hahtalekin was chief of the main Paloos group who lived at the confluence of the Palouse and the Snake, and his followers, like those of Husishusis Kute, opposed the idea of war. Hahtalekin was also known as Taktsoukt Ilppilp [Echo or Red Echo]. He was in the buffalo-hunter class, and reckoned a brave and discreet warrior.[4] The confusion in the Paloos chieftaincy was brought about by General Howard's ignorance of their personnel. The General betrays his animus where he speaks of the man he supposed to be the leader of the whole group, ". . . a wily chief-

---

[3] War Singer (Camille Williams) contributed the following information:
"Husishusis Kute had three brothers. Their names were, Wesims, Husishusis Kute I, Husishusis Kute II, and Yusyus Tokekazein. Husishusis Kute I was elected chief of the Paloos band after the war with Cayuse and other bands. He took part in this war. When fighting with troops near Cheyney, Washington, he got so thirsty he ran to the lake or large pond. He lay down on his belly to drink. The troops fired a cannon on the Indians but didn't hit anyone. The cannon ball touched Husis' head while drinking. That knocked him into the water unconscious. He was pulled out by other warriors. Next day or two his hair come off his head. His hair was clipped short above his ears. He was bald for a long time. When the swelling left him, he told his warriors that he was going to take the name of Husishusis Kute." [Bald Head]

[4] The Paloos were closely amalgamated with the Nez Perces in both language and environment, and the only logical reason that can be advanced for their having been thrown with the Yakimas in the Treaty of 1855, is that they owned an empire of the finest of lands, coveted by the treaty makers for the whites. The Paloos did not realize the swindle until too late, and therein was the just cause for their joining in the Yakima War, 1855-8. Koolattoose, properly Klahtoosh, was the only member of the tribe to sign the treaty (if he did sign) which they repudiated. They declined to lead a reservation life. Strong and hardy, home-loving people, they stood on a par with the Nez Perces with whom they were widely intermarried. The two tribes should have been placed together by the treaty.

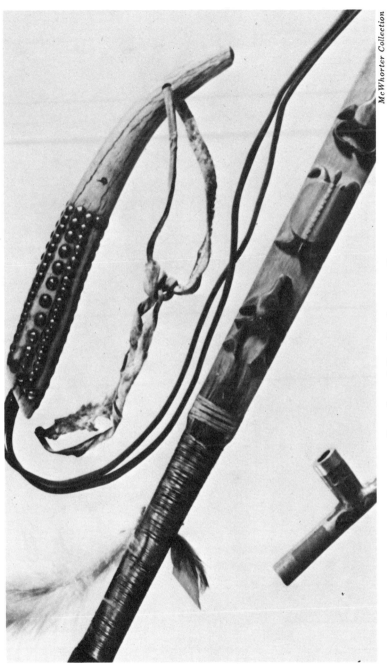

CHIEF JOSEPH'S PIPE, PIPE STEM, AND QUIRT

OLLOKOT

This picture was taken at Walla Walla, Washington in June, 1877, immediately before the outbreak of the Nez Perce war, according to W. C. Painter, who saw the picture taken. Ollokot was a brother of Chief Joseph's.

tain about the age of Young Joseph [Ollokot]. It could be said of him in the words of Scripture, his heart was deceitful above all things and desperately wicked."[5] According to Nez Perce tradition, Peopeo Moxmox appealed to General Howard as follows,

"Husishusis Kute has a religion unlike that brought by the white people. He has a drum to beat in worship same as myself. When he locates I want him next to me at Potlatch Creek. Settle us all on one side of Lapwai, and the new religious people on the other side. Then there will be no interference."

Toohoolhoolzote was freed on pledges from Chiefs White Bird and Looking Glass for his good behavior.[6] There is a native story to the effect that a contingent of young men from the White Bird and Toohoolhoolzote bands, fully armed, mounted, and chanting a war song, were on their way, resolved on a desperate attempt to rescue their spokesman, when forestalled by his release.

Returning to Portland, General Howard wired Division Headquarters, May 21,

Non-treaty Nez Perces constrained compliance with orders of government. Thirty days allowed to gather scattered people and stock.[7]

---

[5] Howard, *Nez Perce Joseph*, p. 19.

[6] Howard, *Nez Perce Joseph*, p. 69; *My Life and Experiences*, p. 257. War Singer avers he never heard of such pledge being made. Of his release he writes, "As the Chief stepped from the Guard House, he was hailed as 'bride' by the other Indians, because he was wearing a white shirt given him by some soldier. It was a custom that a newly married woman would always get a new dress from relations of her husband. General Howard does not mention how long he held the Chief prisoner, nor why he did not arrest Ollokot for talking the same words spoken by Toohoolhoolzote."

[7] *Rep. of Sec. of War*, 1877, I, 117.

Fundamental Causes of the War

Religion played its role in bringing about the wholly unnecessary conflict of 1877. With the primitive and weak, land was religion. With the civilized and strong, religion was land and more land, obtained after the ancient Joshua procedure. Howard clung to Smoholla's doctrine of an Indian resurrection to drive out the whites as a primary cause of the war. Later he wrote of the prewar period:

> This fanaticism is kept alive by the superstition of these "dreamers," who industriously teach, that, if they continue steadfast in their present belief, a leader will be raised up in the east, who will restore all the dead Indians to life, who will unite them in expelling the whites from their country, when they will again enter upon and repossess the lands of their ancestors.
>
> Influenced by such a belief Joseph and his band firmly declined to enter into any negotiations, or make any arrangements, that looked to a final settlement of the questions pending between himself and the Government.[8]

Howard attributed the acceptance of the whole of Smoholla's teachings to the Nez Perce Dreamers, but he had never broached the subject of a reappearance of deceased Indians who would assist in the recovery of their lands, to Joseph or the other leaders. This is regrettable, and the only inference is that he had accepted unquestioningly Agent Meacham's erroneous statement attributing the origination of the Dreamer cult to Smoholla. Smoholla's doctrine of resurrection did not "take" among the Nez Perces.[9] A letter to Many Wounds telling of General Howard's sweeping indictment, brought this prompt and terse response, "No such story was told among the Nez

---

[8] Howard, *Nez Perce Joseph*, pp. 32-3.
[9] See above Chapter V, p. 76.

Perces. Never heard nobody say that before the war
or after the war. This is all bull!''

James Mooney, in his *The Ghost Dance Religion*,
commenting on the Nez Perce War, declares, "As is
generally the case with Indian wars, it originated
with the unauthorized intrusion of lawless whites on
lands which the Indians claimed as theirs by virtue
of occupancy from time immemorial."[10]

This intrusion by lawless whites was indisputably
encouraged if not authorized by both civil and Fed-
eral officials, all glaringly in the open. There was no
secrecy about the influx of stock rustlers and settlers
into the Wallowa Valley. The movement of whisky-
mongers and gold pirates in the Salmon River basin
was not hidden nor did the tent city of Lewiston, with
its boasted twelve hundred souls, spring into existence between two suns. While the crime of 1863 was
the embryo of the pillages and local politicians, it
was incubated and hatched in the government's ter-
ritorial-expansion nest. Surely a blindfold justice
slept on the pinnacled crags of the Clearwater, while
vulture-beaked greed wasted the piteous remnant of
a once-splendid people.

The Nez Perces Prepare to Move

The deeply wronged Nez Perces, with no other
alternative, proceeded to the arduous task of round-
ing-up their far-ranging stock, horses and cattle, a
half year's task crowded into a thirty-day limit, an
injustice for which no legitimate excuse has ever, or
can ever, be offered. Added to all this, loomed the
certainty of loss from lack of adequate pasturage on

---

[10] James Mooney, "The Ghost Dance Religion, and the Sioux Outbreak of 1890," *Fourteenth Annual Report of the Bureau of American
Ethnology*, 1892-93, II, 712.

the greatly contracted reservation. The drowning of thousands of animals was sure to be followed by the starvation of vast numbers. The Grand Ronde and Salmon River valleys were the best stock range the Nez Perces had, freest of snow. The Snake River Valley was climatically good, but so broken and steep that their stock could not get over it.

Stalled by river floods, a vast herd of cattle were being held on the far side of the Snake, when the herders left to protect it were attacked by whites, and the cattle driven off.[11] This charge was confirmed by Peopeo Tholekt of the Chief Looking Glass band, who could tell little about the incident except that a large bunch of cattle were lost. There are well-authenticated stories of cattle and horse thievery with no interference from state or county officials and winked at by the military stationed at Fort Lapwai "in the interest of law and order." It was during this month preceding hostilities that a herd of two hundred cattle, left in the Grand Ronde country, were driven away by the two Owsley cattlemen. This drove was but a small part of the vast numbers left there. Approximately two hundred pack-horse loads of cured *kouse* roots were left cached in the Grand Ronde because of the potential dangers incurred in crossing the Snake at floodtime, cached to be moved at a more propitious time. This vast store of food was later destroyed by the military. While the men rounded up the stock on the range, the aged, the women, and the children of the five bands gathered at their ancient tryst, Tepahlewam, [Split Rocks or Deep Cuts] where the women harvested and cured the stores of camas adjoining Tolo Lake.[12]

---

[11] See Helen Hunt Jackson, *A Century of Dishonor* (Boston, 1887), p. 131.

[12] The Nez Perce name for this historic lake was Eewahtam [Small Body of Water, such as a miniature lake or pond]. For the history

The moving of the cattle blocked by the high water which prevailed at that season, the riders, with the exception of the few who remained to watch the herd to prevent straying, also retired to the Split Rocks rendezvous. It was after this that the light guards beyond the angry swift-flowing Snake were overcome by an outnumbering band of cattle thieves and the entire herd driven away. This open outrage was further fuel added to the still smoldering fires engendered by "showing of the rifle" at the peace council.

SIZE AND STATUS OF NONTREATY BANDS IN 1877

Because government sources and partisan writers have so overestimated the number of warriors engaged in the 1877 struggle, it seems expedient to look briefly into the following of the chiefs, naming them in the order of their numerical strength, followed by a brief description of each.

Chief Joseph's Band

Chief Joseph's following, officially reported to be about fifty-five males,[13] may have been close to sixty, and was reckoned the largest of the five bands constituting the Nez Perce malcontents. They were called the Kammooenem or Pammuienem.[14]

---

of how it came by its name, Tolo Lake, see Appendix I, p. 52, in *Yellow Wolf*. This historic lake and the region known as Tepahlewam were within the domain of Chief Heyoom Ilppilp [Red Bear], son of Chief Many Wounds, the "Bloody Chief" of Lewis and Clark fame.

[13] *Rep. of Sec. of War*, 1877, I, 115. See Chapter X, pp. 150-51, for further analysis of the size and composition of Joseph's following.

[14] This place name is derived from *kammoo*, a hemp weed growing along a certain section of the Snake River, from the fiber of which an especially strong cord and fishing lines were made. These manufactured articles were designated by the same name borne by the growing weed. *Nem* means a designated place on Snake River. Thus Chief Joseph's band was identified as *Kammooenem*, literally "people of Snake River."

Contrary to Indian custom, history has accorded Chief Joseph unqualified pre-eminence over his four associate chiefs.[15] Joseph, the youngest of the five and the only one among them not a buffalo hunter—and therefore inexperienced in tribal or other forms of warfare—would inevitably be barred from the war leadership of the whole group.[16] The source of his historic fame must be looked for elsewhere. Pure circumstance coupled with the outstanding natural ability of Chief Ollokot, his younger brother, had much to do with his fame. Ollokot was at many times his monitor and guide.

Also, the Wallowa was more remote and isolated than were the holdings of the other nontreaty chiefs whose lands were so early overrun by the swarming gold seekers that there was not the chance to contend against encroachments that Joseph's location afforded him. Joseph saw and took advantage of his situation and his gallant fight against military-protected banditry won for him not only brilliant renown among his own people, but the admiration and sympathy of all justice-respecting peoples. The leadership he displayed in the days just preceding the war plus the glamor of his surrender to Colonel Miles assured him canonization in the annals.

But his unwarranted fame as a military leader is regrettable. The bare facts in Chief Joseph's

---

[15] Chief Joseph's native name, *Heinmot Tooyalakekt*, has had several English renditions, but that of "Thunder Traveling to Loftier (mountain) Heights" seems the most correct. This conclusion was reached after long and close Nez Perce contacts. The translation, "The Sound of Thunder Coming Up From Water" (McBeth, *History of the Nez Perces*, p. 94), would seem to smack of ambiguity, since no syllable of it appears to denote water, which in Nez Perce is *coose* or *cooze.*

[16] See *Yellow Wolf*, p. 218. Only once does Yellow Wolf speak of Chief Joseph as giving anything like an order. When he returned from Colonel Miles' camp where he had been held a prisoner, he said to the warriors, "I was hobbled in the soldier camp. We must fight more. The war is not quit!"

career were sufficient without fictional embellishment by friendly, overzealous writers. It may be startling to many, but Chief Joseph was not a military genius. In Indian society, a "war-chief" or foray leader must be wholly self-made by acts of daring and heroism in contact with the enemy. Joseph had never accomplished these things. He had been in the buffalo country only once as an adult, and had never joined any war party in hostile territory. Chief Joseph was preeminently a man of peace.

In all contacts with the enemy, it devolved upon the chief or leader to announce any contemplated advance or attack on an opposing line or position. Not once during the entire war did Joseph, according to the warriors interviewed, ever pretend to assume such a role. Chellooyeen [Bow and Arrow Case (Phillip Evans)] and Lahpeealoot [Two Flocks on Water (Phillip Williams)] were both of Chief Joseph's contingent throughout the war. Quoting Bow and Arrow Case: "Indian commanders always made announcement before attack or battle. Joseph never did that. Joseph had not the fighting blood in him, as none of his ancestors were warriors. Ollokot was a better warrior. If Joseph had been given the command it would be known just where, what place he was given the command. The war came on suddenly."

Quoting Lahpeealoot: "Joseph had no experience in war, and therefore the warring Indians would never have given him the command. I never heard Joseph make announcement, even in camp, to the warring band. Nor did I hear any of the chiefs directing the fighting. Experienced warriors did the directing at such times; as when Rains and his men were killed."[17]

---

[17] See below, pp. 501-7, for further discussion of Joseph's leadership. Also see p. 249 and p. 254 for the part he played at White Bird Canyon.

Never did Joseph lead in battle. He well understood and respected the traditional tribal laws, and it is unjust to his memory as a towering primitive diplomat to ascribe to him utterly fictional achievements. Even had he aspired to war leadership, such aspirations would not have been tolerated by the tried and seasoned warriors. He was not even in the war council until the one where the issue of surrender was discussed.

This discussion of Nez Perce chiefs would be wanting should it fail to do homage to the marked ability of Joseph's younger brother. Chief Ollokot[18] was conspicuous throughout the trouble brewed by the treaty of 1863. While Joseph, as elder son, inherited the father's mantle under racial and tribal custom, Ollokot, through sheer intellectual ability, became a dominant force in the shaping of his brother's policy.[19]

In 1877 the young chief was a striking figure in the prime of life, standing six feet two inches in moccasins, with the trim, erect build of an athlete, with a vivacious, though determined eye, revealing

---

[18] *Ollokot*, variously spelled, is of Cayuse origin, a lost language which had practically disappeared by 1851. (The tribe was placed on the Umatilla reservation by the Walla Walla treaty of 1855.) The English rendition of the name is uncertain. In one instance, during the course of the investigation, it was given as "tanning" or "skin tanning." Many of the older Nez Perces thought that it meant "frog." With the Yakimas, proper, who are of the same linguistic family, the Shahaptian—which embraces the Cayuse, Nez Perce, Walla Walla, Paloos and Umatilla, *ahloquaht* is "frog."
After the death of the father, Joseph was often called "Old Joseph" and Ollokot "Young Joseph," especially by the whites.

[19] [See above, pp. 152-54. See below, p. 196, where Ollokot joins with Joseph in attempting to restrain the young men bent on precipitating war. See pp. 243-44, where Ollokot's role at the battle of White Bird Canyon is discussed. His leadership of the warriors at the Big Hole (see p. 396), and at Camas Meadows (p. 418) indicate the position of leadership he assumed on the field. Joseph himself attested this position of leadership in his speech at the surrender, where he gives, as one of his reasons for yielding: ". . . He who led the young men is dead." (See p. 498) (Ed. note.)]

joviality and good will, but holding a glint that betrayed the sleeping tiger within. Even the most bitterly partisan writer cannot point to a single crime chargeable to either of the brothers during the entire course of the trouble. All the Nez Perce spoke highly of Ollokot's bravery and warrior ability. In short, he was the chief warrior in Joseph's band, as well as Joseph's advisor.

White Bird's Band

Chief White Bird's following was second in size to Joseph's, and did not exceed fifty able-bodied men. This group was known as the Lamtama (as belonging to Lahmotta,[20] by which White Bird Canyon was designated). While the canyon has been named in honor of Chief White Bird, his name was more correctly Peopeo Kiskiok Hihih—"White Goose."

Having reached his seventies, Chief Peopeo Hihih was the oldest of the five nontreaty chiefs. Standing just short of six feet, well proportioned, with a splendid physique and stately bearing, he commanded attention wherever seen. A medicine man, and boasting a long line of noted warrior ancestry, his status and influence with his following was pronounced. As a buffalo hunter and experienced in tribal warfare, he held an honored place in all councils. He was mild in temper and in speech. The charge that he was an advocate of war had no foundation in fact.[21] Being

---

[20] The English definition appears to be of a dual nature. One is "wishing for more," the other, "bothered," "tired," "weary," or "restless." Strangely enough there appear to be grounds for the two definitions. See *Yellow Wolf*, p. 50. The canyon was a resort to be longed for, which was offset by the laborious trail of ingress and egress, hence the other definitions.

[21] Typical of the charge made against him is that found in R. Ross Arnold, *Indian Wars of Idaho* (Caldwell, 1932), p. 115.

well past the warrior age, he took no part in the fighting until the last battle, where he handled a gun from one of the rifle pits. The story that he took part in the Salmon River forays was denied by every warrior questioned. On the trail during the great retreat, he and Joseph appear closely allied, both riding in the camp contingent composed of old men, noncombatants, women and children. But in the end, there was a parting of the ways, for White Bird scorned surrender and his disdain for General Howard knew no bounds.

The Looking Glass Band

Chief Looking Glass was third with his Alpowai band. According to a member of the band, the late Chief Peopeo Tholekt, this group did not exceed forty men. They counted about twenty guns, several of them shotguns belonging to half-grown boys. His solitary village and cultivated gardens were on the Clearwater River. For an Indian, he was highly respected by the whites.

Looking Glass was almost six feet tall, well proportioned, with features denoting strength and tenacity of purpose. He was truly a commanding figure. Mrs. Frances Monteith said of him, as well as White Bird and Toohoolhoolzote, in a letter to the author: "Looking Glass and White Bird were fine looking men. The first-named apparently in his early forties, while White Bird was a man of considerable age. Too-hool-hool-zote was old, fat, and ugly and quarrelsome looking. All (three) were malcontents, always! They were responsible for war by refusing to go on the reservation."

Ippakness Wayhayken [Looking Glass Around Neck] inherited his father's name, where the latter as second signer of the Treaty of 1855 is recorded as Appushwahite. The Crow Indians called the son "Arrowhead," or "Flint on the Neck," so named from his "habitual wearing of a flint arrowhead suspended from his throat."[22] Interpreter Williams writes, "His own tribe called him Allalimya Takanin." His enviable reputation as a warrior had been greatly enhanced three years prior to this war, when, with his following, he joined the Crows in a victorious battle against the aggressive Sioux.[23] It was this prestige that gave him the leadership of the great retreat destined to be unique in the annals of Indian warfare. It was a leadership that has been unduly praised, and which proved the utter undoing of the patriots, assuring for all time the silent, undying hatred of the war party for the very memory of this leader's name.

Toohoolhoolzote's Band

Toohoolhoolzote was fourth with a following of thirty men. While this band could be classed as buffalo hunters, it had the usual quota of overage individuals. Veritable mountaineers, this band inhabited that wild fastness of mountain wilderness lying between the Snake and Salmon rivers.

Chief Toohoolhoolzote has gone down in history as a morose and querulous "cross-grained growler,"[24] while an old pioneer dubbed him as, "A fighter from hell!" The description of him given by Interpreter Williams, who often heard him discussed by his war associates and others, follows.

---

[22] T. B. Marquis, *Memoirs of a White Crow Indian*, (New York, 1921), p. 129.

[23] *Ibid.*, pp. 89, 97, and 128. This battle took place in 1874, at Pryor's Fork, a tributary of the Yellowstone.

[24] Howard, *Nez Perce Joseph*, p. 64.

Toohoolhoolzote was a tall, heavy man, but not fat or big-bellied, nor was he ugly looking. He was supposed to be the strongest man of the tribe. He was known to carry two grown blacktailed bucks to his lodge, from where he killed them, traveling afoot over the roughest of steep mountain country. No other man was ever known to accomplish such a feat. I was once told, by an old man, that Toohoolhoolzote went on a drunk and became bothersome and some of the Indians thought to quiet him by tying him up. Eight men got hold of him but could not get him down, and were obliged to let him go.

Apparently, had the chief been so inclined, he could have given General Howard unlooked-for exercise when he and Captain Perry led him out of the Lapwai council,[25] for his Herculean strength was still great despite his declining years. He proudly traced his lineage through a century of illustrious warriors who were never known to turn back from the foe. We shall tell later how this Dreamer patriot fought and how he died. As an orator, his influence over the various bands was pronounced. But sound evidence is all against the charge that he favored or counciled war.

The Paloos Band

Chief Hahtalekin was the fifth with his Paloos contingent of sixteen men, counting himself, all of the buffalo-hunter class. The Paloos were reputedly heroic fighters. The tribe lost its vast domain in the Walla Walla treaty of 1855, retaining only a meager residue at the confluence of the Snake and the Palouse, where a member of the clan still resides (1944) as caretaker of their ancient cemetery.

This Paloos contingent comprised two groups, the second known as the Wawawai band, whose habitat

---

25 *Ibid.*, pp. 66-7.

was about fifty miles up the Snake River from where the Palouse enters it. The leader of this group was Husishusis Kute [Naked Head], a vivacious Dreamer exponent.[26]

Bow and Arrow Case, who was a warrior of tried courage and ability, when asked through Interpreter Many Wounds for his opinion as to the comparative rank among the patriot Nez Perce chiefs, replied:

I think Looking Glass was the highest because he was a war chief. He stayed in Montana most of the time where there was war continually. When a small boy I saw his father, who was always taking lead in Montana and buffalo country. This convinced me that Looking Glass was a true out chief. His father signed the 1855 treaty.

Toohoolhoolzote and White Bird criticised the Christian religion. Chief White Bird did no fighting until the last battle, where he did some shooting from a rifle pit.

Then next came Chief Joseph and Ollokot, brothers, and most active within the tribe. Ollokot was a leader at the capture of General Howard's mule train.

Casting up the number of warriors in each band, we find in the patriot ranks 191 men including the aged and those incapacitated for bearing arms through disability or lack of manly courage. Among all the warring tribes the numerical preponderance of women over men made polygamy necessary, if eventual tribal extinction was to be avoided. Hence, in many of the tepees, there were two or three wives living in harmonious unity. (In this matter of harmony, tribal laws were imperative.)

It was from this aggregation of about six hundred,[27] with its preponderance of women and children

---

[26] See above, pp. 171-72, for more detailed discussion of Husishusis Kute.

[27] The Nez Perces computed their number at about six hundred. General Howard's estimate was about seven hundred men, women, and children.

[The editor was able to compile a list of the names of over 155 of (less the Paloos band which did no fighting in Idaho) that General Howard estimated 325 warriors opposing him in the Clearwater Battle,[28] and the about [including the Paloos contingent of sixteen] four hundred warriors, encountered by Colonel Gibbon at the Big Hole, as evoked by that magician of the pen, G. O. Shields.[29]

Thirty years after the war General Howard, depicting the Dreamer force gathered in White Bird Canyon declared: "They probably had at that point as many as five hundred Indians bearing arms, many young Indians from other tribes had joined them, delighted to take a hand in the war that Joseph was going to conduct."[30]

This claim by General Howard that there were alien warriors in the Nez Perce ranks was vehemently denied by all surviving warriors. Yellow Wolf, who was in every fight of the war declares that the "actual fighters numbered less than fifty," and that he could "give names of them all."[31] When told of General Howard's claim as to their number, he exclaimed:

No other tribes helped us. They were all against us! Nobody joined us at White Bird Canyon. Never joined us anywhere. All of every chief's band were Nez Perces. Only two I knew who were not Nez Perces. Owhi, the Yakima, joined us in Montana. He went with us from there, but he was not of the fighting men. The other one was Seeskoomke

---

these warriors from McWhorter's notes and the Indian narratives. The identity of these 155 can be established, and in most cases something is known of their role in the war. It should be added that this list includes males who on one occasion or another bore arms, but were not necessarily considered real warriors by the tribe. (Ed. note.)]

[28] *Rep. of Sec. of War*, 1877, I, 124.

[29] G. O. Shields, *The Battle of the Big Hole*, p. 16.

[30] Howard, *My Life and Experiences*, p. 243.

[31] *Yellow Wolf*, p. 43.

[No Feet] who had one hand and both feet gone. Once a slave, I know not what tribe he belonged. Many tribes and most of our own people were against us.[32]

Thus it is seen that the veritable foreign legion which legend has ascribed to Chief Joseph resolves itself into one camp follower and one pitiful ex-slave minus both feet and one hand.

General Howard has also claimed that "at least five hundred warriors," allies of Joseph, "renegades and wild roamers of the Columbia" under Chiefs Smoholla and Moses, had been turned from joining in the threatened war, when they were informed in council at the Yakima Indian agency that the trouble had been settled and the Nez Perces had agreed to move to the reduced reservation.[33] All this was a chimera of the General's imagination. Neither Chief Moses or Smoholla ever contemplated such a move, nor did the Nez Perces at any time solicit their aid.[34] Nor can it honestly be contended that war was in any sense contemplated by the Nez Perces themselves until after the stormy Lapwai council, and then by the young hotspurs only. Not one of the five chiefs advocated armed resistance prior to the unfortunate raids on the Salmon River interlopers, and even then, as will be shown, Chief Joseph advocated delay until an attempt at reconciliation could be made with the soldiers when they put in their inevitable appearance.

---

[32] *Ibid.*, pp. 52-53; 125-6.

[33] Howard, *Nez Perce Joseph*, pp. 81-84.

[34] Press, ink, and time have lent themselves to the creation of a fantastically fallacious story of a blood relationship between Joseph and Moses, and a sanguinary battle fought by them in a vain endeavor to determine the chieftainship.

CHAPTER XII

THE FIRST SALMON RIVER FORAY—THE INDIANS TELL THE STORY

JUNE 12, 1877, FOUND THE NONTREATIES STILL lingering at their ancient rendezvous, Tepahlewam, with but forty-eight hours between them and removal to the reservation by armed force. Among the young men camped there was Wahlitits, who will be remembered as the son of Chief Eagle Robe, killed by Larry Ott.[1] The boy had now reached full manhood, an athlete with the trim faultless form of an Apollo, attained by the early, rigorous, self-disciplined training customary in his tribe. He had scaled almost inaccessible mountain crags and canyon walls, swum daily across the Salmon River and back for five consecutive winters.

Nez Perce legend boasts that he was unsurpassed as a long-distance runner and in wrestling had never met his match. His strength was prodigious. Entering a corral of trapped wild horses he would throw his lariat, necking two of them in its loop. Then with the rope half-circling his waist, he could stand against the horses' most frantic plunging. One of his chief amusements was to chase a band of wild horses into the Salmon River, and, stripped to his breechcloth, swim out and mount the most spirited among them and swim it ashore, where despite its

---

[1] See Chapter VIII, p. 122, and McWhorter, *Yellow Wolf, His Own Story*, pp. 43-4.

WALLOWA LAKE, OREGON

The beautiful valley in which this lake sets was occupied through a broken treaty with the Nez Perces. It was the ancestral home, and burial place, of Old Chief Joseph.

wet, slippery coat and frantic cavorting, he would ride it as long as he wished, then leap to the ground without losing his footing.

Mild tempered, and generous to a fault, he was prone to deeds of charity, but was an opponent to be shunned when fully aroused. He was never known to use bad language of any nature, was a favorite leader among the young men, and a dangerous leader, as was proved those critical days. However, he was not addicted to strong drink. Such was the son of Chief Eagle Robe, the young warrior destined to ignite the torch of war in June of 1877.

Although the young men were deeply perturbed and resentful of the role their people were being forced to play, it was probably not so much their resentment as an urge to pay a last and final farewell to their ancient and semisacred Tepahlewam that caused them to stage a war parade on that day of ill repute, the thirteenth of June. In this ceremony, the column of horsemen was brought up by two warriors mounted on the same steed, riding at a distance in the rear, guarding the most dangerous spot from possible enemy attack. Only the bravest would assume this position regarded as a post of honor. In actual warfare it was indeed an exposed and dangerous role.

In this parade, Two Moons rode at the tail of the main column, also a post of supposed peril, and the double riders behind were Wahlitits and Sarpsis Ilppilp, the latter the son of Chuslum Moxmox [Yellow Bull] of White Bird's band. These rear riders were first cousins, or brothers in Indian parlance. Wahlitits was mounted in front and when passing through the village his horse stepped on a spread canvas covered with *kouse* roots drying in the sun. Seeing this, Heyoom Moxmox [Yellow Grizzly

Bear]² spoke in angry derision, "See what you do! Playing brave you ride over my woman's hard-worked food! If you so brave, why you not go kill the white man who killed your father?"

Stung by this open reflection on his courage, the young rider replied in an even tone of voice, "You will be sorry for your words."

One version of this parade episode has it that a small child became endangered by the hoofs of the horse ridden by the two rear guardsmen, and the father, already embittered with jealousy because Wahlitits had paid too close attention to his comely wife, took occasion to openly upbraid him for "playing brave" while the murderer of Eagle Robe still lived untouched by the son. This taunt, some claim, proved the spark that brought war.³ This story was branded pure fiction and of white origin by the older Nez Perces. Also the oft-repeated tale that the guardian riders in the farewell parade, whisky-imbued and reinforced by a third companion, started immediately on their mission of revenge, is an error. Instead Wahlitits brooded, Indian fashion, over his wrongs and contemplated redress. On this score Camille Williams writes:

> When parade was over, Wahlitits cried, after crying he was heard to say, "Reason I didn't want to kill the murderer of my father, because some of my tribesmen are wealthy with stock and I don't like to see them get robbed."
>
> The following story I got from Mrs. John Minthon was, that while John Minthon [Swan Necklace] was still in bed the morning after the parade, Wahlitits came and told him

---

² According to the Indians, Yellow Grizzly Bear, a member of the Clearwater band, took no part in the Salmon River raids. He never fired a gun during the entire war. He was exiled, returned to the Nez Perce reservation, and was buried at Kamiah.

³ See, Will Cave, *Nez Perce Indian War of 1877 and Battle of the Big Hole* (Missoula, Montana, no date), p. 7; and Francis Haines, *Red Eagles of the Northwest* (Portland, 1939), p. 241.

to follow him outside. He did and was asked to ride behind on his horse. Few Indians might have observed this as it was early in the morning, but no one knowed where they were going. Fired by bootleg whiskey is false. Wahlitits and Sarpsis Ilppilp never used intoxicating liquors.

If the departure of the three that morning was observed by any of the Indians, they recognized that Wetyetmas Wahyakt [Swan Necklace] was to act as "horse holder." Their goal was the scene of the killing of Chief Eagle Robe, their purpose was to avenge his death on his slayer, Larry Ott. But that worthy, taking alarm, had fled to the Florence mines, where he was later seen garbed as a Chinaman and panning gold with them.[4] Balked thus of their prey, they determined to pay their respects to Richard Devine, an elderly man living alone on the Salmon River some eight miles above the mouth of Slate Creek.

It was nighttime. Wahlitits' wife was living on the opposite side of the Salmon at Horse Shoe Bend, and he called across to her in the darkness and told her where they were going, and for what purpose they had come from Tepahlewam. It is doubtful whether Swan Necklace was fully aware of his friendly captor's intentions until this announcement was made.

Devine, their first victim, had won for himself an unenviable reputation among the Indians for his implacable hatred of them, ending in his murder of the crippled Dakoopin under circumstances of inexcusable malignance. His general attitude toward Indians was one of irritation. He had some ground fenced, but no Indian ever trespassed by entering

---

[4] Under date of June 30, 1877, Larry Ott's name appears in the list of Colonel Ed McConville's company of volunteers. *Fifteenth Biennial Report of the Board of Trustees of the State Historical Society of Idaho*, 1935-36 (Boise, Idaho, 1936), p. 56.

the field. Yet Devine was prone to set his vicious dogs on any passing Indians, and also threatened them with his rifle. Arriving at their goal, the avengers left their mounts in the care of the horse holder and entered the house. War Singer writes:

Divine [Devine] was not in bed when the two Indians entered. He was surprised for no Indian was ever in his house. He was killed with his own gun. After killing, the three men started down and arrived at John Day ranch early morning and staked their horses in oat field so the whites would be attracted to that direction so to be easy killing and it was. The owner, Henry Elfers first came and noticed the horses staked in the field. He came to the horses swearing. Sarpsis was about to jump up and shoot him, Wahlitits told him to keep still, to let him come closer. When he was about a rod away, Elfers noticed a gun, turned and ran back. Wahlitits started after him and grabbed him and downed Henry. Then Sarpsis caught up to them and shot Elfers dead. Two killed, one white man got away. He afterwards married Mrs. Elfers.

The avengers had appropriated Devine's rifle and ammunition, and it is said, a fine horse. They went to the home of Elfers and secured additional arms and ammunition but offered no violence to the women. Elfers had also won the ill will of the Indians. Among his other faults, he emulated Devine in harassing passing tribesmen by inciting his vicious dogs to attack them, at the same time making a display of arms.

In contrast to the treatment meted out to these Indian-haters was that accorded the Wood family of the same district. Charles B. Wood had a small store and always dealt squarely with the Indians. The three raiders, resplendent with feathers and red flannel strips in their hair and with more face paint than usual, called at the Wood residence. Sarpsis Ilppilp, as spokesman, requested Mrs. Wood to fix them up a lunch. When asked where they were going, they replied, "Up little Salmon, hunt horses!" The lunch was given and they rode away. The next day they returned and meeting G. F. Cone, another resident of the area, they asked if he knew the horses they were riding. Suspecting something was wrong, Cone replied, "Yes. John Day ranch horses. You buy?"

"No, we kill men, take hosses and guns! Injuns make big fight. You go home! You go home tell Wood, tell your boys to stay home and Injuns not hurt them. You ride out on range, maybe people see and shoot you!"

A few days before this outbreak Alamoot, an Indian, had borrowed a horse and saddle of Mr. Wood, who naturally never expected to see his property again, but three nights later, after a stockade had been built, the families gathered in, and the guards posted, Alamoot crept up and left the saddle on the store porch and turned the horse in the pasture field.[5]

There are some interesting features, hitherto unearthed, connected with the fiery deeds of these two young men in their abrupt opening of hostilities. It appears that Swan Necklace was, after an old tribal custom, practically kidnapped, and was, therefore, unaware of just what might be ahead of him. He was a strong lad of seventeen and a grandson of the murdered Eagle Robe, his mother being Wahlitits' sister.

During the second night out, the party recrossed the White Bird divide[6] but the two warriors re-

---

[5] The above information was taken from the Wood family records, and transmitted to the author by Mrs. Anna G. Norwood, daughter of Charles Wood.

[6] This historic mountain appears to have no recorded name. In *Yellow Wolf*, p. 43, it is designated as "Mahsamyetteen" [Buzzard

frained from entering the Tepahlewam camp. Instead they stopped on Thorn Creek, a small unmapped stream known also as Round Willow, so named from the willows growing in a peculiar rounded form. Their stop was about three quarters of a mile from the summit of the divide, and some miles from the village itself. This precaution was to prevent their deeds being attributed to a conspiracy on the part of the entire band. However, they did dispatch Swan Necklace to acquaint the village with their deeds on the Salmon and of their intention to return there the following day to even up additional scores. Most likely this was done to afford possible sympathizers an opportunity to join them if they wished without embroiling the peaceably inclined tribesmen with the military. They solicited no aid, and, their deeds being wholly of their own volition, they reasoned that by holding aloof from the village they alone would be accountable to the civil and military authorities.

Camille Williams said:

When the three men, including Mrs. Wahlitits, who had joined her husband at Horseshoe Bend, arrived at Round Willow, Wetyetmas Wahyakt [Swan Necklace] was sent ahead to Tepahlewam camp to tell the news of the killing of whites up Salmon River. He rode a roan horse that was taken from Elfer's ranch, and while riding toward the camp he noticed that everybody he met, also women digging *kouse,* and lots of these women left their *kouse* already sacked and headed for their camp excited when Swan Necklace arrived at Tepahlewam camp and told the news of the killing. And Hemackkis Kaiwon [Big Morning] rode the roan-colored horse around the whole camp, telling of the killing of white men up Salmon River, and showing

Mountain], and was so called by Many Wounds, whose family was of White Bird's band. But many of the Nez Perces never knew it by that name, and the early settlers and the Forestry Service knew it only as the "White Bird Divide." War Singer would write "Buzzard Mountain," *Masktsam Kisppaliya.*

them the roan horse as proof. It wasn't long after when the two Indians and the woman were seen riding toward camp, singing war song. When they arrived in camp, Wahlitits told other Indians of the killing and told them that he was not inviting them to join this trouble. Chief White Bird never rode through the village to urge the other Indians to join in the war. It was Two Moons that rode through the camp and urged every able-bodied man to join these two men in other forays. The camp broke up same hour, some leaving for their homes.

Thus it would appear that General Howard is in error when he represents White Bird as advocating war.[7] According to all the warriors interviewed, White Bird was outspokenly opposed to any resort to arms, notwithstanding both official and lay reiterations to the contrary. He could foresee the tragic consequences.

The annals are all agreed that Chief Joseph was absent from camp at the time of the Salmon River foray. It appears fitting at this point to introduce the narrative of Wetatonmi, the wife of Chief Ollokot, who had accompanied Joseph on his expedition to the cattle herd beyond the Salmon River.[8]

I was born in the Montana buffalo country in midwinter, about January. I was a married woman when the war broke out, and had one child which died. My husband was Ollokot, brother of Chief Joseph. Before marriage my name was Tahmokalona [or Tahmokalah].

We were camping at what is now Tolo Lake, named for an Indian woman. In June, it was a favorite camping place because of the camas harvesting.

From there a trip was made across Salmon River. Several men and two women went. The men were Chief Joseph, Ollokot, Half Moon, John Wilson, and a young man whose name I do not remember. The sixth was Welweyas, a half-man-and-half-woman, who dressed like a woman. The

---

[7] Howard, *Nez Perce Joseph*, pp. 105-6.

[8] The time of this interview was October, 1926.

women were Hophop Onmi [Sound of Running Feet], daughter of Chief Joseph, and myself.

We stayed on the Salmon a few days, and then came back. We had about twelve horses packed with beef. Nearing the home camp, we saw a rider coming, running his horse. The men say to each other, "He must have news to tell us."

It was Two Moons coming to meet us. He said, "War has broke out. Three white men killed yesterday!"

Wahlitits and two others had done these deeds on Salmon River. We call the place Tipsusleimah (name of an edible root) on John Day's Creek. All the men followed Two Moons back to camp, leaving us women to follow with the pack horses. When we reached camp we saw the tepees all down, and the horses were being packed to move to Apaschesap [Drive In] on Cottonwood Creek. Chief Looking Glass and his people had been gone a couple of days to their old home camp on the Clearwater. Chief Joseph and Ollokot rode among the people trying to stop them from moving. They called out to them, "Let us stay here till the army comes! We will then make some kind of peace with them."[9] But the people would not stay. After some confused shifting, all moved but two tepees. These tepees were Chief Joseph's and his brother's. They were watched closely by the warriors. They suspicioned that we would move to Kamiah or Lapwai. Three men were with them. Wetyetmas Yahonyeen [Three Feathers] and Yahtteen Cilu Kitaniyin [Metal-Eyed

---

[9] Colonel C. E. S. Wood, Howard's adjutant during the campaign, agreed with Indian sources as to Chief Joseph's attitude at the outbreak of war. He wrote the author March 4, 1928, "I took charge of Joseph at the time of the surrender, and his account—confirmed by Yellow Bull and others from time to time—is that he intended to go on the reservation as agreed at the Lapwai Council, but some of his young men nagged and inflamed each other and started out on their career of murder on Salmon River the very last day of allotted time, and he knew then that fight was all that was left to him. The facts all support this. He was across the Salmon River at White Bird Creek at the end of the 30 days allowed him. That is, he was practically on the reservation. The cattle herd was on the other side of the Salmon, and he had gone across to butcher a steer. His wife was expecting to be confined and he wanted to stock up with provisions.
"The 30 days were consumed in gathering herds, cattle and ponies, and moving up from Wallowa Valley, Oregon to White Bird Creek, Idaho. Everything confirms the story that the outbreak was a sudden act by some young men discontented with Joseph's submission, and possibly inflamed by the resentful Tohule-hulezote." Naturally Colonel Wood holds to the common misconception that Toolhoolhoolzote was an uncompromising advocate of war.

Crane]. Next day we also moved to Cottonwood Creek. Of course the two brothers, Chief Joseph and Ollokot, had not decided to fight. Instead they were coming to the reservation. But they had no chance for such move. From Cottonwood, next morning, all Indians went to White Bird.

The story of Chief Joseph riding through the camp with a six-shooter in either hand threatening any warrior who attempted to take the warpath is pure hokum. There was no such grandstand play. From all warrior statements, it is confirmed that Joseph was far from being a two-gun man.

It would seem well at this point to refute another widespread error in connection with the expedition for beef, graphically described by Wetatonmi. The story goes that the beef was wanted for Joseph's wife who was about to be confined, and that Joseph's daughter was born four days later, accompanied by the roar of the White Bird battle. This legend is not true and the evidence is most conclusive. Yellow Wolf, who was of Chief Joseph's household, when asked the place of birth, replied promptly, "Tepahlewam! Before moving to White Bird." This fact has been verified by elderly women who went through the war. Williams writes, "I found out that Chief Joseph's daughter was born while he was across the Salmon River for beef." Later he added:

Reason Chief Joseph and others made the trip across Salmon River was, that Apis Wahyakt [Flint Necklace] made a verbal will a year before the war, that after his death, his brother, Heyoom Bakatimma, should invite 10 men to go and kill 11 head of beef. So Bakatimma invited the following named men, Chief Joseph and Bro. [Ollokot], John Wilson, Yahtteen Cilu Kitaniyin, Teetouton, Lelooskin, Eoye Kam [Shell Rock], Tipyalana Kiki, Welweyas [the freak man, means "coulee"] Yoomtis Kunnin [Grizzly Blanket].

News of the outbreak spread rapidly and women who were digging roots in the hills, abandoning their harvested stores, mounted and raced for home. The young Nez Perce fighting spirit became thoroughly aroused, and with its unleashing, the flame of war with its ever-attendant horrors flared to its zenith.

It was a war that Agent Monteith had sedulously courted. As early in his incumbency as June 15, 1874, he officiously wrote of alarming conditions among the nontreaties. He was incubating trouble. It was a war that General Howard had invited by "showing the rifle" in a peace council, a war that claimed the lives of 141 enlisted men and volunteers, and more than forty civilians; a war that exacted ninety-three Nez Perce lives on the field of battle, one third of them women and children; a war that later caused the death of treble that number amid the slime of malarial poison swamps in faraway prison camps. It was a war that cost the government $1,873,410.12, and was totally devoid of glory for our government, a war to bring the blush of shame to the cheek of every justice-loving American.

All of this General Howard and Agent Monteith could have averted by the concession of an additional thirty days for bringing the widely scattered stock within the bounds of the shrunken Nez Perce reservation, a full season's task. How piously inhuman, how foreign to churchly pretensions! The Dreamers never had a friend at court.

The breaking of Tepahlewam camp was the end of an epoch. This ancient domain inherited by Chief Red Bear, of other years, was held on a par with Lahmotta, the veritable capital of the once-dominant Nez Perce nation. Tepahlewam was never to see the raising of another tepee pole.

It is a credit to the patriotism of Chiefs Joseph and

Ollokot that they did not break with, or desert, their fellow bands as they may apparently have contemplated during the first surge of panic that pervaded the camp with the startling news of the killings. There was but one member of Joseph's band to be found in the subsequent raids. Lahpeealoot, originally of the Canyon band, was in the second sally.

NARRATIVE OF TWO MOONS

No truer insight into the temperament of the nontreaty or Dreamer chiefs and their following at this period of the trouble can be had than was given the writer by Two Moons in October, 1908, with Silas Whitman as interpreter.[10]

It is not for me to read the white men's books, but I have been told that many of them contain the talk of lies. The enemies of the Nez Perces, only, have written of the trouble that started at Tepahlewam. I am glad that I can now tell my side of how it came about.

I was of Chief Joseph's band. He did not want to fight while some of his young men were willing to stir up a war. But it was all because General Howard talked the rifle when in a peace council. This caused some of them to ride wild one day when Chief Joseph and Ollokot were absent from camp. But the war grew from the rifle at the council, and the big waters in the Snake and Salmon Rivers.

I have told you something of the wars and battles we had among ourselves, between the different tribes

---

[10] At the beginning of this interview the interpreter said, "Two Moons says to tell his white friend that he had a good sleep last night, and is now ready to give him his part in the war with General Howard's soldiers, if wanted to do so." The object of informing the public on the Nez Perce side of the trouble was explained, after which the interpreter continued, "Two Moons says he will give you the story after he first has a smoke." Filling a small stone pipe with a mild preparation of aromatic leaves and bark with a light sprinkle of tobacco, the old warrior sat smoking in silence for a few minutes, then returning the pipe to its pouch, he rose to his feet and took up the trend of his story.

wherein the safety of our homes was not concerned. But now, I will give you a far different story. I will tell you how, because we loved our ancient home and did not want to leave it war was brought to us, wherein we did fight, losing many of our best warriors, women, children, and old men. How our land in the Wallowa Valley, the Salmon River, and elsewhere was taken from us, and how my people were sent to the swamp marshes of Kansas and the Indian Territory to die. I will tell you this, that you may write it down as my side of the trouble we did not start or bring about.

General Howard called the Indians to a council. In that council he told the leading men or chiefs of the tribes [bands] that all the Indians living along the Snake River and other places outside the later-formed reservation, must move at once thereon. He said, "I will give you thirty suns or one moon, and if you do not mind these orders, I will take my soldiers and drive you in!"

This was the language that hurt the Nez Perce feelings. It was as if you make the statement, "You shall be shot to pieces by my soldiers, if you do not do as I tell you." Guns must not be talked in peace councils. Only in war talks must arrows be spoken.

Big waters were in the Snake and other rivers. It could not be done, this moving stock and property across to the reservation in so close-worded time, but if let alone, the Indians decided to try doing so. But stock would be lost because of mad water and short time.

During that spring the Nez Perces gathered in camp at Camas Prairie which is in state of Idaho. It came June, and the Indians were having a good time, gambling the bone game, horse-racing and different sports. At this time Chief Joseph and his brother

Ollokot, with others, went over the Salmon River to kill beef.

It was while in their absence, three young men, who had obtained bootleg whisky, rode to the Salmon waters. Their names were Sarpsis Ilppilp [Red Moccasin Tops], Wahlitits, and one still younger man named Wetyetmas Wahyakt. Over there, the two older of these young men met an old white settler, a bachelor, who was rather mean. Any time the Indians visited to have a talk with him, they were driven away. He killed one crippled man. The Indians never had done any wrong to him, but after the foregoing talk by General Howard at the peace council, they were angered. The young men said, "Since guns have been talked by General Howard, we shall have to stir up a fight! We must stir up war for General Howard!"

They killed this white settler. The bachelor settler was a stockman. They took a stallion that he kept, and it was brought over to Camas Prairie to show what they had done. It was night when the youngest came to camp.

Just then that same night the chiefs held a council, putting the question to one another, "Shall we mind General Howard and go to the reservation? Shall we bring out all our stock from the Salmon River country, everything else we have, all the property along the river? It will take quite awhile to do this and the waters are at this time big!"

The best warriors were not in the council. Wahchumyus [Rainbow] and Pahkatos [Five Wounds] had not returned from hunting the buffalo. Some said, "We shall not have war." Other talks, "We may have war brought to us." An old man, also named Rainbow, was asked to tell what should be done. Should we fight or not fight? This old warrior stood up and talked this way, "You people are wrong, speaking of war! A small bunch of Indians yourselves, you are hardly strong enough to put up a war against the great number of whites. You cannot make any kind of fight with only rifles against so many whites with big guns. Wait until the summer comes, so the rest of the Indians shall gather at Weippe, a sun's camp-move east of Kamiah Valley. Then we shall have a big council of all the tribes. We shall then find out what to do! If most of the people say 'Let us not fight,' then we will not fight! But if soldiers come and most of us say fight, then we shall put up a war! This can be decided later."

This was the statement from old man Rainbow.

While having this council, someone called from the next tepee, "You poor people are holding council for nothing! Three young men have come from White Bird country, bringing horses with them! Horses belonging to a white settler they killed. Killed yesterday sun! It will have to be war!"

The next morning, I, Two Moons, stepped from my tepee and at that minute Chief Joseph and his brother and others came in sight from bringing beef from Salmon. They were riding, driving loaded pack horses.

I, Two Moons, jumped on a horse and met them. Told them the whole story. The happenings of the three young men in the Salmon country. How they had killed the older stockman, and how they had brought the horses, anxious to put up war.

Chief Joseph and his brother made no reply regarding war. They rode silently, but swiftly to camp. Reaching there, we found most of the tepees down, camp broke and many of the people getting ready to move to their homes on Clearwater River,[11] while

---

[11] The Indians bound for the Clearwater were the bands of Chiefs Looking Glass and Hahtalekin, the last named being Paloos.

others were moving to a camping place on Cottonwood Creek where once had been a hard battle with
the Bannocks.

I, Two Moons. . . . continued at Camas Prairie.

During the night at Camas Prairie, we were
greatly disturbed by whites. They did not shoot at
us, nor did they speak to us, but they were gathered
around our camp. Finally one gun was fired through
a tepee.[12] When anyone went out to speak to them,
they would ride away, galloping their horses out of
our sight into the darkness. They kept doing this
until the break of morning. We were alarmed and
did not sleep because of it. Coming daylight, we
followed the other Indians down to Lockyah[13] above
the little town now there, called Stites.

So I, Two Moons, then took down my tepee, and
started back to Camas Prairie, thinking, "Just as
many of you Indians as want to follow me can do so."
While traveling back to Camas Prairie, I concluded
to go to White Bird. I would get out of the way of all
trouble. When I reached White Bird, there were
quite a few Indians following me. . . .

§

NARRATIVE OF WOUNDED HEAD

An extract from the story of Husis Owyeen [Wounded
Head] is apropos at this point.

I was camping with my family at Camas Prairie,
along with other Nez Perces. My little boy was sick
and I was always at the couch of the child.

During this time, I heard talk among the people

---

[12] This shot passed through Joseph's tepee, and was answered by
Yellow Wolf's rifle. (See McWhorter, *Yellow Wolf*, p. 46).

[13] *Lockyah*—"This means wood built across watercourse keeping
back all fish and salmon from running this dam made of small sticks."
—Many Wounds.

of the whites putting up a war against our tribe. Knowing not on what reason this talk was made, I was questioned and asked questions regarding going with the tribe. I refused. Every time I refused to go in the fighting. Next sun, while holding the sick baby, my wife said, "Someone calling you outside. Go see what they want!"

I handed this little boy to my wife and stepped outside the doorway. Three men were going away from my tepee. Reaching a grass spot, they laid down. I went and laid down by them. They asked if I had a gun, and I told them, "No." They said they had one good gun. I told them I had a bunch of good horses and I would let them pick one for the gun. They said they would put off the subject till the next sun when they would bring the gun for me to examine.

Next morning I got my saddle horse and ride after my band of horses, drive them in for selection of choice for the gun. Coming back with the herd, I rode down to the camp and at a distance I saw crowd of people around my tepee. I wondered what had happened. I thought by this the child of mine must have died. On coming near, one of those three men came riding out from the tepee, holding a good, shining gun. On coming close, he shouted to the crowd, "This is the gun Wettustolalumtikt[14] has bought, and now belongs to him. The horse he is riding belongs to me."

I rode up to him, then passed on to the tepee. He rode around the camp announcing I had bought the gun for purpose of going to war. I got down from my horse and went inside the tepee. My wife said,

---

[14] [A name by which Husis Owyeen was known before he acquired the appellation, "Wounded Head," during the war. It means "last time on earth." (Ed. note.)]

"You are an awful man, buying a gun preparing to go to war! See the child sick in bed! What is wrong with you?"

I said to her, "I did not buy the gun for purpose of going to war. I buy the gun so that, luck and life permitting, during the summer we can go to the mountains and look for game. That is the only reason I buy the gun. The gun will be mine, but not for the war. Maybe we will go to the mountains now, for I do not want to go to war with the rest of the people!"

During that hour, camp was broken and moved some miles below Camas Prairie. I spoke to my woman, "We will not go anywhere! We will stay right here!"

But Eapaleckt Ilppilp [Red Cloud] came and told me, "You will have to go with the rest of the people! It will not do for you to camp here and be slaughtered, all of you, by the soldiers! There is now a war at hand! You must go with the tribe!"

Hearing this from my old time warmate, I prepared to go with the rest of them, and did go. During this same sun, not the next sun, but that very time the war broke out.

I moved camp, going to the place where the company stopped, and the war talk went on. I did not want to go fight, but I camped at the spot where the rest of the people camped. The next day Elootpah Owyeen [Shot in the Belly] said to me, "They are fighting near Mount Idaho! Let us go see what is going on!"

We both got our horses and went out there that same sun. A little way from the town, we noticed a small band of Indians ahead. They were watching the whites in every direction. We stayed but a few minutes with them, then started back to camp where we came from. The next sun from this the camp broke. All decided to go back to Camas Prairie. All went, but I followed slowly. The band was ahead some distance, when looking back toward the Cotton-wood, I saw a distant troop of whites, who seemed to be a scout, come toward Camas Prairie. I then drive faster to gain Camas Prairie where the tribe had gone. Reaching there no tepees had been set up. The people were still horseback and the pack horses standing under their loads. If they had intended stopping, they now changed their thoughts. The band traveled on to Lahmotta, where we camped and re-mained all the next sun.

§

CHAPTER XIII

THE SECOND SALMON RIVER RAID

THERE IS AN ELEMENT OF HONOR IN THE ACTIONS OF the two outlawed avengers who attempted to avoid casting guilt on their fellow tribesmen by staying aloof from the camp. However, as morning broke, they were joined at their rendezvous by sixteen[1] of their associates, burning with a spirit of revenge against those at whose hands they had suffered unrequited wrongs. These young men had been brooding over General Howard's show of force in a peace council, followed immediately by open seizure and imprisonment of their chosen speaker for no greater crime than "showing his heart." This latest affront, added to past bloody atrocities, proved too much for the young hotspurs who accepted the challenge in the only manner they knew; and the early-morning gathering at the Round Willows tryst resulted.

It is only fair to the Indians to call attention to the fact that the outrages against women and children did not occur until after the raiders became beastly drunk on whisky found by the barrel at Benedict's

---

[1] Howard very fairly places the number of recruits added to the original three at "about seventeen." *(Nez Perce Joseph,* p. 103) But the hysteria in Idaho at the time is exemplified by James W. Poe, who in a letter of June 18, 1877, addressed to Governor Brayman, states that the returned Indians which he understood to be a small band, were joined by the entire band which he placed at two or three hundred who continued their bloody raids towards Mount Idaho. *(Fifteenth Biennial Report of the State Historical Society of Idaho,* 1935-36, p. 90).

store-saloon located on the lower reaches of White Bird Creek. That atrocities were committed by a few of the young Nez Perces, no one pretends to deny. But whisky was at the bottom of all of them.

It has been generally conceded that this band of avengers was made up wholly of young men, which is correct with but one possible exception. The evidence seems very conclusive that Chuslum Moxmox [Yellow Buffalo Bull] the father of Sarpsis Ilppilp, and also a member of White Bird's band, was among the recruits. A buffalo hunter and a warrior of some distinction, he had been with Chief Looking Glass at the Crow-Sioux battle on Pryor's Fork, and leadership would naturally fall to him.[2]

The Harry Mason Incident

The raiding party, thus augmented, did not tarry but recrossed the mountain into White Bird Canyon. Among this day's victims (supposedly) was Harry Mason who had only a few months before used a blacksnake whip on two unarmed Indians without any known excuse. According to the Indian version, he was met now in the road by the raiders, who jeered and teased him for what he had done. They toyed with him much as a cat plays with a mouse before devouring it. They twitted him about his former bravery in using a whip when he had the advantage over his victims. Then the Nez Perces ordered Mason to run, which he did, only to be brought down by an arrow from Strong Eagle's bow. Whether or not it actually was Mason who was killed at this time is open to question, since some claim he was killed in his home. But in any case, the body of this man was left where it fell.

---

[2] See Appendix I, pp. 558-59.

Soon after this killing, Samuel Picket, a Nez Perce lad in his teens, together with his mother, Tipyeak, and his aunt, Emma, came along the road from Rock Creek, with a few pack horses loaded with oats. Near the White Bird store, Samuel had found a small buckskin bag of gold dust, which he tied to his saddle. Continuing on their way, they came upon a dead man and a straw hat lying close by. Samuel, bending from his saddle, caught up the hat and placed it on his head. Before reaching their destination, they learned of the outbreak and the killing of the man. The mother told Samuel to throw the hat away lest they be suspected of the crime. Riding hard, the bag of gold dust became bothersome flapping up and down against the saddle, and the mother instructed Samuel to drop it, which he did. It would seem that the arrow must have been removed from this man's body, or the nature of his death would have been obvious to passers-by.

At the Benedict Store

Meanwhile the raiders proceeded down the White Bird to even up scores in that area. Among those slated for vengeance, Samuel Benedict, merchant-saloonkeeper, stood first. He had no Indian friends nor had he fostered any good will among them. According to the stories told, his favorite game was short-changing Indians. A reputable old tribesman of the Looking Glass contingent complained to the writer, "This store man always cheated Indians. Maybe a poor woman with only a little money want buy pound of coffee, thirty cents; or maybe two bits worth of sugar. Buy only one of these and hand him fifty cent or maybe one dollar, she never get change back. That store man all time keep all the money."

Of this same White Bird merchant-trader, General Howard says:

> In August, 1875, Samuel Benedict, who then resided with his family at the mouth of White Bird Creek, killed an Indian. The circumstances under which the killing took place were as follows:
>
> Late at night, several intoxicated Indians came to Benedict's house and demanded admission; and upon being refused, commenced breaking the doors and windows of his residence. The wife of Benedict and her two children made their escape, under cover of darkness, through a back window, waded White Bird Creek and found shelter in a neighboring house.
>
> Benedict fired, and killed one Indian and wounded one or two more. He is accused of having sold liquor to the Indians[3]

Very probably this story of Howard's was Benedict's version, for the Indians tell quite a different tale. Their account was that the trouble happened in broad daylight, and that Sarpsis Ilppilp was wounded but not seriously, the bird shot striking the back of his head.

It is not known whether it was before or after this incident that the body of Motsqueh [Chipmunk] showing bullet wounds was found close to Benedict's place.[4] Chipmunk was a young fellow who excelled as a purloiner of small articles. While he and two companions were in Benedict's store, he deftly concealed a bottle of whisky under his blanket and got away with it. Before riding any great distance, the group consumed the liquor. This only whetted their appetites for more, and Chipmunk was urged to return and slip out with another bottle. He refused, pleading that he would be detected and killed. But his inebriated companions, who had swallowed the

---

[3] Howard, *Nez Perce Joseph*, pp. 101-2.

[4] This and succeeding incidents are wholly from the Nez Perce version.

greater portion of the liquor, insisted that there was no danger, that he alone possessed the power of secrecy and would have no trouble since no one had ever been able to detect his tricks of theft. Still Chipmunk refused. He pled that his *Wyakin* had instructed him to steal but once; that he knew he would be killed should he disobey. It was only when the now-crazed drinkers drew their knives that Chipmunk gave in and turned back on his ill-fated errand. This was the last time he was seen alive. His two companions were blamed for the part they had played in the mystery. Later a search uncovered Chipmunk's ill-concealed body showing bullet wounds as if made with buckshot, for which Benedict was now to atone with his life, as Chipmunk's body was found not far from his place.

At this late day no listing of the war parties' victims in sequence can be made with any degree of accuracy. Concerning the second day's raid, General Howard states:

... On their way (to Salmon River) they shot and wounded J. J. Manuel and his little girl, killed James Baker, and upon arriving at Benedict's place, they discovered Benedict in the attempt to escape across White Bird Creek. They fired at him, and he fell dead. At the same time, they killed a Frenchman named August Bacon. On the following day, June 15, they killed Mrs. Manuel, William Osburn, and Harry Mason. This is the time when Joseph is accused of participating.[5]

The same author says of Mason, whom he mentions as among the murdered:

Another citizen, Harry Mason, whipped two Indians early in the spring. A council of arbitration met to decide who was in fault. Mr. Elfers, a white man, (I believe chosen by

---

[5] Howard, *Nez Perce Joseph*, p. 103.

the aggrieved Indians) being a member of the council. The decision of the council, as one might have predicted, was unfavorable to the Indians.[6]

Of this episode Interpreter Williams had this to say:

> The Indians did not select Elfers to sit on the case of Mason's outlawry. Knowing him to be their uncompromising enemy they would never have selected him as claimed by General Howard. He was there to decide in favor of Mason and, of course, it was fixed up that way from the first.
>
> Elfers was an old enemy. He opposed prosecuting Larry Ott for killing Chief Eagle Robe; declaring openly, "He should not be prosecuted for killing a dog."

The war party had proceeded to Benedict's place at a swift gallop. As they drew near, Benedict and another man, August Bacon, ran from the building and made for a foot-log or bridge spanning the stream. Some claim there was a third man, who may have escaped. Sarpsis Ilppilp shot Benedict, whose body dropped into the creek to be borne away on the swollen tide, never to be recovered.[7] His companion was killed as he reached the opposite bank, where he fell near an outbuilding of some kind. The Nez Perces had no account of any other killings at this place. No women or children were molested there.

There was a second store at the mouth of the White Bird, so it appears the raiders did not tarry. They hurried on to settle scores held against its proprietor. But they were too late. Evidently alarmed by the gunfire at Benedict's, the merchant and two other

---

[6] *Ibid.,* p. 102.

[7] The manner of Benedict's death has never been known to the whites, but for a verification of the complete disappearance of his body, see Robert C. Bailey, *River of No Return* (Lewiston, 1935), p. 205.

persons were seen in a boat midstream of the flood-swollen Salmon, pulling desperately for the opposite shore.[8] The Indians let them go. Benedict was the one the war party was seeking, and he had fallen before the rifle of his shotgun victim of other years. Both stores were looted and wrecked, goods destroyed, scattered, or carried away. Gold dust found in the cash boxes, although legal tender, was taken out and sprinkled on the ground.

Had it not been for Benedict's whisky, which, one old-timer assured the writer, must have run into the hundreds of gallons, the darker atrocities of the outbreak would never have occurred. This old-timer further declared, "I can show you the grave of a young man who went late one evening to the isolated camp of a young Indian couple and getting the drop on the husband, tied him up and forced his attentions on the wife during the night. He was one of the so-called 'innocent' victims of the war party."

The Manuel Party

Lahpeealoot [Geese Three Times Lighting On Water (later known as Philip Williams)], the only member of Chief Joseph's band with the raiders, says of his part in this second day's foray:

I was furnished with a bow and a few arrows, and somewhere above [present town of] White Bird we chased a white man who was mounted with a small boy riding behind him. I used an arrow drawn on the man but it struck the boy on the arm and he cried. When I heard that pitiful

---

[8] There is obvious confusion in the listing of some of the war parties' victims. While the Nez Perce raiders tell of witnessing the escape of this party by boat, James W. Poe, in a letter to Governor Brayman, names H. C. Brown, a merchant, as killed in this locality. *(Fifteenth Biennial Report of the Board of Trustees of the Idaho State Historical Society,* 1935-36, p. 90.)

voice, I turned my horse and backed away. Not used to killing, it hurt my feelings to hear that little child crying.

Later a rancher named Jack was killed and Wahlitits gave me his gun.[9] This killing was on White Bird Creek.

It was the Manuel party that the young bow-and-arrow warrior had encountered. The girl was mistaken for a boy. David B. Ousterhout, member of Company R of Captain Randall's Volunteers, told the writer that Jack Manuel was a saloonist at Mount Idaho.

Much has been written relative to the mysterious case of Mrs. Manuel, whose fate has been widely speculated upon. Most sources agree that she died from a knife thrust when her home was entered by drunken Indians, and that her body was cremated when the house was later burned. This was contradicted when several men "carefully raked over the ashes without finding any trace of human bones." This in turn was impugned by the finding of Mrs. Manuel's earrings along with a fragment of a skull.[10] Then incongruous with all of this is the confession of Yellow Bull, who (with the usual stipulation that his story not be divulged until after his death) told how Mrs. Manuel was held a captive for a month, until the retreating Nez Perces had passed over the Lolo Trail into Montana, where, in camp one night, "she was killed and dragged into the brush."[11] The incredible part of this story is that the month's retention as a prisoner is solemnly placed after the finding of the earrings and skull fragment in the ashes of the burned house. So much for Yellow Bull's story.

[9] J. J. Manuel was wounded through the hip, but there seems to be no reliable account of his having been killed. See Arnold, *Indian Wars of Idaho*, p. 151.

[10] Bailey, *op. cit.* pp. 188-90.

[11] *Ibid.*, p. 190.

Of the various accounts of the Manuel tragedy, none was more vicious than that hatched by Ad Chapman, who laid the crime directly at Chief Joseph's door, at the chief's own dagger-point.[12] This imputation of a crime of which he was wholly innocent, darkened Chief Joseph's entire life. The charge of murder proved a "haunt" that would not down, a shadow which even the grave has failed to obliterate.[13]

The Nez Perce version of how the only woman victim of the outbreak met her death is quite different. Red Wolf was carrying her on his horse, seated behind him, when she snatched the knife from his belt and attempted to kill him. He struck her,

---

[12] Chapman was a low-principled scoundrel, wedded after the tribal ritual to a Umatilla woman. Speaking the Nez Perce language fluently, he became General Howard's interpreter throughout his Nez Perce campaign and later accompanied the Nez Perce group into exile as interpreter.

[13] For example, this letter is found in the *Appendix* to the *Congressional Record* (v. 84, pt. 14, July 18, 1939, p. 334), written by a Christian Lapwai Nez Perce to Representative Usher L. Burdick, at the time a monument to Chief Joseph was being considered. "One other important point. Chief Joseph was not the man which history would place before the educational institutions as has been suggested along with the erection of the memorial. He is guilty of wantonly killing a white woman, Mrs. J. Manuel, while he was under the influence of liquor. On June 15, 1877, the chief and two companions, also under the influence of liquor, visited the home of the Manuels on White Bird Creek, where friendly Indians were keeping guard over the wounded Mrs. Manuel and baby with the understanding that the woman would be given aid in escaping to the white settlement. Joseph proceeded to wrangle over the succoring of the enemy white woman, and when the friendly Indians remonstrated, the chief reached out with a dagger and plunged it into her breast, killing her almost instantly. General Howard had heard of this soon after the war, but he refused to believe it. There is an old warrior living today who was present when the killing took place, and it has been generally known among the Nez Perce that Joseph committed the deed."

A kindly worded letter from the author to Mr. J. M. Parsons, author of the above charge, asking for the identity of the old warrior who witnessed the knifing of Mrs. Manuel was silently ignored. By now, the old warrior is safely dead. That Chief Joseph held aloof from the whisky-crazed Salmon River raiders was declared by every warrior interviewed. "Joseph had one good thing about him. He was a temperance man." (Kate McBeth, *The Nez Perces Since Lewis and Clark*, p. 98.) This from his most bitter spiritual enemy!

felling her to the ground, and she died from the fall. If Mrs. Manuel's earring was found in the ashes of her burned home, most evidently she had been carried there (and very probably she had) before life entirely departed. Black Feather [sometimes referred to as Black Eagle, and known among the whites as Jefferson Green] still living at this writing [1942] is a man of splendid repute. Of Chief Joseph's band, he was in the boy-warrior class and lays no claim to battle achievements. In an interview he declared with marked earnestness, "Chief Joseph was not of the party that did killings on the Salmon waters. Nothing of such charge was ever made against him at that time amongst any of the Indians. It is all a bad lie."

Readers of Nez Perce Indian lore, are, in general, familiar with the thrilling story of how Frederick Brice, an Idaho prospector, was able—through the magic which his emblematic cross-tattooed breast worked on the Indians—to rescue the wounded Manuel child, and of his weary, hungry tramp with his helpless, suffering burden before reaching safety. But the story has never been told from the Indian viewpoint. Knowing that Whylimlex [Black Feather] was a principal in this truly striking episode, he was prevailed upon, in September, 1931, to relate the incident which is here given in his own words.

It was on the White Bird River and the sun was about there [indicating midforenoon]. A white man named Jack lived near, but of course he was not there at that time. He had been driven away, but his place was where I was heading for.[14]

I looked around and saw three Indian men sitting on the ground in a circle smoking. I walked down a slope going

---

[14] The man referred to is J. J. Manuel.

to them and came close to some bushes near the riverbank. I stopped and stood still for I heard something like a person crawling through the brush. I did not know who it might be. I threw my eyes in that direction and waited. Soon a person came to view and I recognized a white man. I saw on his left arm a child that he was carrying. I knew his face but not his name. Not a real young man. I do not expect he is now living.

That white man nodded his head at me, a "how-do-you-do." The first words I understood him say, was "Will you kill me?" I answered, "No."

I had a gun, a rifle. I turned and walked to the three men smoking. Close behind me came the white man with the child on his arm, his right hand bracing it. When I approached near the smokers, the one facing me, Loppee Kasuny [Two Mornings], an oldish man, sprang up pointing his gun ready to fire, trying to make a shot past me. One of the other men, all of them past middle age, spoke to Loppee, "Hold there! Do not shoot! Can you not see child in his arms?"

I turned to the white man. He was almost against me, and that was why Loppee Kasuny could not shoot quick. He might hit me. The white man stood without speaking. I motioned him to the bushes. To beat it! Which he did!

When he reached the thicket, he turned again and nodded to me, then disappeared in the brush. I saw him no more. I now said to Loppee, "If you shoot the man, who can care for the child? Would you carry it?"

That is all the story. Nothing more to tell.

Somewhat surprised that no mention had been made of the tattooed cross which all white accounts have indicated figured prominently in saving Brice from death at the hands of the Indians, I interposed, "Did you see a picture painted on the white man's breast? A strange sort of painting?" To which came the prompt reply, "No, I saw no paint, no picture on his breast. He showed us no markings on his body anywhere."

Interpreter Williams pronounced the story of tattooing having saved the man's life as "fishy." The

Dreamer Nez Perces did not worship or recognize such a sign in their religion, though they were very used to seeing paintings and markings on the body.

Elias Darr, Union veteran of the War Between the States, had a blacksmith shop in Grangeville and did considerable independent scouting during the outbreak on the Salmon waters. In an interview, he made the following comments on the Manuel tragedy, "This woman, who was loved by everybody, was never heard of afterwards. Inquiry among the Indians, after the war was over, failed to reveal any account of her whatsoever. Her small child was found by an Irishman—who saved himself by exposing the cross tattooed on his breast—and carried to safety, as narrated in history."[15]

Weyah Wahtsitskan, a warrior known to the whites as John Miles, said of the Manuel tragedy, "On Salmon River a man we knew as Jack was killed and his wife disappeared. We had no need to war against women, and none of us knew what became of this one. She may have drowned herself in the Salmon River. Nobody seemed to know."

The Norton-Chamberlain Party

After the opening of hostilities, the Nez Perces had scouts and sentinels on all of the Camas Prairie trails and the stage road leading to Lewiston, in order to intercept, as far as possible, messengers and dispatch bearers sent out from the scene of disturbance. A wagon-freight train, known to be en route

---

[15] See Arnold, *Indian Wars of Idaho*, pp. 152-54, and diverse other publications. Fantasy has been allowed free rein with the Brice episode until some of the depictions are lugubrious. It is possible that the warm-hearted prospector, using his wits, capitalized on the potentialities of his mystic decorations when elaborating on his thrilling experiences.

from Lewiston, was awaited by these intercepting parties in the Camas Prairie region. This was the outfit conducted by Wilmot and Ready, which met with disaster. Had it not been for the whisky contained in this train's cargo, probably the ghastly outrage on the Norton-Chamberlain wagon would never have been made. Had these people remained in the Cottonwood House, it is very probable they would not have been molested.

Of the Norton-Chamberlain disaster, Elias Darr gave the following as his part in the rescue of the victims.[16]

The Norton party had reached to within four miles of Grangeville when the attack was made.[17] Both horses shot down, Norton killed and others of the party wounded, they remained all night in their exposed position, the Indians for some cause, not rushing them. Before the attack, or about the time of the onslaught, a lad of twelve years was let down from the tail of the wagon and told to try to make his way to Grangeville with the news of their plight. This boy told me afterwards of his experiences that night out on the open prairie. He ran, dodging the Indians as they galloped about over the plain, laying down in the grass whenever they drew near. Their horses actually leaped over his body as he thus lay hugging the ground. The next morning an object was seen on the hill above the town, and parties rode out to investigate. It was this boy, who told them the story of the attack.

All was excitement and a few of us hurriedly saddled up and rode to the rescue. I had a pony which I knew nothing about as to its running quality, but I threw on the saddle and hurried away. Reaching the wagon, the other boys dismounted, stripped the harnesses from the dead animals and harnessed up two of their saddle horses which were known to work. I remained on my horse and kept a lookout

---

[16] [For a typical account of the Norton-Chamberlain incident, see Howard and McGrath, *War Chief Joseph*, pp. 136-38. (Ed. note.)]

[17] [Like all other settlers in the area they had heard of the forays and were attempting to flee to safety. (Ed. note.)]

for Indians. Soon I saw them coming, a band of the Indians, and I called to the men, "There they come boys! Get out of here quick!"

Some of them started to bring Norton's body when I yelled, "Let it alone. They cannot hurt him any more!"

They mounted and were off. I dropped in behind, but I was soon left far behind. My pony was no runner, and it seemed to me that that wagon and its few mounted guards had wings. The Indians were gaining on me rapidly. I had a good carbine and seventy-five cartridges in my cantenises [Cantenisses: saddle pockets]. I unfastened the flap of the cantenises and got out a few cartridges. If overtaken I would dismount and sell out as dearly as possible.

A short distance ahead I saw a formation of rocks, on which, if I could reach, I thought I could successfully stand the Indians off. I reached the rocks all right, and being in sight of Grangeville, the people were aroused and by the on-coming wagon and were rushing out mounted and afoot. The Indians withdrew without putting up a fight. I was not particularly disappointed, however, that there was no occasion for firing a shot.

One of the Chamberlain children, a girl, we found with its tongue partly severed. The smallest child, a mere baby, was sitting between Norton's knees, and the other one was found out on the prairie. The older child recovered, but the smaller one died.

Mrs. Chamberlain was wild and we had to run her down and surround her before we could make her believe we were friends.

Lew Wilmot was not of this rescue party, nor had either of the little children a knife run through its neck pinning it to the ground, as you tell me Wilmot said was the case. Neither was the child carried out of the White Bird by the Irish prospector mutilated in any way.[18]

After his story of the attack on the Norton family,

---

[18] In a copy of George Hunter's *Reminiscences of an Old Timer*, found in the library of the late D. V. Vincent, Spokane, Washington, is the following marginal note written by Lew Wilmot, "I found this (Manuel) child and I think its head was struck on the ground and its tongue bit off. But a knife had been stuck through its neck into the ground."

Darr went on to give a graphic description of the occurrence that may well be regarded as the prelude to that lamentable tragedy.

Lew Wilmot and a man named Ready were freighting, each with a wagon and trailer and four-horse team. They had barreled whisky for the saloon in Mount Idaho, and were crossing Camas Prairie when they heard the Indians. It was in the night, not long before the Norton attack.

Wilmot, who had a good rifle, wanted to put up a fight, but Ready was of a different mind. So, unhitching their teams, they mounted the swiftest animals and dashed away, the loose horses following. The Indians, on coming to the wagons, were satisfied with the prize, and gave no further attention to the two fleeing men, who escaped.

You know what happened then, for you are acquainted with the Indian character and their unrestrained appetite for ardent spirits. Doubtless it was this whiskey that caused the horrors that overtook the Norton refugees within the next hour or so.[19]

A STATEMENT OF J. G. RAWTON

There were two graphic happenings in the Camas Prairie district at this time, which, aside from being brought out by Yellow Wolf,[20] appear to have received little or no notice. The narratives are here given as received from two of the actors in the drama. In August, 1930, J. G. Rawton gave the following statement.

---

[19] There seems to be no mention of this whisky cargo in the annals, but Darr's statement is confirmed by J. G. Rawton, citizen volunteer, who in reply to an inquiry wrote, "P. H. Ready and Lew Wilmot were crossing the prairie from Cottonwood to Mount Idaho, with freight wagons. They fled before being attacked, and the Indians followed them a short way but did not catch them. The freight was being hauled for Wallace Scott and Sam Weiller of Mount Idaho, and there was whisky in the freight, but I do not know how much, and it was not recovered. Nothing in the wagon was recovered."

A Mr. Markham informed the writer, "When Wilmot and the other freighter abandoned their wagons they were chased within a quarter mile of the Markham home, and the Indians could have killed all of us had they wanted. The chase seemed more for sport than any desire to kill."

[20] See McWhorter, *Yellow Wolf*, pp. 47-49.

There were twenty of us scouting around under Captain George Shearer.[21] We were about two and one-half miles southwest of Grangeville, and I was sent off to the left. I saw Indians robbing Ab Smith's house, he and his family being absent. I know not how many there were, and so hastened to report to my squad. But one was seen, and he mounted, appeared to be on the lookout from the front yard. There proved to be but three of them, and when we drew in sight the other two were mounting their horses.

My position threw me in the lead as we made a rush for the house about a quarter-mile away, and I had a good horse, which held his place throughout. Two of the Indians escaped but the third had a slow horse and we rapidly gained on him. At a distance of about two rods I took a shot at him, and then drew my six-shooter and fired twice, horses running at full speed.

Wellington Clark, a young man in his late teens, ran his horse alongside the Indian, who threw his gun to his shoulder, drawing on Clark at only a few feet range. Clark threw himself to the side of his horse, and whirling, dashed back. I could never understand why the Indian did not shoot, for he could not have missed his aim.

The Indian abandoned his horse and made off on foot. A heavy man, his progress was slow. Ben Morrison, Ad Chapman and others dismounted and fired from the ground. The Indian fired only one

[21] Colonel Redington writes in response to inquiry, "The Captain Shearer you mention was Major George Shearer, who held the rank of major in the Confederate army. The last time that I saw him was at old Camp Howard, near Grangeville, Idaho, where Lieutenant Farrow's scouts were encamped on their way to the higher Salmon River mountains, campaigning against the Sheepeater Indians . . . He was a fine conversationalist, and it was a real pleasure to talk with him. He was well spoken of by everybody that I ever heard mention his name."

shot, but I do not know at which one of us it came. I saw John O. Barker dodge down in the grass as if he heard the ball. It was only a moment when the Indian dropped, falling on his back. Indeed, I think that his back was broken by one or more shots, for he made no struggle to raise himself. Clark and I kept on after his horse, a small animal. It was checked by stepping on the bridle reins, and we soon secured it and brought it back.

In the meantime, Shearer, who carried a fine double-barreled shotgun, which he had borrowed, ran upon the fallen man, and would have been killed had the prostrate man not been so far gone. He brought his gun to bear but could not hold it in position. It wavered, describing a half-circle, and dropped to his opposite side. I think that this was but a dying effort, and that the rifle fell from lifeless hands.

Captain Shearer discharged both barrels of his gun into the Indians' inanimate body, and then broke its stock over his head.

Our captain took the Indian's gun. Some of the men wanted to scalp him, but Ben Morrison and I said, "No!" The Nez Perces had scalped none of our people and we would not scalp theirs.

[In reply to questions, Rawton continued.] Yes, these Indians were robbing the house, but I know nothing of what they were taking out of it.

No, I do not remember if any cartridges were found in the Indian's gun.[22] But I know that he fired only once during the entire scrap and we chased him about half a mile.

---

[22] The victim had but one cartridge. See *Yellow Wolf*, (pp. 48-49) where he says, "I saw his body myself, all covered with blood. He had many gunshot wounds, eleven in all. His head was crushed, was all over blood."

The white man you speak of as being killed later near where the Indian was killed was Charley Horton, and we supposed that his death happened one or two days later. It was three or four, possibly five or six, days before his body was found. . . .

On the evening of June 13, we received news of the outbreak on the Salmon River, and the settlers were called in, Horton with others. The next morning before it was light, Horton, who was a young single man of about thirty-five or forty years, started home. . . .

John Adkinson found his body up near his farmhouse. Adkinson believed that Horton, doubting about the Nez Perces being on the warpath, was permitted to ride up to a squad of warriors and was shot from his horse.[23] He was lying up near the mountains, about a mile and a half to two miles from where the Indian had been killed by our volunteers, under Captain Shearer.[24]

§

---

[23] For the Nez Perce account of this killing, see McWhorter, *Yellow Wolf*, p. 49.

[24] Darr told this story of these events, "The day after the Norton tragedy, in scouting around, we saw four Indians robbing a house which had been deserted by the occupants. We started for them, several of us. The Indians did not see us, and the word was passed to keep silent and we would get some of them. But one of the men could not hold his yap and let out a yell.

"The Indians, thus alarmed, mounted and broke away. There was a twenty-acre field, fenced, and the Indians went around this field, pursued by the man.

"I had a fine running horse, and I left the party, cutting across to head or intercept the Indians. I knew nothing about a ten-foot ditch which lay in my path until I was right up on it. Putting the steel to my horse, he cleared this ditch completely, and on we went. I soon saw my chance.

"One Indian, rather poorly mounted, was falling behind his comrades. I drew steadily closer, but I withheld my fire. I came up within twenty feet of him, and then fired. He was hit, but hung onto his horse and turning, snapped his Henry rifle at me twice. The bore in that gun looked as large as a hat-crown to me. The other boys, coming up, opened fire, and the Indian went down. He was on his

The Story of Lew Day's Ride

When the news of the outbreak was brought to Mount Idaho by Arthur Chapman, Lew Day volunteered to carry the news to Lapwai, and started immediately on the long ride. Of what followed, Mr. Rawton wrote:

As Day was going up the mountain after passing Cottonwood, he met three Indians in the road who shot him. I do not remember how many times he was struck but I think twice. He turned his horse and rode back to Cottonwood. The people at the tavern got in a wagon and started for Mt. Idaho, but the Indians overtook them about three miles from Grangeville, and fired on them. I helped to bring in some of the dead the next morning. Day, who did not leave his horse when attacked on the mountain, was killed there.[25]

Another version of the interception of Day on the stage road, which strengthens the claim that the Indians were interested only in preventing dispatches from going out, is this:

William Stuart and three or four other men were packing flour from Lewiston to the firm of Grasteen

---

feet instantly, menacing us with his rifle and running alternatively. He was hit more than once, but still he kept going, threatening us with his rifle. I rode closer, dismounted, and fired from on foot. The Indian fell and did not get up.

"George Shearer now came up and emptied both barrels of his shotgun into the Indian's body, and then broke the stock over his head. Some of the men wanted to scalp him, but I objected, and others joined with me. He was not scalped.

"The Indian had a repeating Henry rifle, which I took. Shearer borrowed it from me and that was the last I ever saw of it. The Indian was a middle-aged man."

David B. Ousterhout, Company B of Captain Randall's volunteers, in telling of this occurrence said, "I was with the men, among them Elias Darr, attacking the Indians supposedly robbing the vacant house. One of them was killed. We had him surrounded, and all of us were shooting at him. George Shearer broke his gunstock over the lifeless Indian's head. Shearer was the first man to reach him after he fell."

[25] See the accounts in Howard, *Nez Perce Joseph*, pp. 104-6; and Arnold, *Indian Wars of Idaho*, pp. 154-61.

and Bernard, traders at Mount Idaho. They encountered a party of perhaps a score of Indians, but were in no manner molested, although the packers were unarmed save for the traditional six-shooters at their belts. They had gone on but a few hundred yards when they heard rifle shots in the rear, and looking back saw Day come dashing down the road. They hurriedly cut the lashings of their packs, letting the loads drop to the ground, and made all speed for Mount Idaho.

The fact that Day was not even pursued indicates the truth of the Indian's contention that their aim was solely to prevent communication between various enemy points. Most of their killings were in the nature of reprisals, the worst of which were indulged in only after whisky had been obtained from the captured freight wagons.

Number of Victims

The estimated number of the war party's victims differs. General Howard places them at fourteen,[26] while James W. Poe makes the count fifteen,[27] and Ad Chapman says there were twenty-two.[28] When one weighs the three-days' carnage and murder of the few Nez Perce avengers against nearly two dozen years of murdering and thieving by gold seekers and cattlemen, surely the balance must break in favor of the Indians.

---

[26] Howard, *Nez Perce Joseph*, pp. 102-5.

[27] *Fifteenth Biennial Report of the State Historical Society of Idaho*, 1935-36, p. 90.

[28] *Ibid.*, p. 50.

Friends Among the White Settlers

That there were amicable relations between the Indians and the better class of whites was indicated on several occasions. One woman among these settlers told the author many years later, "The Indians were better, as Indians, than the white men were as whites." There are occasional rifts in the wall of partisan hatred which reveal a happier side. Edison Briggs was one of a surveying crew, and, when the war broke out, was engaged in running lines through the Cottonwood country under his uncle, Major Truax, government surveyor. Briggs was riding at night, headed for Lewiston, when he ran into one of the Nez Perce road vedettes or war parties. His bridle was seized, his horse stopped. A lighted match flashed on his face, followed by the ejaculation, "Eeh! Briggs!" He was told to "Hurry on! Watch! Be careful! Maybe you meet Nez Perces who not know you." Young Briggs reached his destination without being molested further, indicating the patrol was only of a local nature.[29]

While the bitter racial animosity ran high as always, not all the settlers were arrayed against the Nez Perces. There were a few who, fully cognizant of the deep wrongs under which the tribesmen were smarting, covertly sympathized with them, even to the extent of lending them material aid. The Indians deeply appreciated such friendships and not one of the white friends of these Indians was in any way molested. Red Elk, an intelligent tribesmen of fine repute, relative of Chief Yellow Bull, who became a chief after the close of the war, told the following as we sat about a campfire one October night in 1926.

---

[29] This information was given the author by Harry M. Painter, ex-lieutenant of the Washington State Guard.

My father, Red Elk, was brother to Yellow Bull, who became a chief after close of the war. I had seen only ten snows but I remember many happenings of those days, as if only recent.

Not all the whites were against the Nez Perces. I know two men who lived up Slate Creek, who were our best friends. They were not squaw men (as men with Indian wives were called). They had white wives. Rich men, they showed us strongest of friendship. All along they let the Indians have ammunition and other supplies for hunting. They often gave us beef or flour, and we remembered them with gifts of Indian-made goods, and sometimes with jerked venison and salmon.

One of these men was Wood. He lived there many years. He was a wealthy man, owning horses and cattle. The other one was Josh—I do not remember his last name. Both made a good living off the Indian lands; and both had strong friendships with all the Nez Perce Indians. These men were not troubled when the war broke out. No Indian molested them in any way. Wood had a son we know as Jack. He had a hardware store in Grangeville in later snows, but sold out and disappeared.

Wood saw the Indians coming after they had killed some whites. He stopped them and said, "Tie your horses and come in. We will have a talk."

Chief Yellow Bull, Sarpsis Ilppilp, Wahlitits and others were in the bunch. They went into this white man's house as requested. Men, who were working for this man, got scared. They thought to be killed. The friendly white man spoke to Yellow Bull, "I know you people! For many years I have known you very well. Also, I know the actions of the whites toward you. The government is cheating you of your lands. You Indians have been enduring wrongs for many years. While you have remained peaceable, not so the whites. You have lost good horses and cattle by thieving white men. Miners have taken possession of your country, digging out your gold. Your people have been killed; many of them. Now you are making resistance. One thing I want to tell you. Stay here around Snake River. This is a rough country. Do not leave it! Here you will always have good food. Get ready! Meet the soldiers and fight them."

They then shook hands, saying good-by. The white man spoke final words to them, "Boys, I hope you good luck!"

It was not long afterward that the soldiers came and fighting commenced. Chief Joseph and others wanted to stay in the Snake River country and fight it out there, but they were overruled. Then came the long ride over the Lolo Trail toward the buffalo country, and the Canadian border. You know the rest of the story. It was at this same time, when the good, rich man was helping Indians on Slate Creek, that, if the people around Lewiston, and other places, saw the dust of wild horses, they would say, "There is Chief Joseph! Indians are out on the warpath."

Had all the whites been like those few friends on Slate Creek, there never would have been war. They were not scared. Warriors passed by their homes, nighttime and daylight. They were never afraid. Indians all knew them to be friends.[30]

Again, touching the cause of war, the deductions of the late Phillip Evans seems apropos. Chelooyeen [Bow and Arrow Case] was of Chief Joseph's band, formerly of the Canyon Nez Perces. In August, 1932, in an all-too-brief interview, he said in part:

When Rev. James Hayes (Nez Perce) was in Washington City, he was asked what caused the war of 1877. He explained, and cited the Larry Ott case, who killed an Indian chief for his land. The son remembered how his father was murdered after he had given Ott part of his gardenland, and he went on the warpath to kill Ott. Not finding him, other bad and disliked white men were killed, and then came war. Hayes believed Larry Ott's killing of Wahlitits' father, before he, the son, was full grown, was the real cause of the war. I concur in this opinion.

But the real blame rested on the government. Had Ott been punished instead of upheld, Wahlitits would never have gone on the warpath. As it was, he and his associates killed others who should have been hanged by law, but who were never arrested or punished. Only after the war party became crazed by the white man's whisky, did the innocent white people suffer.

I was not at the Lapwai council when Chief Toohoolhool-

---

[30] Red Elk died Halloween, 1930. See *Yellow Wolf*, p. 140.

zote was arrested for speaking his mind. When the Indians came back from the council, I understood that General Howard had named thirty days for all the Indians to get on the lesser reservation. It seemed that people balked. Everybody agitated; moving and in great confusion. I went to Mount Idaho, and when coming back I met a man with the message that there was talk of war. When I heard this my feelings were those of a strange sensation.

This was about a mile from Grangeville, and all the way to the camp at Tolo Lake I felt strangely. I saw everybody ready to go. Women and men on all sides, hurrying, excited. My heart went back to the past.

These are my own people! I will not remain alone. I was not scared of anything. After that time, after my mind was made, when there came the call at any time, "We are attacked!" I felt ready for the fight. Never afraid. . . .

I belonged to Chief Joseph's band. I lived in the wintertime at White Bird, and in summer we had a place on the Little Salmon, this side of Weiser. We wintered once in Imnaha. I was raised mostly at Tolo Cave.[31]

Here as if old memories had been reawakened, the narrator paused and sat for some moments gazing silently out over the scene that is rich in lore of the famous legendary Kamiah monster. There was a tinge of pathos in his voice, as the old patriot continued: "My native country! You tell the government that I want my old home given back to me! I am now old and I want to die and be buried where my ancestors lived and are now returned to Mother Earth."

---

[31] Rocky Canyon. Philip Evans died here.

CHAPTER XIV

THE BATTLE OF WHITE BIRD CANYON

THE FIRST NEWS OF THE SALMON RIVER OUTBREAK
to reach General Howard was brought by two
Christian Nez Perces of whom the General writes,
". . . These Indians were much excited. They arrived
at Lapwai about noon. The name of one was Pu-ton-
ah-loo, and the other was an Indian lad of perhaps
fourteen years."[1]
    In October, 1926, Many Wounds arranged an in-
terview with the younger of these Indians, Nat
Webb,[2] in which he said:

I was about fifteen years old, living with my rich father
at Webb (now Fountain Station). A lot of us were camping
with the Chief Joseph Indians, when three young men went
out and killed some of the whites. The next morning John
Lawyer, Wepttaschite [known as Mitchell], and myself
started with the news to Fort Lapwai. Reaching near my
father's place, we met Joe Broncheen, a half-blood French
and Nez Perce, who was acting interpreter for five soldiers,
who were heading for the Salmon country. They turned
and brought us to General Howard at Lapwai, who sent us
on to inform Agent Monteith of the trouble.
    We had left the Indian camp not to return. Had our
object been known, we would not have been permitted to
leave. I am the only one of the three riders now living.

---

[1] Howard, *Nez Perce Joseph*, pp. 92-93; *Rep. of Sec. of War*, 1877, I,
119.

[2] "Nat Webb" was a white cognomen derived from *Nat Waptas
Tamana*, the name of his father, a well-to-do stockman who did not
join the war party nor did he go against them. He flatly refused to
scout for Howard. Nat Webb died about 1937, according to Camille
Williams.

This message, announcing hostilities, was confirmed a few hours later by dispatches to Howard from L. P. Brown of Mount Idaho. The spark from the rifle shown in the Lapwai council had burst into flame. The war was now on!

SERGEANT SCHORR'S NARRATIVE

General Howard took action. He ordered Captain Perry of the First Cavalry to take his own Company F, and also Company H under Captain Trimble, and proceed at once to the scene of the disturbance. Together the two companies aggregated ninety-nine men, all that were then available, and since Captain Perry's company was minus officers, Lieutenant Bomus and Lieutenant Theller, both of the Twenty-first Infantry, were detailed to his command.[3] After an all-night ride the cavalcade reached Grangeville the evening of the following day.

Here Captain Perry learned of the Nez Perce whereabouts: that they had fled to their ancient stronghold, Lahmotta, the White Bird Canyon. While General Howard had ordered the command to the scene of the outbreak to protect the distressed settlers from further depredations, it appears that Perry, once in the field, was swayed by the ever-voluble Ad Chapman and others who urged him to follow up the "cowardly Injuns" and administer a crushing defeat before they could place the raging Salmon between them and their pursuers.[4] Perhaps the vision of a cherished brevet had

[3] *Nez Perce Joseph*, p. 98; *Rep. of Sec. of War*, 1877, I, 120. Of these troops, Mrs. Angie B. Bowden writes, "As a small girl I saw Captain Perry and Lieutenant Parnell at the head of their respective companies ride away from Walla Walla, for Fort Lapwai, shortly before the battle of White Bird Canyon, in which so many were destined to give up their lives. Captain Perry was a tall, handsome man and very arrogant. Lt. Parnell was a splendid appearing man and very likable. The two men, of very different types, Colonel Perry was a conceited West Pointer, while Colonel Parnell was an experienced soldier who rose from the ranks, and they despised each other. Parnell had been a commissioned officer in the Crimean War."

[4] Of the wisdom and justness of Captain Perry's White Bird raid, the following from Sergeant Schorr is of moment. "Here is an item I would like to mention concerning the volunteers in the White Bird Canyon fight. If Colonel Perry had not listened to the volunteers, not a man would have been lost, as Perry was ordered to protect the

something to do .with the Captain's decision to pursue and deliver an early morning surprise attack on the camp while its "savage" occupants were still sleeping, unconscious of their pending doom. Eleven enthusiastic citizen volunteers,[5] who chose George Shearer as their captain, joined the regulars. After a few hours rest, supper, and feed for the horses, the gallant cavalcade set out upon its march for the canyon rendezvous of the unsuspecting "hostiles." But that momentous night ride can best be told by actors in the field. Sergeant John P. Schorr of Company F, Twenty-first Cavalry, wrote the following to the author.

We understood it was a settled fact that the Indians were to come on the reservation by the 15th of June, 1877, (and) as I happened to be on guard on the 14th and during the night apparently all indications pointed that way, for all night long the Indians were passing back and forth which was only a ruse to make it appear as if they were making preparations to come on the reservation. But that was only to deceive us and by the 15th we received news they were on the war path.

On the 15th, Corporal Sytle, myself, and another private whose name I cannot just now recall, were sent on detached service to find out the reason why the Red Devils never came on the reservation. But we did find out pretty quickly for when we got 12

citizens of Mount Idaho and Grangeville, in connection with which he was called before a Court of Inquiry as you know. They (the volunteers) urged Perry to hurry before the Indians could escape across the Salmon, for they were 'cowardly and would not fight.' When too late we found the reverse to be the true facts.

"The few volunteers who went with us, saw but little of the fight. They were the first to break and run. None of them were killed, and only two slightly wounded.

"One, Sergeant Fuller, brought the report to Fort Lapwai that we had all been massacred."

[5] W. R. Parnell, "The Battle of White Bird Canyon," in Brady, *Northwestern Fights and Fighters*, p. 100; Howard's report, *Report of the Secretary of War*, 1877, I, 120. Fuller gives the number of volunteers with Captain Perry in his White Bird expedition as about fifty. (See Fuller, *History of the Pacific Northwest*, p. 226). For additional data see McWhorter, *Yellow Wolf*, pp. 15-16.

miles from Lapwai we met a messenger from Mt. Idaho telling us to turn back. Indians on War Path, and that he had a message for the commanding officer at Lapwai. Arriving at the Fort we found Troops F and H, 1st U.S. Cavalry, all mounted and fully equipped ready for action, commanded by Captain Perry, 1st Cavalry, Captain Trimble, and 1st Lt. Parnell of H Troop. Lt. Theller of the 21st Infantry was attached to my F troop.

"We left Fort Lapwai about 8 P.M. on the 15th, and rode all that night with a short rest to get a bite to eat for man and horse. We then again took up the march and on 16th June, we saw the many depredations committed by the Indians such as killing of horses, and robbing prairie schooners and burning down ranches and I guess the Red Devils were pretty well filled up with fire water. Among their plunder we found an empty whiskey barrel with the head knocked out. Whiskey is not good for anybody, so imagine how it befuddled their heads.

Here we threw out our advance guards and noon on the 16th found us at Cottonwood or Norton's ranch where we saw more of their dirty work; household goods strewn about the place and by some miracle the ranch [house] escaped being burned down, for some one of them set an open trunk of papers and clothing afire and it so happened the lid was shut down and smothered the fire. Here we had another short rest, then off again for Mt. Idaho, arrived there about 10 P.M. and with about four hours rest found us in the saddle again.

At 2 A.M. we were rousted out of what little sleep we could catch in the saddle where a halt without dismounting had been ordered. We were near entering the White Bird Canyon to make a surprise attack on the Indians at daybreak. But let me state right here, we were to have the surprise of our lives.

As we reached the crest of the mountain at the head of the White Bird Canyon, there came from the timber, just off to one side, the shivering howl of a coyote. That cry was an Indian signal, enough to make one's hair stand straight up.

In going down into the canyon a Mrs. Benedict with her two small children were found in the brush almost starved and in rags as they had been hiding from the Indians for several days. The husband and father being killed and their ranch [house] burned to ashes along with all others in the canyon. Mrs. Benedict really pled with our officers not to go any further as we would all be massacred, which came very near being the case.

Out of our ninety men, thirty-three were killed in almost less time than it takes to tell,[6] for the Indians were well provided with magazine guns and it was a miracle that any of us escaped. We never got a chance to bury our dead until a week later. But I did manage to cover the body of my buddy. . . .

After the lightning-like routing of our force, I managed to find a mount for Mrs. Benedict; but in the excitement I forgot to hand her the bridle reins. I placed the children on . . . trooper's mounts. . . .

It turned out that Mrs. Benedict fell into the hands of the Indians, and being a kind-hearted woman she won the friendship of the women and was not detained. Two years later I heard that she was at Walla Walla with her children.

§

[6] Howard gives the losses as thirty-three enlisted men plus Lieutenant Theller killed. *(Rep. of Sec. of War*, 1877, I, 120.) [Ed. note.]

Captain Perry had made a night march of sixteen miles to White Bird Canyon, where he knew the Indians were. But his hope of falling upon the Nez Perce village unawares was doomed from its very inception. Alert Indian scouts had discovered him at Cottonwood, and his movements had been under close surveillance until the troops arrived at Grangeville, where the spies left him to warn the White Bird encampment.

Topography of White Bird Canyon

It is important at this point to note the topography of the region that Captain Perry was so blithely entering. The trail does not strike the upper White Bird Canyon proper, down which the creek boisterously cascades on its way to the Salmon River. Instead the trail enters a dry canyon at the foot of the mountain which is bordered on the east by a low butte-like range, linked with an extensive broken terrain, dividing it from the canyon proper. The dry canyon in question is hemmed in on the west by an uneven waste, skirting the great mountain range locally known as the White Bird Divide, which reaches out from the north.

When visiting the old battleground in August, 1932, with Many Wounds, the author was shown a spring, at or near the entrance of the trail to this dry canyon, marking an ancient Indian camp ground known as Penenwes Pah [Coming Down to Open Place, or Coming Out from Thick Brush]. This is some four miles from where the battle was fought. Farther down the canyon, at no great distance, is a second watering place called Mahal Koos [Grasshopper Water (now known as Grasshopper Spring)]. Here was another Indian camping place known as

Overlooking the Whitebird Battlefield

SERGEANT JOHN P. SCHORR, COMPANY F, FIRST CAVALRY, U.S.A.

tamer, mounted and hurried to the encampment with the news of the near approach of the soldiers. The sober men in the camp were immediately alert and preparing for the fray. Doubtless many a half-drunk was whipped into sobriety.

WOUNDED HEAD'S NARRATIVE

What was happening among the Indians at their campsite as the soldiers approached can best be learned from warrior Husis Owyeen's unfinished narrative.

During the first evening after our removal to Lahmotta, a small party of three young men went back toward Camas Prairie to watch if the soldiers followed after us. I knew not a thing of all this. I was drunk that night. Next morning they missed me, and I must have lain out all night in the bushes where one woman found me. My wife said to me, "What are you doing here? Everybody has gone for the fighting."

"Where is my horse?" I asked her. "Tied out there; your best horse!" she answered. I jumped on my horse and hurried away without my weapon. Not all had guns and one must have taken mine, the rifle I had traded with the horse. I overtook an old Indian and I asked if he had my gun. He pulled out an old-time pistol with one bullet and the last powder and cap in place. I took it and went on.

I came to a soldier thrown from his horse. Perhaps he was wounded. I rode up to him, but instead of receiving me and asking me questions, he pointed his gun and made to shoot me. As he raised his gun I drew the old pistol with its last bullet. I shot first and he fell backwards and did not move. The bullet struck between his eyebrows.

I jumped to the ground and took his gun and belt

of cartridges. I left the dead soldier the old pistol as a present. Laid it on his breast.

I now rode swiftly to join in the battle with my soldier-gun. But I was too late. The fighting was all finished on the field. I saw the retreating soldiers were too far away for me to catch up with them.

The whisky had ruined my chance for good fighting. But I did round up a few soldier horses to divide among the Indians. In doing this we came upon two soldiers hid, who appeared wounded, but put up a fight. We left them dead and brought away their guns and cartridge belts. One of my partners now said. "The soldiers are too far ahead of us. It is getting late. No use chasing them!"

We now turned back toward camp lower down the White Bird. While going on the trail I looked back and saw a bunch of Nez Perces. They called to me, "Look ahead to the hillside. See what is coming toward you!" I looked. It was a white woman making her escape down the hillside. I rode to her. She made a sign that I do not kill her. I motioned her to get on the horse behind me. She did so and I turned back to the trail where the other Indians met me. I asked them to take charge of the woman, but they refused. With the woman I rode on down the trail, but not in view of the camp. I continued along the hill out of sight of the rest of the people, down to the gulch where I stopped. I think she was scared when I told her to get off to the ground. I instructed her to escape with her life, and I shook hands with her. She went and I rode back to camp.

That was one good thing I have done for the whites. When I returned from my wanderings after this war, this very woman was still alive. She had asked in the meantime about the Indian who let her escape that day in the gulch. She was a very great friend to me, and the first time I met her after my return she gave me six dollars as a present. She used to live at the mouth of the White Bird, but I have forgotten her name. She often told me to come to her house and she would treat me like a brother. Growing old, like myself, she is now dead.[12]

§

Wounded Head said he was drunk. There were a great many drunken Indians in the Nez Perce camp the night of the sixteenth and morning of the seventeenth. Black Feather, who figured in the dramatic rescue of the Manuel child by Patrick Brice, declared on this score:

> I was drunk the night and morning of the battle as were a great many of the young men and even the older men. But I was not counted as a warrior, never entered into the real fighting. Yes, I had a gun after the White Bird fight, and so did many others who made no great use of them. When we did shooting it was a good distance and from close hiding. I never went ahead of a brave man, I followed. I never made myself a brave man. Never did anything of worth.

Had it not been for the barreled whisky contained in the freight wagons captured by the Nez Perces on Camas Prairie, it is probable that Captain Perry's command would not have escaped from the canyon.

Howard has given a confusing description of the opening of the White Bird battle, wherein Captain Perry, as he descends from the mountain summit

---

[12] It should not be inferred from the foregoing that the narrator was conceited, as the pronounced use of the personal pronoun might imply. Wounded Head had been requested to portray his own personal achievements, what he saw and did; and the Indian speaks only of that in which he is strictly concerned. The cool, calculating courage of Wounded Head on the field of battle has been attested by his contemporaries in arms, while his veracity has never been questioned. He died at his home on the Lapwai reservation, 1912. The white woman he befriended was, of course, Mrs. Benedict.

into the canyon, observes "light smoke from the Indian camp," and sees men emerging slowly from
their lodges, each wrapping his blanket about his
neck as he moved among the horses changing them to
better grass, or relieving the "night watchman" with
the herd.[13] In reality the village was completely
hidden from the approaching troops nor was it visible
from any part of the battleground. Strangest of all,
Howard mentions the Indian scouts high on the trail
riding down to camp at sunrise, after the chiefs had
discovered the approaching enemy by the aid of a
glass, a glass that every warrior questioned declared
they did not possess.[14] The General's graphic description of Chief Joseph's spying on the approaching
enemy, vetoing a proposed flight across the Salmon,
ordering preparation for the coming battle is interesting, but pure fantasy. When we realize that not
forty-eight hours had elapsed since Joseph and Ollokot had been closely guarded by their tribesmen lest
they desert and surrender,[15] the General's picture
of the great Chief's activities is despoiled of its
classic glamor.

Captain Perry states that he reached the summit
of the divide between Camas Prairie and White Bird
at midnight, where he halted waiting for daylight.
At dawn they proceeded down a narrow gorge which
widened later. It was here that Lieutenant Theller
and eight men were detached as an advance guard
and the command was directed to load.[16] All this,
according to General Howard, had occurred prior
to any alarm being conveyed to the Nez Perces or

---

[13] See *Nez Perce Joseph*, p. 110.

[14] *Ibid.*, pp. 111-12.

[15] See above Chapter XII, 199, and *Yellow Wolf*, p. 45.

[16] David Perry, "The Battle of White Bird Canyon," in **Brady,**
Northwestern Indian Fights and Fighters, p. 114.

leaders, despite the midnight howl that more than one trooper reports. Yellow Wolf's disposal of the warrior force pending the enemy attack is more logical and understandable by far than that advanced by the military technicians.[17] Howard goes on to tell how Ollokot betrayed panic at the first sight of the enemy and urged immediate flight beyond the swirling flood-swollen Salmon.[18] This is completely foreign to the make-up of the young leader, novice to war that he was. Howard's claim that old White Bird led and directed his young men during the battle is also without factual basis.[19] White Bird could no longer maintain the warrior pace. Chief Joseph was in the fray, but not as a commander.

A Peace Mission

There can be no doubt that as the troops approached the Nez Perce leaders still hoped that somehow peace might be effected and war averted. Ollokot, whose influence extended over a wide circle of associates, urged the warriors to comply with the

[17] See *Yellow Wolf*, pp. 55. Abraham Brooks, full-blooded Nez Perce (Christian) Indian who served as scout for General Howard, at a hearing held at the Nez Perce Agency in 1900 for the purpose of establishing claims for pay for such service, testified in part, "I went up with the soldiers to White Bird before I had a uniform. Jonah Hayes went along, and when I started and got above the fort at Jonah Hayes place, I saw Jonah, Wish-tas-kat, Yu-wish A-kaikt, Frank Hushush, Joseph Albert, Joe Rabusco (interpreter), Amos Wap-she-li. These went along with us to confer with the hostiles to attempt to stop them from fighting. We rode all night to Grangeville, where we met Colonel Chapman and twenty white soldiers. We went with 100 white men and ten Indians to see Joseph's band, who commenced shooting just as soon as Colonel Chapman opened fire on them. We, the Indians, had no guns and could not take part. Some of the Indians, after this fight, went to Mount Idaho and some came back to Lapwai." ("Claims of the Nez Perce Indians," *Senate Executive Document No. 257*, 56th Con., 1st Sess. p. 84).

[18] Howard, *Nez Perce Joseph*, p. 112.

[19] *Ibid.*

ruling of the chiefs and older warriors, not to fire the first shot should fighting ensue. The young chief wanted first to learn the intention of the soldiers. The Indian's first gun is supposed to have been fired only in answer to challenging shots from the whites. Had Captain Perry obeyed his commander's orders to halt at Mount Idaho, war would have been remote.

Warrior movements just prior to and at the opening of the battle differ markedly from those described by General Howard and contemporary writers. White accounts have never indicated that the Nez Perces sent a commission of six, carrying a white flag, to meet the troop commander on a mission of peace. The leader of this party, Wettiwetti Howlis [Vicious Weasel] was a man of splendid repute, known to the whites as John Boyd. This peace mission had strict instructions not to fire unless first fired upon. They were fired upon by the red-handed Ad Chapman of the volunteers, who had boasted that he could "whip the cowardly Injuns" himself. It is significant that after this Chapman was well cared for not only throughout the war, but until the release of the Nez Perces from exile eight years later. This ignominious disregard for an emblem that has ever been held in reverent respect by all civilized nations, was not mentioned in the military reports of the day. Both Captain Perry and Lieutenant Parnell appear purposely vague in their descriptions of the opening of the battle. The traditional account of the first shot, the first volley, is conspicuously absent,[20] yet how could Chapman's act have been kept from General Howard's knowledge?

THE NARRATIVE OF TWO MOONS

Two Moons, waiting with others at a more southern point for the appearance of the soldiers, confirmed that

---

[20] See Brady, *Northwestern Indian Fights and Fighters*, pp. 102-115.

the first shot was heard from beyond the buttes to the north. Of the morning's events, Two Moons, who arrived at White Bird camp after nightfall the evening before, gave the following account.

When I reached the White Bird camp, I found a great many Indians had followed me. Not only that, but the people I had left at Cottonwood Creek had come straight to White Bird. Came in daylight, while I and my wife did not arrive until growing dark. News was spoken that soldiers would come and it would be war.

Next morning every man of our party got up early to go bring in his horses. We would all go back to Camas Prairie or on to the Clearwater River where we had left Red Owl and his people. But my horses had gone so far up the mountain side that I had trouble finding them. Bringing them down, I found everybody but my brother, Sewattis Hihhih [White Cloud] had gone up the canyon to meet the soldiers. My brother had waited for me. Too late to escape the soldiers, I now took my best running horse and a good running pony and hurried to where the battle was to be fought. I saw five Indians standing holding their horses. I gave them a scolding. I said to them, "Why are you men standing here? Why do you not go to fight? This is the very war we have so long talked about, considering if we should be forced to war. Now is the time for you people to fight! General Howard is upon us with his peace-talked rifle! The fighting is now here!"

One of the men answered, "If that is the case, we are ready! I did not know I was among the warriors, or was into such trouble. But now we will have to take it as it comes!"

I joined with the others, among them Yellow Wolf and my partner, Otstotpoo [Fire Body], an old-like man. There was a gun report to the north and soon, right away, we saw a man wearing a broad, whitish hat and riding a white horse coming fast from the north. He was on high flat land along a rock-topped ridge lying just west of us. That rider was Chapman, a known bad man. When he saw us he fired across at us but his shot was lost.

Several, maybe twenty, soldiers followed close after Chapman. There was a bugler and when the party all stopped, this bugler rode a little ahead of them. He began calling orders on his trumpet. Otstotpoo said to me, "You now watch! I will make a good shot and kill that bugler!"

He did make the long-distance shot, and dead dropped the bugler from his horse. Chapman and his soldiers whirled and rode rapidly away from there. They did not give Otstotpoo a chance for another shot. He had fired the first shot from our side and killed. I fired the second shot but did not kill. It was good to get the bugler who called the General's orders to his fighting soldiers.[21]

Two Moons was in charge of the gallant sixteen that struck Captain Perry's left flank with such disastrous results.[22] Of the conflict in general at this stage, Two Moons paints a vivid picture.

---

[21] Sergeant Schorr, writing of his experience at the Fort Lapwai barracks gives the following striking incident. "The medicine chief, To-hool-sote, who seemed to be the most obstinate, refused any and all proposals made by General Howard, who finally had said Chief confined to the guard house, and it so happened—rather a coincidence —that Trumpeter Jones of my troop was in durance-vile at that particular time, and the Chief and Jonesy became quite friendly while together, and I remember our Trumpeter made the remark, after gaining his liberty, that if the Indians did go on the war path, they would not harm him. Strange though it seems, that he should have been the first picked off by an unseen sharpshooter. His horse was also killed during the ensuing battle, and a week later we found his stall mate with saddle and saddle-bag and bridle still on him but minus the saddle blanket."

[22] For another account of this see McWhorter, *Yellow Wolf*, pp. 57, 58.

After Otstotpoo killed the bugler, we ran our horses to where the fighting was getting under way. There were about sixteen of us and we struck the soldiers' left flank. Those soldiers, some of them in citizen clothes, were on a low rocky butte, other edge of the regular soldiers. They did not stay there any time, and I, Two Moons, hardly saw them at all.[23]

I, Two Moons, saw Sarpsis Ilppilp, Wahlitits, and Tipyahlahnah Kapskaps, all three wearing full length red blanket coats and two of them on fine-looking grey horses, come riding side by side at head of the charge. Those three warriors came through that wild charge and mixing up the soldiers, untouched by the hail of enemy bullets. They did not pay attention to enemy bullets that must have been as hail about them. Shooting from horseback, these three noted warriors drove the soldiers back. Never stopping, the soldiers gave way before them. Turned and rode hard from that deadly mixing. After this battle these three men were known as the "Three Red Coats."

It was a wild battle and quickly over. Soldiers seemed poor shots. No Indian was touched by a bullet in all of this battle. In other parts of the field two warriors were light wounded but none killed anywhere.

The soldiers were now riding hard in an effort to escape with their lives. With the other warriors, I, Two Moons, and Otstotpoo mounted our horses and set out chasing the soldiers. Not so young as in other snows, we followed only part way up the mountain.

---

[23] Relative to Chapman's sudden leave-taking Sergeant Schorr writes, "As for Ad Chapman, after our first encounter I lost sight of him. He was all that we ever pictured of him.

"It was the soldiers' right flank where the main Indian charge struck hardest. Many of the Warriors hung to the side of their horse so as to hide from the enemies, but not all of them did so."

Coming behind the hard-riding soldiers, General Howard's Christian Nez Perce scouts seemed to edge in below the troops and above us. But I did not want to drop any of these enemy Indians, not at all.[24] I kept calling for them to keep away from the soldiers. Away from our bullets!

Gaining the next hilltop, one of these scouts turned his horse and came out in the open. I scolded him! I said, "What you doing against me? If I was mean enough I might have killed you. Go! Let me do the fighting. Keep away or I might happen to drop you!"

That Christian Indian scout hurried out of sight. Soon my brother met me. He was quitting the chase. He had captured a roan horse which he brought to me. He said, "Let us now go home and rest till to-morrow."

We returned to our White Bird camp that evening. I know not what other boys did in that fight. I am only giving you of my own, what I, Two Moons, did and saw as facts.

§

Of the two notable charges made by the Nez Perce horsemen which threw Captain Perry and his cavalry into panicky flight, Weyahwahtsitskan (known to the whites as John Miles) who was an eyewitness and participant in the fight, said:

It was a truly startling scene. Unlike the trained white soldier, who is guided by the bugle call, the Indian goes into battle on his own mind's guidance. The swift riding here against the troops was done mostly by the younger men.

---

[24] Abraham Brooks in his testimony at the time of the claims dispute says that there were ten Nez Perce scouts accompanying Captain Perry's force in the White Bird raid. ("Claims of the Nez Perce Indians," *Senate Executive Document No. 257*, 56th Congress, 1st Session, p. 84). Jonah Hayes, Nez Perce scout with Captain Perry states in his testimony that ten had enlisted and that "Abraham Wa-tsin-ma joined us at Cottonwood, making eleven." *(Ibid.,* p. 81)

All the warriors, whoever gets ready, mount their horses and go. In this charge against the soldiers' right flank, Wahlitits, Sarpsis Ilppilp and Tipyahlahnah Kapskaps were the first to start in the charge, all of the three wearing full-length red blanket coats of same make and pattern. These coats were to show their contempt, their fun-making of the soldiers, to draw their rifle shots, of which they were not afraid.

Other warriors follow after them riding singly, and many hanging on the side of their horses, shielded thus from the soldiers' sight. There is fast shooting and wild yelling and whooping as the horsemen stream by, an occasional horse shot down.

It is a bad mixup for the soldiers. They do not stand before that sweeping charge and rifle fire of the Indians. Their horses go wild, throwing the riders. Many of their saddles turned when the horses whirled, all badly scared of the noisy guns. Soldiers who can, remount, and many without guns dash away in retreat. It was a wild, deadly racing with the warriors pressing hard to head them off.

Chapman under his big hat, who came first afront the soldiers, was now going back, still afront the soldiers. This running war continued a long distance.

The warriors charging the soldiers left flank were just a small force. Some of them middle aged and some quite past that time of life. They routed the volunteers from a rocky butte. Not all the warriors of this band had guns. Chapman must have skipped early in the fight, for none of those left-flankers got sight of him.

None of the chiefs, Joseph, White Bird, or Toohoolhoolzote, were in this charging fight. Joseph did some fighting but he was not with either bunch of the charging warriors. He did no leading.

While it is true that the Nez Perces evinced a military skill that was astonishing, the claim that they had drilled in modern cavalry tactics, in anticipation of war, will not hold under close investigation. They were trained horsemen, as were all buffalo-hunting tribes, and doubtless they had, in their warlike sports, maneuvers not unlike some of those of the cavalry, with whose tactics they had become more or less familiar around the various frontier army posts. But that army cavalry tactics had been adopted by them in actual warfare can be regarded as absurd.

Yellow Wolf, when asked about the claim by certain writers that the cavalry was thrown into utter confusion by the Nez Perce stampeding a band of wild horses through their ranks, replied:

Such was not the case. We had no use for wild horses in battle; did not have them with us. Maybe the soldiers thought the horses we rode were wild horses, for oftimes we could not be seen. We hung to the side of our horses, on opposite side from the soldiers when flanking them or wanting not to be seen. No wild horses were used at White Bird, Clearwater, or any other fight. How could we have managed them and all the shooting going on?

Some of the actions ascribed to this battle are pathetically ludicrous. Theodore Swartz, said to have been the volunteer shot in the knee while defending the rock-crowned butte that had been assigned to them on Captain Perry's left flank, told how he was watching some movements on the hillside or bluff above him, when, happening to glance below him, he saw an Indian at his very stirrup, in the act of shooting him. But he was too quick for the "Redskin," and whipping out his six-shooter, sent a bullet straight between his eyes, killing him instantly. Bravo! Not an Indian was killed in all that battle.

Quality and Size of the Nez Perce Fighting Force

As fighters the Nez Perces could hold their own with any other tribe, including the Sioux. In former years they had often gone to the Sioux country to fight, and would return home laden with war trophies, captured horses, blankets, and Sioux scalps.

As to the size of the Nez Perce force, Howard said in his official report that the warriors were double Perry's force in numbers.[25] Later he wrote that they outnumbered Perry three to one.[26] Following this same pattern, one historian places the Nez Perce force at over three hundred warriors.[27] This numerical superiority attributed to the Nez Perces over the troops in this and subsequent clashes is without basis. Even when the unarmed men, and those with only bows and arrows and antiquated firearms are counted as warriors, the Indians were outnumbered two-and-one-half to one.[28] Taking inventory, certainly the two troops of cavalry, carrying forty rounds of cartridges to the man, with their full complement of commissioned officers and a volunteer auxiliary, far outclassed their semi-naked "savage" adversaries except in fighting efficiency.[29]

[25] *Rep. of Sec. of War*, 1877, I, 120.

[26] Howard, *My Life and Experiences*, p. 285.

[27] C. J. Brosnan, *History of the State of Idaho* (New York, 1938), p. 136.

[28] See McWhorter, *Yellow Wolf*, p. 56, for a discussion of Nez Perce armament. See Chapter XI, pp. 177-85, above, for a discussion of the number of fighting men the Indians could put in the field, estimated at 191 men.
[Perry's force, plus the volunteers and Indian scouts, totalled 120 men. It was McWhorter's belief that the Indians seldom used anywhere near their full fighting force, which at this time totalled 151 as they had not been joined by the Looking Glass band. It seems probable, but not certain, that only 45 warriors participated in the engagement (as indicated by McWhorter) when the fact many had no arms this early in the war is taken into account. (Ed. note.)]

[29] A striking example of warrior nonpreparedness in the White Bird battle is revealed by the case of Tipyahlahnah Elassanin [Roaring or Thundering Eagle]. Of fine physique, and a man of few words, he was known to the whites as George Comedown. His story goes:
"I was about twenty-one snows of age and unmarried when the war broke. The first battle was on Sapalwit [Sunday] early in the morning. Many of the young men were drunk but, never a whiskey drinker, I was cold sober.
"I had a rifle, an old-time musket loaded from the muzzle. Not a

Military Incompetence

Captain Perry, extolled by Howard for "meritorious conduct in this battle,"[30] was confused to such an extent that he mistook 7:00 A.M. for 7:00 P.M.[31] Frank Allen, who saw service with Colonel Hunter's volunteers later on in the war, declared of the raid:

> That Canyon invasion by Captain Perry was badly planned and a complete failure in its execution. Cavalrymen ride with loose cinches, and theirs were not tightened up before the descent into that death-trap.[32] At the first volley from Indian guns, the horses whirling, many of the saddles

good gun for meeting soldiers with breech-loading army guns. In going to the place selected for the battle, no one warrior waited for another. So stripped for war, I mounted my horse and rode swiftly along with the strung out riders, some of them carrying bows and arrows only. Soon the soldiers started firing. After making the first shot with my old musket, I found that I had left the ramrod down at camp. Having no way to reload the gun I thought, 'I will get a rifle somewhere!'

"I was still holding the musket when about eight soldiers were surrounded. Because of lacking ramrod I missed firing at these soldiers. But they were all killed and I made for one of their guns, and with it I got a cartridge belt, but it was quite empty. I now had two guns and gave the musket to another man.

"The battle was of short duration. Across a draw we saw a horse and made for it. I reached it first and found it wounded. A soldier's horse. One man took the saddle and bridle.

"That was the first real battle, and what I saw and all that I did for a fact. The real fighting was all over before I had a gun that could be loaded, but nothing to load with. It was no use for me to follow after the soldiers, so did not cross the mountain in the pursuit."

[30] *Rep. of Sec. of War*, 1877, I, 120.

[31] See Parnell, in Brady's *Northwestern Indian Fights and Fighters*, p. 106. Relative to Perry's confusion at the White Bird field Colonel [then Lieutenant] Bailey wrote the author: "I heard no reports nor surmises of suicide at the battle of White Bird Canyon. I had direct from Colonel [then Lieutenant] Parnell the story of Perry's confusion when they met after the rout at the head of the canyon, and Perry wished to hold there until dark, when Parnell looked at his watch and said, 'Captain, it is now only seven . . . or thereabouts . . . in the morning, and we cannot hold that long.' And Perry replied, 'My God! I thought it was near night!' "

[32] In regard to the charge that the troopers went into the fight without readjusting cinches loose after the long ride, Sergeant Schorr replied: "So far as I know, we looked after the cinches, as it is a darned poor cavalryman that neglects to cinch his horse properly."

At the site of the village occupied by Looking Glass's band, which was destroyed by
Howard's command at the beginning of the war; left to right: Many Wounds,
L. V. McWhorter, Yellow Wolf, Peopeo Tholekt.

turned, pitching the riders to the ground. The commander was timid and he was aware that his men were none the bravest. Aside from all this, that later affair at Cottonwood, when he refused to go to the aid of Captain Randall's volunteer party, spelled cowardice.

Elias Darr, while not of the voluntary contingent participating in this expedition, commented on Perry's management of the encounter:

In that fight the troops had ridden far, and the commanding officer did a very foolish thing in entering the canyon without first having it scouted. The troopers did not even recinch their saddles, which should have been ordered before making the descent. This neglect proved most disastrous. At the first fire from the Indians, the horses whirling, many of the saddles turned, dismounting the cavalrymen. There was where the heaviest casualties occurred.

Chapman, who was greatly instrumental in influencing Captain Perry to undertake the night venture which proved so disastrous, was conspicuous for his broad brimmed white sombrero and white horse. Chapman, always wanting to be the head of everything, was far in the lead of all in that mad race from the canyon to the higher mesa.[33]

Nez Perce Casualties

The Nez Perces suffered no fatalities in the White Bird battle, and but two actual disabilities. Chellooyeen [Bow and Arrow Case] was wounded while in a death struggle with a soldier, of which he says:

I was wounded about forty feet west of the monument (erected to an unknown soldier) that stands at the foot of White Bird grade. Two soldiers were there afoot, all the

---

[33] Elias Darr was a Civil War veteran, having enlisted at sixteen in Racine, Wisconsin. Assigned to the Fourth Wisconsin, he saw service at Vicksburg. He was commander of Mead Post, G.A.R., Yakima, Washington, where he died at the age of eighty-eight on January 27, 1928.

others on the run up the hill. I was shot at close range and did not know I was wounded.[34]

I caught the soldier and his gun. He spoke to the other soldier, but I did not understand his words. I soon had him on his back, and I hear someone saying to another, "Be careful! Don't shoot each other!" I didn't know what killed the soldier. I heard no gunshot. He may have been killed with an arrow. When I got up with the gun, a friend who had no gun asked me for it, and I handed it to him. It may be that he had only a bow and arrow and had killed the soldier.

I recognized Chief Joseph's voice at the time the warning was given to be careful about shooting. Ollokot and the man who asked me for the gun had come to my rescue. It must be that one of these three killed the soldier.

My wound was on the right side, at the waist. I did no more fighting until the Big Hole battle.

The Nez Perces did not outnumber the soldiers, volunteers, and their Indian scouts. Two of these last were captured, but they were not harmed, as one of them had a father in our camp. They returned to Lapwai about two days later. Otstotpoo's shot that killed the bugler was the first shot fired from our side. Before the White Bird fight, Ollokot told the Indians not to fire first. He wanted to learn the intentions of the soldiers. The first Indian to fire a gun was supposed to be Yellow Bull. But his was not the first shot of the battle. He was in another part of the field from Otstotpoo, and from where I was wounded. He was in the charge against the right flank.

Espowyes, the other wounded warrior, was the Auskehwush of Yellow Wolf's narrative.[35] He was shot in the side of the abdomen when he seized the muzzle of a gun and endeavored to draw it from beneath a soldier lying prone on his stomach, either

---

[34] McWhorter, *Yellow Wolf*, p. 60, states that Bow and Arrow Case was wounded while wresting a gun from a soldier.

[35] The name is a sample of various pronunciations and spellings, including "Auskehwush," "Askeeis," and "Ashhawus," interpreted as "prying open" or "heavy weapon." In the Walla Walla language it is said to mean "thread" or "small cord." Another meaning given by one interpreter was "light in the mountain."

killed or feigning death. The wound proved not to be of a serious nature. His mother sang medicine songs over him and he recovered.[36]

In connection with the wounding of Espowyes, is the brief narrative of Kowtoliks which follows.

I was at the White Bird Canyon village when word was brought by the scouts, "Soldiers are coming!"

I then got my horse and mounted. Not to fight, for I was too young, only fifteen years old. I wanted my horse either to run from the soldiers or to see the flight, should it go well with the Indians.

The soldiers came on, and soon there was fast shooting. The Nez Perces were too much for them. They began to run back the way they came. With other boys, I rode up the hill after the soldiers had been driven away. We followed the flight. We saw dead soldiers lying about on the ground. One man I noticed flat on his belly. I saw that he wasn't dead, and it looked as if he was holding a gun under him. We boys had no gun, and we were afraid of him.

Coming where we could see ahead, there were three soldiers going afoot. Before that we had seen four, and I believe that the missing one from this bunch was the one we had seen lying on his belly.

I saw no dead Indians, but I did see three who were wounded. They were Espowyes, who escaped to Canada and later returned to Lapwai, where he died; Moositsa, who died in exile; and Chellooyeen.

Moositsa [Selish for "four blankets"], an unarmed youthful onlooker, had his thigh seared by a bullet which drew no blood. Pitching from his horse, his wrist was cut on a rock, giving rise to the report that he was wounded.[37] Moositsa was one of the unarmed young men who helped to swell the Indian horde to "three to one" of Captain Perry's force.[38] Armed

---

[36] McWhorter, *Yellow Wolf*, p. 60. Yellow Wolf's mother also joined in the singing.

[37] *Yellow Wolf*, pp. 59-60.

[38] Howard, *My Life and Experiences*, p. 285.

with one of the captured guns, Moositsa was in all of the subsequent fighting, surrendering only to die in exile.

Mutilation of the Dead at White Bird

The stories of the appearance of the battlefield and the mutilation and burial of the dead soldiers left on the White Bird Canyon after the battle, can be best related by those who were present.

Of the appearance of the White Bird battlefield, Wetatonmi, wife of Ollokot said:

It was following an early breakfast the first morning after our arrival from Cottonwood, when we heard news that we were going to be attacked. The Nez Perce warriors took stand to resist the enemies. The place I will not try to describe. It was above and quite a ways from our camp. Of course this confident army did not have strength to stay the Nez Perces and there was a quick retreat. The warriors pursued after the fleeing soldiers. I rode out over the battlefield with other women, and I saw dead soldiers, many of them. I did not try counting them but there was a good many.

On the twenty-sixth of June, ten days after Captain Perry's defeat, General Howard with 227 troops and twenty volunteers, reconnoitered the White Bird battlefield and buried the dead.[39] Under date of June 21, 1877, from Fort Lapwai, General Howard sent this dispatch to his Portland headquarters relative to the White Bird disaster, ". . . Prisoners state that the wounded were killed, making loss thirty-three and bodies not mutilated."[40]

Nonetheless, stories of atrocities committed on

[39] *Rep. of Sec. of War*, 1877, I, 120.
[40] "Claims of the Nez Perce Indians," *Senate Executive Document, No. 257*, 56th Cong. 1st Sess., p. 17.

the dead by the Nez Perces are legion, and this from the pen of Lieutenant Eugene Wilson of Captain McConville's volunteers is a sample. "On arrival at White Bird Canyon it was found that although more than a week had elapsed, the dead were still unburied and that disagreeable task was performed by the volunteers. The squaws had badly mutilated the bodies, as was their wont, making the duty a most disagreeable one to perform."[41]

In response to inquiry, Sergeant Schorr who has been quoted before, wrote, "I would say, so far as the dead at White Bird, the only one I buried, my buddy, was not stripped of clothing, although some were partly stripped. So far as I know, after they stripped the dead of firearms and equipment, the Nez Perces made a hasty get away."

The late Colonel Harry L. Bailey, who as a second lieutenant, Company B, Twenty-first Infantry, was with General Howard through the Salmon River and Clearwater campaign, wrote the author, "I have told you of helping to bury the thirty-three dead of our own troops, ten days after the Perry defeat at White Bird Canyon, and that no real sign of scalping was apparent, and even the bodies were not left wholly naked, trousers and shirts unremoved. I saw one body that was not stripped of any part of clothing."

Penahwenonmi [Helping Another], the wife of Wounded Head, declared: "I rode out over the field with other women and saw dead soldiers lying about. None of the dead showed disfiguring knife cuts. No one knifed those dead soldiers. There were many white friends of the Indians over in that country where the trouble started. The war should not have come."

<hr />

[41] Eugene Wilson, "The Nez Perce Campaign," MS., Washington State Historical Society Library.

Colonel Bailey has this explanation of the genesis
of the scalping stories:

My own company buried eighteen of the thirty-three
bodies which had lain ten days exposed to the elements,
the hot sun by day, until they were swollen and changed
into awful shapes, too dreadful for our eyes and olfactory
nerves, so we had to run a distance every little while during
the making of the shallow graves in the rocky soil with
entrenching bayonets, and trying to find enough of our
scarce blankets into which to pull the bodies for a semblance
of decent interment.

I did not see the body of the brave and unfortunate Lieutenant Theller, though it was eventually found, and is now
buried at San Francisco.

Of course we were ever on the lookout for sudden attack,
and one body of a cavalry soldier gave us some anxious
moments, for it was thrust so hard into a small hawthorn
tree in the full and life-like position of firing that we did
not approach without guns cocked until near enough to see
that the poor fellow was also dead and swollen beyond
recognition. He must have worried his foes very greatly
for his body was torn and torn with bullets. It was very
difficult to remove that body.[42]

---

[42] This account by Colonel Bailey of finding a trooper's body jammed
into a thorn thicket in such a lifelike attitude, explains the myth,
widely circulated that Sergeant Gunn's body was found propped up
under a thorn bush and in such a position as to appear reaching
for berries overhead, so placed by the Indian women in "heathenish
mockery and fun-making of a dead foe." In connection with this
illusion in regard to Sergeant Gunn's body, John Lynch, Company F,
First U.S. Cavalry, told the author, "I was of the White Bird Canyon
burial party and I saw no mutilation, whatever, of the dead. On the
contrary we found Sergeant Gunn's body lying on an Indian blanket
under the scant shelter of a thorn bush with baking flour plastered
over his bullet wound, this to stay the hemorrhage."
Doubtless this use of flour gave rise to the following transverse
deduction as given me by a Mr. Pomeroy, who claimed to have been
a volunteer with the burial party. He declared, "Sergeant Gunn's
abdomen had been ripped open and a bunch of wild flowers stuck in it,
which were blooming as nice as you please."
It is significant that in 1908, a score of years before the foregoing
revelations, the interpreter, Thomas Hart, a full-blood Nez Perce,
volunteered the following in a discussion about the Indian women's
having desecrated the White Bird soldier dead. "They found Sergeant
Gunn in a sort of washout away from the traveled path. They brought
him out to the side of the trail, and laid him on a blanket, their own

We heard the stories of mutilation and scalping as did the general public, but in the light of later information and inexperience, I am sure there was no mutilation, and that the appearance of scalping was due to the falling off of the decayed hair.

In contrast to the testimony of reputable army men who had buried the dead, that all evidence of scalping was lacking, this is an example of the tales that have found their way into the histories of the period: ". . . the last act of Whitebird before he retired with the braves into the canyon was most defiant. Shouting derision at the soldiers, he shook at them a bunch of scalps which were tied to a pole."[43]

An After-Battle Incident

A tragedy which followed closely on the burial of the White Bird dead has been uncovered only recently. The following excerpt is from the diary of Private Frederick Mayer of Company L, Twenty-first Cavalry, which reads in part,

---

blanket. On this they carried him to a thorn bush and placed him in the shade where not so hot. There they left him on the blanket and went away, went off and did not bother him. Next morning they went to see him and found him dead. They thought, 'Soldiers will bury him.' They did not take their blanket."

[43] Brosnan, *History of the State of Idaho*, p. 206. (Copyright, 1935. Courtesy of Charles Scribner's Sons.) According to all warriors interviewed, Chief White Bird because of his age took no part in the fighting until the last battle. There, in despair and desperation, he handled a rifle in one of the defensive pits, where marked physical exertion was not required. Yellow Wolf stated that White Bird, Looking Glass and Joseph were the "Same as General Howard," that is, they did no fighting of moment. Along this line, a brief comment of Camille Williams is of interest. He writes, "I am opposed to invented history as there is enough of it in this country. I glanced over an Idaho history for schools the other day, and read about the White Bird Canyon fight, where it says Chief White Bird had a pole with scalps of soldiers tied to it, which he showed to the retreating whites. This is all lie! Chief White Bird was not in the fight, and no soldiers were scalped.

"I saw in this same history a picture of Chief Moses of the Okanogans, and under it was written, 'Chief Joseph.' "

JUNE 29TH. Marched down the canyon to bury the dead.
. . . This was the most sickening sight I ever seen. . . . We
could not handle the bodies, but had to dig a hole by the
side of each, and roll the body in with shovels and cover
it with earth, and on top of it stones to keep the coyotes
(prairie wolves) from digging them out again.

JUNE 30TH . . . Camped in White Bird Canyon near
Salmon River. Pvt. Reed, Troop "E", 1st Cavalry, shot
through the shoulder by Infantry Picket by mistake. Lieutenant Woods, 21st Infantry, aide de camp, mistakes a
soldier for an Indian and shoots him. He belonged to the
4th Artillery.[44]

Since Lieutenant Woods of the foregoing was obviously Lt. C. E. S. Wood of the Twenty-first Infantry, he was sent a copy of the above paragraphs,
which elicited the following reply,

I am afraid it would not do to make history from the
diaries of soldiers. I remember the incident you, or rather
Private Mayer, refers to. I was in camp with my company
D of the 21st Infantry, Captain Pollack commanding. But
it is a long time ago and I do not remember the details distinctly. My impression is that the man who was shot was
killed and not just shot through the shoulder, as Private
Mayer says, but however that may be, I am glad to assure
you I had nothing to do with the sorry affair. I was sound
asleep in my blankets till awakened by the shot and the ensuing excitement. As I recollect this unfortunate incident,
one of the guard, being relieved from picket duty, was
approaching the campfire, wrapped in a blanket. An officer,
I forget which one, was sitting beside the fire with his
rifle across his knees. He had fallen asleep and being suddenly awakened by the steps of an approaching figure,
wrapped as he was in his blanket, mistook him for a hostile
Indian and half-dazed by sleep, fired instantly, almost auto-
matically. I thought I remembered a military funeral, when
we buried the body, but am not at all sure of this and also
I seem to remember a Court of Inquiry which exonerated

---

[44] *Seventeenth Biennial Report of the Board of Trustees of the
Idaho State Historical Society*, 1939-40, (Boise, Idaho, 1940), p. 28.

the officer who fired the shot, as unaware of what he was doing. I am sorry I can contribute nothing more definite and of more value than my assurance I was not the shooter.[45]

Of this same incident Colonel Bailey wrote in a letter, December 7, 1933.

A song of doggerel for the campfires was the howling of coyotes or forest wolves, because settlers had told us that the Nez Perce war cry was the Coyote Howl. And, I must say, we had some almost unbelievable cases of such "war cries," as though we were actually surrounded by a thousand warriors.

Once, for instance, when I was away out from the main command as an outpost, with half dozen men, and it was surely expected that the camp would be attacked at any moment, there was a solitary cry came from off to one side of us. After a minute an answering cry came from the opposite side, and then from the other side. Then deep silence for half an hour, when all hell broke loose on every side of the whole command, exclusive of my outpost.

Then, again deep silence for some minutes. I had just arranged my little outpost along a big log for defense, when there came a single shot in the midst of the main command. Then a few lights were seen moving about, but no other sign of life there. My young mind imagined every kind of disaster; such as a sudden silent rush upon the tired soldiers and every throat cut.

No other sound until morning, when I took my guard, as previously ordered, to meet the head of the column for the day's march, but all the way, until I met one of my comrades, Lieutenant Duncan, I could not fathom the strange silence of our usually lively morning march. The Lieutenant told me that a Lieutenant of Artillery had shot one of the privates who was stirring for some purpose, and that the poor fellow had lingered in painful but brave resignation until morning, when he died, forgiving the wretched Lieutenant, saying that it was an unavoidable accident.

I had to be with that Lieutenant for days afterward, at another post, and so far as I know, he was never the same man again. Such are some of the side sorrows of war.

---

[45] Letter, C. E. S. Wood to L. V. McWhorter, March 12, 1941.

CHAPTER XV

THE ATTACK ON THE LOOKING GLASS BAND

ONE OF THE MOST UNNECESSARY CRIMES COMMITTED
under the aegis of the United States Army during
the Nez Perce war was the wanton attack on Looking
Glass's Clearwater village, July 1, 1877. This band
had consciously severed its connections with the hostiles before the battle of White Bird Canyon, and was
peacefully camped at its homesite within the bounds
of the Nez Perce reservation, when unprovoked assault by troops and volunteers drove these Indians
into joining the warring bands.

Looking Glass Attacked

Quoting from Howard's official report:

... The evening of the 29th positive information is obtained that Looking Glass, who, with his people, had stood
aloof from the hostiles, had been furnishing reinforcements
to them of at least twenty warriors, and that he proposed
to join them in person, with all his people, on the first
favorable opportunity.

His grounds for cultivation lay near the mouth of the
south fork of the Clearwater. With a view of preventing
the completion of this treachery, I sent Captain Whipple,
commanding his own and Winter's companies and the gatling guns with instructions to make a forced march, surprise
and capture this chief and all that belonged to him.[1] [After
a night's march, the unsuspecting village was reached about

---

[1] *Rep. of Sec. of War*, 1877, I, 120.

centuries by the Shoshonean tribes, and I was left with but five men. We approached the Snake River and discovered the Nez Perces on the opposite side some three miles above where it is joined by the Salmon River. They were most evidently making to cross the Snake into the Wallowa Valley, but we struck on a ruse that completely changed their course.

A nearby butte formation suggested an idea that was successfully worked. Passing a certain point, we would be momentarily in full view of the Indians, and by methodical spacing of the riders they would, by repeatedly circling the butte, appear an indeterminate body of armed men. The ruse proved so realistic that the Nez Perces turned about and recrossed the Salmon at the point where they were then camped, instead of crossing the Snake into the Wallowa as they had planned.

But Black Feather declared in this connection, "Crossing the Salmon, we saw no whites south of that river. We saw no white men on either side of the Snake River. The chiefs never intended crossing into the Wallowa."

The fact that the Wallowa was never the Nez Perce destination does not detract from the wisdom of Captain Cullen's tactics. And he was not without sympathy for the Indians, for he had declared to his own men that if he were an Indian he would fight for the Wallowa Valley to the last ditch, until carried out dead, before he would give up the ancestral lands that rightfully belonged to him.

Meanwhile General Howard, as noted above, crossed the Salmon River July 1, consuming the entire day in that feat.[5] According to Sergeant Schorr, who as a member of the Signal Corps was stationed on a high peak two miles away, the army had crossed the Salmon by about 3:00 P.M. But noon of that same day the Nez Perces had broken camp

---

[5] *Rep. of Sec. of War*, 1877, I, 120.

and moved twenty-odd miles down the Salmon.[6] This was at Craig's Ferry, twenty to twenty-five miles from General Howard's first crossing of the Salmon. Encumbered as the Indians were with approximately three thousand head of horses, their old and blind, and a preponderance of women and children, they had covered a notably wild stretch of broken, mountainous terrain in a half day's time, and the next morning they were able to recross the turbulent Salmon. All this was done within thirty-six hours from their first camp,[7] and without accident or injury to a solitary soul. Horses were repacked and the families moved to Aipadass, a desert flat where the edible *kous* root flourished in superabundance. Here they spent the night of July 2, the second stop from the White Bird threat. Of this astounding feat no mention is made in Howard's reports. The next morning Red Spy killed Charles Blewett, scout, within rifle-sound of the camp.[8] His fellow scout, William Foster, escaped only to fall later in the day. Red Spy secured a spyglass carried by Blewett, the first the Indians had seen, as confirmed by the late Chief Peopeo Tholekt and other warriors.[9]

This amazing feat of regaining the north bank of the Salmon accomplished by the Nez Perces while General Howard still floundered amid broken mountain defiles trying to determine the direction of the enemy's flight, created alarm in both civilian and military ranks. July 5 the General pressed after the Indians and arrived at Craig's Ferry, only to find that his wily foe had preceded him by at least forty-eight hours. Of his unhappy attempt to cross the Salmon at this point, we read:

[6] *Yellow Wolf*, p. 69.

[7] *Loc. cit.*

[8] *Yellow Wolf*, p. 70.

[9] See Chapter XIV, p. 242, this volume.

The 5th of July brought us to Craig's Ferry, where it became evident that all the Indians had passed back and taken the trail toward the Cottonwood, 16 miles distant. At first I hoped by a prompt crossing to join Perry . . . but having no boats, a raft had been constructed from the timber of a cabin near the ferry.

Our first attempt on the morning of the 6th to cross the river, here a perfect torrent, lost us our raft, which tumbled down the rapids at a swift rate, with all on board, for three or four miles.[10]

Balked and outwitted by his versatile foe, the General veiled his chagrin as he reports, "About this time I ascertained, by Indian couriers that the enemy had already passed from the Cottonwood to the Clearwater, so that my shortest line was to turn back via White Bird Canyon.

"The evening of the 8th my head of column had reached Grangeville."[11]

The failure of the Salmon River expedition was colossal, following as it did the wake of the White Bird disaster. The news columns were burdened with criticism, accusations of incompetence on the part of

---

[10] *Report of the Secretary of War*, 1877, Vol. I, p. 121. Craig's Ferry was known to the Nez Perces as "Luke's Place," residence of Luke Billy or Pahkayatwekin, on the south side of the Salmon. It was his cabin home that General Howard dismantled and transformed into a raft only to have it swept away on the mad river current. Pahkayatwekin was an enrolled scout for General Howard, for pay, and in his testimony in 1900 are found the following statements, "The Indian agent and General Howard said that we would be paid wages and any loss of horses or other losses. When General Howard wanted to cross Salmon River he tore down my house and took the logs to make a raft with which to cross the river with; after that white men took my place and kept it."

". . . lost a lot of apples and fruit trees with my place after the house was torn down. I lost a lot of cattle and horses during the war—about 400 head all told." ("Claims of the Nez Perce Indians," *Senate Document No. 257*, 56th Cong., 1st Sess., p. 117.)

Brevet Colonel W. P. Parnell, who as a lieutenant was with General Howard, states that these cabin timbers were a foot thick, and thirty or forty feet long. (Parnell, in Brady, *Northwestern Indian Fights and Fighters*, p. 130).

[11] *Rep. of Sec. of War*, 1877, I, 122.

the military officials in charge, and reports that the Indian force was being augmented daily by malcontents from other tribes. Military officialdom was worried as even this laconic dispatch cannot hide:

> From various causes the General has been compelled to retrace every step of march he has made since he left Cottonwood two weeks ago. He crossed the Salmon a week after Joseph but not on his trail. In the meantime Joseph's great success has added largely to his force and confidence. . . .[12]

The Attack on the Rains Party

Meanwhile Captain Whipple, returning from his brigandish raid on Looking Glass's peaceful sylvan village on the Clearwater, had entrenched himself on an elevation near the Norton house, now the town of Cottonwood.[13] From this post, on the morning of the third, the Captain dispatched, as citizen scouts, William Foster and Charles Blewett, youths inexperienced in woodcraft, to verify or disprove the rumor that Indians had been seen at the ferry. In this venture Blewett, the younger of the two, lost his life.[14] Events that followed this incident have often been told from the military viewpoint, but never before has the Nez Perce story been told. Quoting the venerable Two Moons:

> After Red Spy killed one of the two white men we knew to be spying on us, a bunch of warriors, only warriors, rode over the hill toward Camas Prairie. They did this to locate

---

[12] Keller, aide-de-camp to McDowell, July 9, 1877, in "Claims of the Nez Perce Indians," *Senate Document No. 257*, 56th Cong., 1st Ses., p. 33.

[13] Cottonwood was named for a solitary cottonwood tree that stood there, aged and hoary. In Nez Perce the word for cottonwood tree is *cupcup*, while *cupcup peen* or *pin* is the designation for more than one cottonwood.

[14] This was Lieutenant Rain's party. See *Yellow Wolf*, pp. 80-83, for the only eyewitness account of this tragedy.

the soldiers we knew to be close. We found them! And I, Two Moons, saw small soldier tents along the gulch where Cottonwood town now stand. Up on the higher ground, the soldiers had dug holes where to hide, bury themselves from danger.

This news was carried to the main body of warriors, and we all dismounted from our horses to prepare for battle. We unwrapped our medicine packs, objects wherein lay our strength and put them on all ready for the fighting. While thus engaged we all sang in low tone our war songs, derived from the Spirit Powers.

All in readiness, the great warrior Pahkatos Owyeen [Five Wounds] led on the right swing, while Rainbow, equally great, led on the left swing. And friends of mine, those two mighty warriors leading right and left, I, Two Moons, followed down a gulch, heading the center charge. We rode slowly, not too fast, and while yet a considerable distance from the soldier camp, we saw that the enemies must have noticed our advance.

A bunch of about a dozen were out on the hillside a goodly distance from their pits and trenches where first seen. Rainbow ordered that we go after these soldiers and we did so. We made the charge. The soldiers whipping their horses, fled for their lives. They struck the main hill or mountain. But it was no use! All were killed.[15]

The rocks where some of them took shelter did not save them from the bullets sent against them. Their horses, guns, and ammunition we took.

After this fight, we did not bother to attack the soldiers where they had made entrenchments for the fighting. Thirteen enemies had been killed that sun, and no Indian hurt. It was well to let the soldiers stay in their camp untroubled.

The story has been told often of how Scout Foster, escaping Blewett's fate, returned to Captain Whipple's camp on a greatly fagged horse, with the startling news of Indians, and the probable fate of his companion. Lieutenant S. M. Rains, with a select troop of ten men, was dispatched under the guidance

---

[15] See below, pp. 284-85.

of Scout Foster to the aid of Blewett if still living, and to ascertain something of the numerical strength of the foe. As Two Moons indicated, the whole detachment was killed.[16]

As Two Moons' narrative indicates, the Nez Perces were about to launch a surprise attack against the main soldier body, when they were diverted from their purpose by sighting the smaller troop riding out from the command. Abandoning their original plan of battle, they pursued the scouting party, a few of whom were killed in the ensuing running fight and eventually all were dispatched.

Two Moons' story was amply confirmed by Yellow Wolf, a participant in the affair, when on the grounds, July 30, 1930. According to his version which coincides with his general statements of 1908, a few of the soldiers were killed east of where the Foster Monument now stands, and at least one other fell farther west before reaching the broken rocks, marking the final annihilation of the survivors. From the Nez Perce version, it would seem that these men had a fair chance of effecting an escape, but for a solitary Indian scout stationed farther up the hill. With horses badly blown, they evidently determined to fight it out with their not too numerous pursuers rather than chance an ambuscade by a possibly greater force. Doubtless, too, they cherished a hope of help from the main body of their comrades in arms.

Yellow Wolf, in his thrilling account of this affair, speaks of a decoy Indian drawing the fire of the rock-sheltered troopers, as they discerned him seeking a precarious shelter behind the slender trunk of a blasted pine tree that stood not far distant in a gulch to the west. This decoy was none other than

---

[16] See Howard, *Nez Perce Joseph*, p. 151.

Strong Eagle of the "Three Red Coats" of White Bird battle fame. When the harassed troopers were seen taking to the rocks, this daring young warrior, keeping to cover, hastened to the gulch in question (then open ground, but now overgrown with brush) where he sedulously held the foe's attention and fire as they were successfully flanked by his comrades. Passing under the eastern lee of the hill, they dismounted and crept well within rifle range of the doomed and unaware troopers, most of whom were killed at the first volley. After a second scattering fusillade, a tall soldier sat leaning against the largest rock, a bullet hole showing directly in the center of his forehead. A clucking sound came from his lips and he "washed his face" with blood oozing from the wound. His fate was debated; some of the warriors favoring that he be permitted to "live if he wanted to," but were overruled because of the seriousness of his many wounds.[17]

No Nez Perce was hurt in this entire fight. The empty shells found at the rocks were those expended ineffectually against the elusive and daring decoy at the blasted pine in the gulch.[18] The fate of the Rains party, as is usual when the white man tells the story, has gone down in history as a "massacre," certainly a misnomer in the true sense of the term. It was a combat between armed forces, of unequal strength it is true, but nonetheless a fight in the open where neither party was expected to ask or give quarter. Captain Whipple had blundered and the

---

[17] Yellow Wolf gives a pathetic and gruesome depiction of this scene. (See *Yellow Wolf*, pp. 71-74.)

[18] The final scene of the Lieutenant Rains tragedy was located on lands now (1943) owned by Mr. Carl Schurra, Section 25, Township 32, N.R.I. West. B.M., Idaho County, Idaho.

price was the loss of a small though splendid body of men.[19]

To a casual reader the incongruity in the varying statements by the two belligerent forces in the Cottonwood embroilment of July 4 and 5 is indeed confusing. Yellow Wolf speaks of but one isolated engagement, wherein a "small bunch of young warriors" were the participants;[20] while white accounts tell of the entrenched soldiers' camp being assailed by not less than two hundred and fifty warriors, who made no impression on their stronghold.[21]

---

[19] Colonel Bailey, then a second lieutenant of the Twenty-first Infantry, writes that the dead had not been stripped, and that Lieutenant Rains' cavalry gloves were still on his hands, that his class ring had not been removed from his finger.

Of this tragedy, Elias Darr says, "I was a courier at this stage of the game. Rains was a fighting fool and with the men was ready to undertake any movement assigned him.

"No one knows just how it happened, but when we arrived on the scene we found Rains and most of his men dead among a sort of rock-pile formation. They had evidently put up a hard fight for there were plenty of empty shells attesting this fact. One man was found killed about half a mile away.

"After the foregoing tragedy, with another man, I was scouting up a canyon and for better observation we divided, one to each ridge on either side of the canyon. In this way a very accurate scanning of the gorge could be made and possible discoveries signalled. After going a considerable distance I was signaled, 'Indians ahead!' With caution, we discovered five of General Howard's Nez Perce scouts in concealment. My partner recognized them all, among them Lawyer. The army officers did nothing when this was reported to them."

Charley Kowtoliks, a lad of sixteen at the time of this fight, when questioned about the Cottonwood fighting replied:

"At Cottonwood I mounted to follow the warriors who went after the party of soldiers seen leaving their camp. My mother told me not to go but I wanted to see the fight. Two of us boys followed, and we came to a soldier who had been shot many times, in head and breast. He raised up and we heard him go 'Kluk! Kluk! Kluk!' [See *Yellow Wolf*, p. 73].

"The warriors were there standing about him, but we saw no other soldiers. We saw him because he raised up.

"No Indians were killed in this fight; but next day Weesculatat was killed in a fight on lower side of Cottonwood. He was riding a swift horse, and the shooting set that horse crazy. He ran toward the enemies and Weesculatat was unable to hold or guide him. Charging among the soldiers, he was killed." (This was the fight with Captain Randall's volunteers.)

[20] McWhorter, *Yellow Wolf*, pp. 75-76.

[21] Perry, in Brady, *Northwestern Indian Fights and Fighters*, p. 125.

The Clash with Captain Randall's Volunteers

Unaware of the Nez Perces' return to the north side of the Salmon, Captain Perry with a light escort left Fort Lapwai the morning of July 4 with a small pack train of ammunition and supplies for the Cottonwood post, and was surprised in the afternoon to meet Captain Whipple arriving with a strong escort including the mountain artillery, to guard against possible attack. As senior officer, Captain Perry assumed command.[22] At 9:00 P.M. Perry dispatched a courier to Fort Lapwai with the following:

> Indians around us all day in force and very demonstrative. Last evening Lieutenant Rains, ten soldiers, and two citizen scouts were killed, and had not Whipple, with whole command, come to our rescue, my little party would have all been undoubtedly taken in.[23]

Of the events of July 5, Sergeant Schorr wrote me of one of the attempts to attack the soldiers:

> It was on the 5th of July that about thirty warriors succeeded in flanking us by a clever ruse. The horses appeared riderless, not an Indian in sight, until after the flanking movement had been completed, when an armed rider suddenly appeared on each of the horses, ready to charge us. Nothing came of the movement, for they were immediately dispersed by our Gatling guns. No casualties on either side.

---

[22] Perry, in Brady, *Northwestern Indian Fights and Fighters*, p. 124.

[23] Perry to McDowell, "Claims of the Nez Perce Indians," p. 30. Regarding this same evening, Sergeant Schorr writes me, "I was careful when out to relieve a sentinel but before he was relieved he says, "John, be careful. Down there is a bush that was not there when I took charge of this post and it seems to be coming closer." So we made an investigation and here pops up a Red Skin and got away before we got a good shot at him, shows how crafty Indians are. He was lying on his belly and moved this bush along."

At the other point soldiers were driven from one pit, taking refuge in a larger one. Of the situation at this time, Wetatonmi, wife of Ollokot says in part:

> We were moving and when near [now] Cottonwood, I heard someone say, "We saw the United States Army finishing up trenches just in front of us!" This was in way of our traveling and soon as we drew near the army fired on us. There was fighting and we women came to a spring where we stood watching.
>
> We left the spring only a little distance when one man, Citskitscuninim, overtook me and said, "Your husband is left near the battle afoot. He has no horse."
>
> I rode back leading a horse for Ollokot. When I came near he seemed under heavy fire. I heard bullets passing me on both sides. Ollokot came afoot, leading his winded horse. I met him and he advised me, "Be careful! Line your horses with the soldiers' firing! Do not stand broadside to them."
>
> I did as directed. Changing his saddle to the fresh horse, Ollokot mounted and we rode away.
>
> In the fighting, at one place, Mimpow Owyeen [Wounded Mouth] was bad hit. When he fell the Indians there retreated. I was not close to that fighting. Owyeen died that evening and was buried next morning. He was the first Indian killed in the war.[24]

The fight referred to in the last paragraph of Mrs. Ollokot's narrative, occurred when Captain D. B. Randall's seventeen volunteers, on their way to aid Captain Perry, were intercepted by a small Nez Perce scouting party within sight of the beleaguered stronghold. In this fray, Captain Randall, an interloper on fifty acres of Nez Perce reservation land,[25] and Ben Evans were killed and two or three others

---

[24] This was Weesculatat, (See *Yellow Wolf*, pp. 76-77) a sample of multiplicity of names. Wareyouh Teepmanin's horse was shot from him.

[25] "Report of Civil and Military Commission to the Nez Perce Indians, December, 1876," *Rep. of Sec. of Interior*, 1877, I, 610.

wounded. It has been averred that the Indians were in this attack in great force,[26] summoned by the traditional signal smoke sent up from the highest butte within a radius of twenty miles.[27] It is significant that no Indian interviewed ever hinted that such a signal was given. There were no distant tribesmen to be so summoned.

LAHPEEAHLOOT'S NARRATIVE

The number of Indians engaged in this fight has been greatly exaggerated by partisan writers. Yellow Wolf speaks of a "small bunch of young warriors, going separately," who tangled with the volunteers.[28] Lahpeeahloot [Twice Alighting on Water] in his story given through Interpreter Williams, corroborates this:

It was two suns after Scout Foster and the soldiers were killed, that the headmen in our camp gave orders that a few young men take their best horses and go watch the soldier entrenchments. Since the main body of warriors must go with and protect the moving camp, we young men, a few short of ten, well mounted, left to guard the prairie road. It was about two miles east of the army entrenchment that we saw several white men coming on an easy gallop.

Unseen, we turned away and dismounted. Leaving one man to hold horses, we ran to near the roadside and lay concealed awaiting the enemy's approach. We would fire on them as they passed.

But they did not pass. One warrior, scouting toward where our horses were concealed back on higher ground, discovered the enemy had swerved off

---

[26] Civilians computed the attacking warriors at 136, according to Amos Markham.

[27] Henry C. Johnson of the volunteers, in a paper prepared for the University of Idaho.

[28] McWhorter, *Yellow Wolf*, pp. 75-76.

to the east and gone by unseen. We ran for our horses and gave chase.

In the meantime another small group of young warriors had intercepted the enemy, but let them pass. It now became a running fight in which we joined, and the whites foolishly dismounted to give battle. There were not more than twelve or fourteen Indians, all young fellows, except Weesculatat, who was more near middle age. Less than two miles away the soldiers could have come meeting them and all made escape. The volunteers, as they proved to be, had fine horses and could soon have met their rescuers.

In the early fighting, Sewattis Hihhih [White Cloud] was wounded in the right thigh and his horse killed.[29] A white man's horse was also killed early, maybe two rods from White Cloud, the horse falling on the leg of its rider. His arm was wounded, or maybe his sleeve was just bloody from his horse. He was released by another white man and both rode away on the same horse. This was early in the fight, just before they dismounted. It seemed strange but Sewattis was pinned to the ground in like manner by his fallen horse.

The fight lasted some time but stopped when Weesculatat was bad wounded. So bad he died that evening.

Soldiers came to help the volunteers after we had gone.

The reason why the white riders, I understand 17 of them, turned to the right instead of keeping the

---

[29] *Yellow Wolf*, p. 77. Sewattis Hihhih was a younger half-brother of Two Moons. Of about the same size and build as his noted brother, he was a fierce fighter, taking part in every fight of the war. Surviving the decimating exile, a member of Chief Joseph's band proper, he died on the Colville reservation about four years after removal there.

road where we lay waiting for them, they became scared. One Indian followed us, staying about quarter-mile behind. He had a red blanket and when he saw the whites coming from a higher point he waved the blanket running his horse right and left. To any Indians within sight, this signal was "Enemies drawing near!" He was a rear guard, but in this case bad. Those whites saw and changed their course. The red-blanket Indian told it all after the fight. Had it not been for him, half of those volunteers would have been shot from their saddles.

§

About ten snows after the war, Lahpeeahloot visited the scene of the fight and found the bones of the two horses killed, still there undisturbed.

Tales of Volunteer Heroism

Among the tall tales of volunteer valor we read, ". . . Lieut. Wilmot fired 76 shots and done as all others did, most Excellent execution, they estimated the number of killed and wounded at 25 to 30 of the Indians."[30]

The Lewiston *Teller* of July 7, 1877, is quoted as saying that one of the volunteers was reported to have fired over sixty shots, and several others over forty shots each, and that Randall continued firing after mortally wounded and up to within five minutes of death. Continuing, "The volunteers say that they know they killed several Indians and wounded many others as they saw the Indians packing off their dead and wounded."[31] Relative to these fantastic

---

[30] L. P. Brown to Governor Brayman in the *Fifteenth Biennial Report of the Board of Trustees of the State of Idaho*, p. 57.

[31] Lewiston *Teller*, as quoted in Lewiston *Tribune*, Sunday, July 3, 1927.

claims of carnage by the guns of the beleaguered volunteers, Interpreter Williams writes:

The Indians numbered twelve or fourteen young men. It appeared very easy for the number to be doubled many times by white writers and the carnage wrought in their ranks by the volunteer rifles is truly marvelous.

Some years ago there appeared in the *Lewiston Tribune* a story told by Major Frank A. Fenn, that 200 Indians fought the 17 volunteers. I was intending to see the Major in person about his statement and tell him that one man, Phillip Williams, who was still living, was in that fight, and told a very different story. But Major Fenn died just at that time. Phillip thought that the Indians and the whites numbered about equal, but there may have been two or three more whites than Indians.

The warring band, camp and fighting men, had gone to the Red Rock spring; passing east of the entrenched troops. The volunteers clashed with the light prairie scouts only, who naturally quit the fight when one of their number was mortally wounded.

It should be noted that it was the close proximity of the troops that caused the main body of warriors to hold so closely to the moving camp. The safety of the families was paramount to every other consideration.

Meanwhile let us turn to Captain Perry's stronghold a mile and a half away in full sight of the beleaguered volunteers. Quoting Captain Whipple, junior officer:

Noticing that there was some commotion at the brow of the hill, where a few citizens had gathered, and that Captain Perry was walking toward me, I turned and met him asking, at the same time, the cause of the excitement. He replied, "Some citizens, a couple miles away, on the Mount Idaho road, are surrounded by Indians, and are being all cut to pieces, and nothing can be done to help them!"

"Why not?"

"It is too late."[32]

---

[32] Howard, *Nez Perce Joseph*, p. 153.

Captain Perry contended that he at first regarded the disturbance as a ruse to get the troops away from their entrenchments but as soon as the facts became apparent he rushed a mounted detachment to the scene. The Indians were driven away and the citizens rescued.[33] Charges of cowardice were openly flung against Captain Perry, on which score General Howard declares, ". . . Much complaint, . . . arose because the officer in command at Cottonwood (Captain Perry) was not more prompt with his relief, whom a court of inquiry, after long sessions and much labor, exonerated. . . ."[34]

---

[33] Perry, in Brady, *Northwestern Indian Fights and Fighters*, p. 125.

[34] Howard, *Nez Perce Joseph*, p. 154. There is no mention of the volunteer fight and its aftermath in General Howard's later book, *My Life and Experiences*.

CHAPTER XVII

THE BATTLE OF THE CLEARWATER

LEAVING THE COTTONWOOD REGION, THE NEZ PERCES moved north to the Clearwater River where a junction with Chief Looking Glass and his adherents was made. General Howard was encouraged to hurl his entire force against the foe while they were yet in the Craig Mountain region. The volunteers would hold them from crossing the Salmon into the wilderness wilds beyond. The General scorned the proposal, declaring his ability to manage his own campaign. Doubtless he remembered the braggadocio of the citizenry who had beguiled Captain Perry into walking into a deathtrap, and how these same doughty knights had hastened Perry's defeat by promptly fleeing the defense of his vital left flank at the first appearance of a charging band of sixteen mounted warriors, not all of whom had guns.[1]

Camp Misery

No doubt this encouraged the General to question the local volunteer auxiliary as essential to his army. Nevertheless there was considerable scouting by the various civilian squads, and the winner of the halo of glory was Captain Edward McConville, who drove ahead to locate and hold the Nez Perces until the

---

[1] See McWhorter, *Yellow Wolf*, pp. 56-57.

arrival of General Howard (he thought), when he was sure they would face unconditional surrender or utter annihilation. But there proved to be a stumbling block in the carrying out of this measure. The behavior of the warriors was such that the Captain took his command to a high hill in the neighborhood where they entrenched.[2] This hill is on Doty Ridge. The Nez Perces called the place Possossona [Water Passing], from a spring in a near-by draw, but it has ever since been known as Camp Misery.

On the ninth of July, General Howard, then at Camp Randall [Grangeville] had sent by courier to General Alfred Sully at Lewiston, a dispatch forwarded to headquarters in San Francisco which said in part:

At five this morning Captain McConville, commanding eighty volunteers, who, with my sanction, made a reconnaisance yesterday toward Kamiah, reports that he has come upon the Indians in force, and asks me to come to his relief immediately. . . . If Joseph will remain one day longer burning houses and bragging of his victories, I will be able to strike him a blow. . . .[3]

Here the General asserts that the reconnaisance by the volunteers was with his sanction, but four years later he averred, ". . . The enterprising volunteers, who had become a little disgusted with the slowness of the regulars, and angered at their own fearful discomfiture near Cottonwood had suddenly left us and started on an independent movement."[4]

2 *Fifteenth Biennial Report of the State Historical Society of Idaho*, p. 66.

3 "Claims of the Nez Perce Indians," *Senate Document No. 257*, 56th Cong., 1st Sess., p. 33.

4 Howard, *Nez Perce Joseph*, p. 154. Under date of July 18, 1877, Keeler, aid-de-camp, sent from Lewiston, Idaho, a dispatch to General McDowell which reads, "I see by the dispatches that you are about to raise two hundred volunteers. This war being substantially over, the regulars at hand and coming will be ample for any probable

Captain McConville would not have rated high as an Indian campaigner. Elias Darr, the free-lance courier, just prior to the entrenching on Doty Ridge had saved the Captain and his command from possible annihilation by warning him of a deadly ambuscade into which he was blindly riding without the precaution of a preliminary scouting. It is said that McConville was visibly affected when the full import of Darr's service burst upon him. But if this was the Rocky Canyon incident of which he speaks in his report to Governor Brayman, his gratitude was short-lived; and he indicates there that he had changed his course prior to the warning from two unnamed couriers.[5]

The story of Camp Misery has been told with many variations. General Howard's nonappearance on the scene was blamed on the inefficiency of his guide, Mr. Chapman, and the army's advance was miles away and on the opposite side of the Clearwater. The Indians made two night attacks on the volunteer stronghold, crawling to within a few feet of their entrenchments. But at no time were the inmates exposed, and the Indians' random shots in the darkness were ineffective. However, they accomplished their main object, to wit, the capture of enemy horses. At their leisure they selected, and drove or led away, every animal that they considered worth the trouble, forty-three head all told.[6] Mr. Cassius M. Day, a member of these volunteers, writes of the attack:

emergency. General Sully, who telegraphed you on June 11th on the subject of volunteers, wishes me to say that he concurs in this view. Volunteers of the character and status of those operating under General Howard would be worse than useless. . . ." ("Claims of the Nez Perce Indians," p. 44.)

[5] *Fifteenth Biennial Report of the State Historical Society of Idaho*, p. 64.

[6] *Ibid.*, p. 66; *Yellow Wolf*, p. 79. A humorous side of the Camp Misery sequel was revealed in a brief interview Mr. Frank Allen granted the author, where he declared, "The few inferior horses left us by the considerate Indians were truly appreciated, although such

Yes, it was a night attack. Colonel McConville was in command, and took first turn as officer of the guard. About 11 o'clock he woke me to take his place. I had only got to the second post when the attack was made. They got most of our horses and I think that was what they wanted.

Most of the horses secured were those taken when the Looking Glass village was plundered. They were returned to their rightful owners who had been driven to join the warring element.[7]

But the Nez Perces were caught unawares. The volunteers had unwittingly held their attention on the west side of the Clearwater from whence the regulars were naturally expected to appear. Just why General Howard should have plunged into the mountainous wilderness on the opposite side of the river from where the Indians had last been seen, and where no trace of them was to be detected, has never been logically explained. That Chapman, his guide, was badly muddled goes without question. The vanguard of the army had passed at least two miles beyond the Nez Perce encampment before Lieutenant Fletcher accidentally stumbled upon it, when seemingly engaged in a little side scouting of his own.[8] It seems ironic that General Howard should come upon and salute the elusive foe with a salvo of artillery at about the hour the dehorsed volunteer heroes of Camp Misery across the river were vacating their stronghold, on the eleventh of July.

---

was not revealed in the general language indulged by the men as a body. Our saddles stacked on the backs of those lank animals were a grotesque feature of our miles of foot padding and entrance to Mount Idaho. It was a hungry bunch of men that the good people, there forting, hastened to feed. They also saw to our remounting, but the hostiles had disappeared from the locality. Our bloodless expedition proved a full-fledged, fizzling joke."

7 *Yellow Wolf*, p. 79.

8 *Nez Perce Joseph*, pp. 157-58; *Rep. of Sec. of War*, 1877, I, 122.

The Onset of the Clearwater Battle

The battle of the Clearwater was on! But, to reach the Nez Perce camp, it was necessary for the army to double back some two or more miles before they could descend the mountain. This move, when attempted, was defeated by the mobility of the foe, and General Howard was forced to give battle on the broad plateau high above, across the river, and away from sight of the Indian encampment. It would be difficult to determine from which side the first rifle shot came, but it probably echoed from Chief Too-hoolhoolzote's vanguard.[9] Mrs. Ollokot, through Interpreter Many Wounds, gave the following account of the battle's onset.

We were camped at Pettahyewahwei [Mouth of Canyon]. It was early noon and after dinner I felt hot and sweaty and went to the river for a cold swim. Just as I got in the water about to my waist, a man came stepping to the bank and said, "We are under a big body of soldiers! An army is approaching on us! Probably a fight will start any minute!"

I got dressed after a quick dip and went back up to the people. I understood the chiefs had said to let the people, the camp, stay where it was for awhile.

Soldiers appeared on the mountain about a mile and a half to the north. A puff of smoke was seen, then came a cannon's boom.

I saw the warriors stripping for the battle. I saw a bunch of them, mounted and led by Chief Toohoolhoolzote, run their horses a ways up the river, where they crossed and climbed the mountain to meet the soldiers. Soon there was fighting up there and the guns were heard plainly. It was then that other warriors left the camp, hurrying to join in the battle. They were led by Wahchumyus [Rainbow], followed on a swift gallop. They had waited to protect the families, had Toohoolhoolzote and his warriors failed to

---

[9] McWhorter, *Yellow Wolf*, pp. 86-88.

hold General Howard's army on the mountain flat. Less than one hundred warriors in all went up against the enemies. Many of the tribe were not fighters.

Thus in this Indian woman's narrative is found confirmation of Yellow Wolf's claim that General Howard's column, two miles long, was for a time successfully held by Chief Toohoolhoolzote's twenty-four picked riflemen.[10] It must be accepted without question that the Indians were taken wholly by surprise, that their camp was nonstrategically located, and that General Howard's move to reach it was a near failure, and that the Indians stalled him for two days on what is now known as Battle Ridge.

COLONEL BAILEY'S STORY

Of this intricate situation, Colonel [then Lieutenant] Bailey writes:

What a blindman's bluff it was for days until at last, seemingly by accident we were forced to fight the Battle of the Clearwater, July 11th and 12th, on ground which may have been chosen by Joseph himself, although I do not now think so. I do know that the citizen scouts and so-called guides took us far around and onto the wrong side of the Clearwater River and almost gave us a defeat.

I had heard citizens tell of brave riding over hill and dale until they had discovered the Indians across the river, and talked to them, and dared them to come over and fight, and my boyish heart was filled with great admiration for our wonderful volunteers. By accident I learned that the good citizens had made a wonderful stone fort on the same side of the river, at a place about nine miles from it (the river). And

---

[10] *Ibid.*, p. 87. Yellow Wolf gives a very complete picture of the Clearwater Battle from the Nez Perce viewpoint, *see*, pp. 85-101.

the fort was away from any supply of water. I do not blame those volunteers, but I have felt sorry that they spoiled my wonderful opinion of them.

We were marching along hoping for anything, if only we might some day finish the hard, hard forced marching, on two meals a day, when along the edge of the bluffs of the river, some of our officers saw Indians on the other side, the side we had left "on information" and at first it was a question whether we might not have come upon a camp of friendly Indians! But after hurrying along for two or three miles, the artillery of one mountain howitzer and two Gatling guns were taken to the edge of a bluff and some shots fired at a very long distance, while the rest of us hurried on, wondering how and where we might get into the attack, and were brought up by an attack at first scattering, and every movement more and more severe.[11]

I do not doubt that they were as much surprised at our attack as we were to find them in their very comfortable old home ground by the gurgling stream, all evidences, after the two days' battle, showing that the camp had long been occupied, and had wonderful stores of supplies.

Intelligent Indians like Nez Perce Joseph would never have chosen to expose their families and such tons of excellent supplies to an uncertain battle.

It seems apparent at this time that the many false directions and idle tales, were the very lucky cause of our striking the enemy in his worst position, where he had so much at stake, and only a chance selection, if any, of a battlefield.

But our choice of a battlefield was mere accident, for we had no water, nor any protection except one or

---

[11] This setback to General Howard's army of five hundred was administered by Chief Toohoolhoolzote's twenty-four warriors.

two small trees, and bare, broken, rocky upland, so rocky even entrenching was difficult.

It is true, I think, that the Indians had made some barricades along the side of their camp away from the river on the opposite side of us, as I saw when we were pursuing them after the battle. I suppose at the time that they had thought we might come to attack them on that side. And yet those barricades might have been made by the squaws during the battle.

The command had (earlier) crossed the Jackson Bridge, and was marching along parallel to the river when the Indians were discovered, and as we had passed the location of their main camp, we doubled back until the halt due to their attack, and the general uncertainty, there being confusion for some time as to "positions" and orders for battle, the troops finding places rather by accident and the form of the ground between the two ravines, the smaller being the first encountered.

The bluffs proved a protection on our river flank, until a few Indians seemed to have succeeded in climbing to our level. Troops were ordered to rout them, which seemed effective to some extent.

The General and his staff soon made a kind of headquarters with the aid of the pack saddles piled in a circular manner, though the protection was very light, except that the position was not so near the hottest fire.

My Company B, 21st Infantry, under Captain S. P. Jocelyn, was on the flank nearest the river, and along the edge of the largest ravine, on the most dangerous front, for we were really surrounded in a short time, so that all sides were fronts.

When the attack commenced along the bluff and edge of the small ravine, the General ordered Captain

Marcus Miller's artillery into that position, who was soon busy on all sides, like the rest of us, when some of his men and some of ours mistaking each other for the enemy, made one of those terrible errors which occur in so many battles, but are generally kept out of the reports. I saw Private Winters of my company wounded, who kept saying that some of our own men had shot him.[12]

I saw that the artillery and my company, and some others, were jumping up and shooting at each other, at a range of one hundred to two hundred yards. Although bullets were flying, I rushed out between the artillery and my own company, yelling, "Cease firing! You are firing into your own men!" Order was soon restored. . . .[13]

§

Of the discovery of the pursuing troops passing over the mesa high above the Nez Perce camp, Peopeo Tholekt said, in part:

It was some days after the destruction of our village that I went to the warring camp on the Clearwater, where Chief Looking Glass joined up the same day. My wound did not prevent me from riding, and next day, with three others, I rode up on the high flats across the river from our camp. We met with big surprise! Soldiers were passing in a long

---

[12] As listed in General Howard's report, "Francis Winters, Private, B, 21st Infantry; conical ball; left thigh; slight wound; flesh wound." (*Rep. of Sec. of War,* 1877, I, 133.)

Under date of September 14, 1877, Fort Lapwai, Idaho Territory, Lieutenant Bailey wrote his father, "Private Winters of my company is here in hospital. He was wounded severely in the hip during our Clearwater Battle of July 11th and 12th. He was near me and had his hat shot off three times, when he concluded to leave it off. His clothing was grazed two or three times, and his cartridge box cut entirely off by a bullet, the leather belt cut as by a knife, as I saw it at the moment it occurred. Rather a hot place, wasn't it? He kept saying that some of our own men had shot him, (and it did seem so to me, tho I told him we were in a shower of bullets all the time). The other wounded men were sent to Vancouver. . . ."

[13] Manuscript of Colonel H. L. Bailey, McW NP 30½.

string of two miles or more. Itsyiyi Pawettes [Many Coyotes] whirled his horse and hurried back down to camp with message that a thousand soldiers were right on us.[14]

A stirring scene was enacted in the near capture of General Howard's supply train by a band of mounted warriors. The tactics of these graceful horsemen were more nearly cavalry style than any exhibited during the war. Of this, Roaring Eagle, a stately young warrior, says briefly:

It was short past noon when some of us made for the place of battle. There was fighting at close range when we got there. It did not appear more than a quarter mile between the firing parties. We were all dismounted when one of the chiefs spoke orders, "Mount your horses!"

There were around thirty of us, all stripped for the battle. When we made the mount the chief called, "Forward!" We made a charge but not as soldier cavalry. In this battle I put myself as a brave man[15] where we stood our ground the best we could. We pushed those soldiers back on the pack-saddle fort, where General Howard stayed with his chief officers, away from bullet danger.[16] But we could not stand before the soldiers' big guns.[17] We were

---

[14] See McWhorter, *Yellow Wolf*, p. 86.

[15] "I put myself a brave man" carries the inference of an outstanding accomplishment on the part of the narrator. But of whatever nature, it was unrevealed. Thundering Eagle was a reticent man who seldom spoke of his war career.

[16] *Yellow Wolf*, pp. 93-94. Apropos of Roaring Eagle's Packsaddle Fort, we again quote from Colonel Bailey's manuscript, "I have just read Wellington, by Phillip Guedalla. . . . Wellington did not follow the general rule of a commander keeping himself as far from exposure of his body as possible, and in after days said he felt that Providence continually protected his life. But General Howard observed that rule so far as I saw. I did not see him leave his shelter in the center to come out on our lines. In fact, he could see plenty for his purposes from his so-called shelter, said shelter consisting of our rations and ammunition and a little bunch of saddles and blankets."

[17] This was the furious onslaught on General Howard's supply train of which he states, "I had previously sent an orderly to conduct the trains within my lines; the fierce onset of the Indians requiring greater haste, Lieutenant Wilkinson, aide-de-camp, being sent brought in the train under cover of Rodney's (artillery) and Tremble's (cavalry) Companies." *(Rep. of Sec. of War, 1877, I, 122; Nez Perce Joseph, pp. 160-61.)*
Of this near capture of their supply train, Colonel Bailey writes,

forced back from that part of the field. The Indian way of fighting is not to get killed. Killed today, there can be no fighting tomorrow.

Such was our teaching, our training from childhood. See everything, hear everything! Let no madness blind you to danger! Remembering all this, it was the big guns alone that drove us back. There were two other companies of warriors but I knew not what they were doing.[18]

The Nez Perces, fewer in number than one hundred warriors had met the oncoming army of four hundred, composed of cavalry, infantry, and artillery and were able to hold this force four times their size in check during the entire first day's fighting. Aside from about twenty-four of Chief Toohoolhoolzote's dismounted band, who early engaged the infantry and held them in check, the first clash was between the cavalry and the mounted warriors as is vaguely indicated in General Howard's report. One body of the Nez Perce horsemen assailed the supply train coming in from the south, while the third company dismounted and, hiding among the boulders, engaged in sharpshooting, to be joined almost immediately by the routed Toohoolhoolzote contingent.[19]

It was at this stage of the fray that General

"It was fortunate that the Indians were so engaged in their battle with us that they did not notice the marching in of our supply train until it had nearly arrived under escort from our hard pressed lines. Further they had us so pent in for some time that we were no means sure we would not be "massacred," as such victories are usually called by our side of the battle."

[18] See *Yellow Wolf*, pp. 86-87. Of the artillery used so successfully here, Colonel Bailey wrote, "My previous comments must show that we found the two mountain howitzers very comforting assistants in the battle of the Clearwater River. I recall distinctly the feeling that I was glad the Indians did not have the use of such guns against us, although cannon are not as dangerous in effect on life and limb as on morale. The Indians, including the squaws, crawled up close to our lines and made good bullet shelters of the many stones on our open battleground and did execution from them, and the howitzers cleared some of them away much to my gratification." (Letter, Bailey to McWhorter, March 3, 1933.)

[19] *Yellow Wolf*, p. 89.

Howard speaks of an Indian who "paraded himself in plain view, beyond our left flank, and beyond the easy range of our rifles. He would dance around, and leap up and down in a strange way, with arms outstretched, swinging, as he did so a red blanket. Doubtless this was done with a view to encourage others to follow him in the bold work of attacking the flank of the position."[20]

Casualties on both sides occurred principally in the earlier phase of the fight. A scattered clump of from three to five trees on the northeast fringe of the field was the scene of the major loss early sustained by the Nez Perces. It was here that Wayakat [Going Across] was killed outright, and Yoomtis Kunnin [Grizzly Bear Blanket] fatally wounded, and Howwallits slightly hurt.[21]

These three daring sharpshooters held an exposed outpost after the rout of Chief Toohoolhoolzote's riflemen, who had been successfully flanked by the enemy and placed *hors de combat*. Grizzly Bear Blanket, though mortally wounded, dragged himself away before the troops occupied the point, and was carried to camp by the women where he died soon afterwards. Wayakat's body remained where he fell at the foot of the largest tree. Three days later, it was buried there by his bereaved mother who returned secretly for that purpose and later rejoined the retreating camp on the Lolo Trail.[22]

The three warriors were sharpshooting from the ground, but the claim has been made that at least

---

[20] *Nez Perce Joseph*, p. 161. The warrior was giving a form of the blanket signal.

[21] See *Yellow Wolf*, p. 98.

[22] Years later the author was able to locate the sunken grave by the stones uniformly placed on it at the time of burial. An additional stone or two was added by each member of our party.

one of their victims was shot from a tree. On this score Many Wounds declares:

All the warriors I have talked with deny that any sharp-shooters were in trees. The three at the clump of trees were on the ground, but soldiers might have thought shots came from among the branches of the trees. If you suspect something you are more apt to find it. Here is how it all was.

Weyatanatoo Latpah[23] was on a point or knoll back of tree from where he could see whole group of soldiers. To them it must have looked like he was up the tree. He must have killed some of those soldiers before he was killed. He made himself brave in battle with the Big Belly tribe.

As soon as the two warriors nearly reached him, one received wound only, the other got fatal shot, because it was an open place. Their names were Wayakat, killed; and wounded warrior was Howwallits.

Sergeant Schorr writes:

So far as I can remember of the trees you mention I thought there were five, and the second one from the East was where this sharpshooter was located, and I remember seeing but one dead Indian when we drove them out of their stronghold.

Of the Indians killed we never found out, but this much I do know, that the Indian sharpshooter, who was afterwards brought down, every time his rifle barked one of the troops fell. This sharpshooter was dislocated from the tree and as near as I know, sent to the happy hunting grounds. I saw him as we passed on our final charge, 2nd days fight, a good looking young Indian lying dead about forty feet from the tree which stood alone right in the midst of our firing line.[24]

---

[23] [It would seem that the Weyatanatoo Latpah [Sun Tied] of Many Wound's story must be another name for Yoomtis Kunnin [Grizzly Bear Blanket]. If not, Many Wounds, not a participant in this battle, was mistaken in the identity of this casualty. (Ed. note.)]

[24] The good-looking young Indian that Sergeant Schorr saw lying dead was in an entirely different part of the battlefield, and will be treated of more fully later on. It was of this Indian that Cassius M. Day of Captain Randall's volunteers wrote me:

"I was told by a man who was in the fight that there was one dead Indian on the Clearwater battlefield; he said the Indian was in a

We lost 40 killed and wounded, all happening in the early hours of the first day's fight. I knew none of them, either cavalry or infantry.

Poor Marksmanship by the Troops

There can be no doubt that those frightened troops wasted their many hundreds of shots on conjured, painted sharpshooters seen in every undulation of the wind-stirred pines. As will later be seen a warrior was killed by a howitzer shot, but not in connection with trees. Of the poor marksmanship of the soldiers and the cause thereof, Colonel Bailey writes:

At this era of our army we had had almost no target practice, and we were like the Indians themselves, with whom poverty and their way of hunting made it the custom to shoot only at short distances,[25] and so not only they but ourselves sent most of our shots too high, as was evident by the showers going overhead until the Indians succeeded in getting within about a hundred yards of us when we suffered our many casaulties, and narrow escapes.

. . . .

tree sharpshooting. A [cannon] shell was exploded in the tree and what was left of that Indian remained on the field and was the only one he saw."

Mr. Day visited the battlefield the day following the fight, of which he writes me:

"I saw what was left of the shattered remains of an Indian who was blown from a tree by an exploding cannon shell. The howitzer had been turned on him, spreading him out over the field."

Comment on the two foregoing items would appear superfluous. Phillip Williams, warrior, who was in the fight, declared that there were but three or four scrub black pines standing within bounds of the real fighting zone, and that they were by far too small to conceal the body of the smallest of men. On the other hand Colonel Bailey writes:

"We saw an Indian in one of the large trees in the big ravine in our front, and after many hundreds of shots he was tumbled down in death. I believe he caused several of our casualties."

Again, "I should have said that without any map at hand I can only give you a general impression of the location of the tree from which was shot that brave who certainly did worry us for awhile, and that perhaps about 100 yards from the edge of our open space, or battleground, towards the big ravine, and about one or two hundred yards from the river bluff."

[25] For a sample of this mode of fighting see *Yellow Wolf*, p. 90.

And they had repeating arms, which our soldiers were not to have for some time because they would shoot all their ammunition away at the first alarm!

.   .   .   .

A number of us saw a poor old horse, probably wounded, standing for some hours out in my front, and I suppose several hundreds of bullets were fired at him without apparent effect. That was one of the lessons I had about our shooting when we had in our army three shots per man per month for target practice.

One can be certain that cayuse drew no Indian shots. It was murderous to send those soldier boys, wholly unqualified as marksmen, to meet such deadly riflemen as the Nez Perces were known to be. As fighters, the warriors soon held Howard's soldiers in supreme contempt. Regiments and companies, where stationed, complained bitterly because of the dearth of target practice even during the training periods. In the Clearwater fight to say nothing of the White Bird shambles the troop shooting was very plainly that of ill-trained gunners.

"Making a Brave Name"

During the day's fighting there occurred an interesting illustration of Indian bravado. To make for himself a "brave name" a warrior galloped within easy rifle range, a goodly length of the enemy battle line amid a hail of bullets, gaining a coveted wound which brought him a worth-while name. Reaching his goal, he turned to regain his own zone when a bullet entered his back just under his shoulder, coming out through the breast.

With a companion he repaired to the river, and, going through a ceremonial ablution which purged the wound of clotted blood, it was bound up and he returned unimpaired to the fight. From that day he was known as Kipkip Owyeen [Wounded Breast]. He fought in subsequent battles, saw the surrender, and was exiled.

A Nez Perce Scout Joins the Patriots

An outstanding incident in the first day's battle of the Clearwater, was the spectacular desertion of one of General Howard's Christian Nez Perce scouts to join the patriots. Joe Albert, known to his tribesmen as Elaskolatat [Animal Entering a Hole], was the actor in the drama. An enlisted scout, he had figured in Captain Perry's ill-fated White Bird invasion, and again in the Clearwater campaign.[26]

Evidently at the Clearwater there was some friendly communication between General Howard's Christian Nez Perce scouts and the Dreamer patriots, for Elaskolatat learned of the death of his father, Weesculatat, who fell in the Captain Randall fight near Cottonwood.[27] The son immediately resolved to abrogate his allegiance to the government and return to his own people. He did not await the dark covering of night, but under the glaring blaze of the July sun, he dashed across the shot-ripped field for the Nez Perce quarters, gaining them safely despite the firing of troops and warriors; the former because of his apparent intent, the latter because of his uniform. Of this incident Yellow Wolf declared,"Elaskolatat came to us because his father was killed in the Cottonwood fight. Immediately after joining us, he went with others in a horseback fight with soldiers and received a bullet wound through the inner part

---

[26] "Claims of the Nez Perce Indians," *Senate Document No. 257*, 56th Cong., 1st Sess., pp. 14-99.

[27] See Chapter XVI, p. 286ff; p. 290 and *Yellow Wolf*, p. 76.

of his thigh, which made it hard for him to ride the Lolo Trail in the retreat. He was a brave fighter."

Horse Blanket (known as Sam Morris), a half-brother of Yellow Wolf, and one of General Howard's scouts, said of the incident:

> It was the first day of the Clearwater Battle. Elaskolatat and another of the scouts went to find their horses. Fast horses that had strayed away, and good horses were scarce. They found them and Elasko said to his companion, "My father was killed over there at Cottonwood, and I must go help those Indians fight the soldiers!"
>
> Then riding very swiftly to the Nez Perce side, he threw off his citizen's clothes and dressed as an Indian for battle. In the evening of that day, he was shot through the thigh by the soldiers.[28]

This ex-scout went through the long retreat riding with his leg bundled, resting on his good leg. The badly wounded would leave the camp early each morning, ahead of the main camp, riding slowly. The horse of each was led by a well man. Elasko could use his hands, bearing his weight very greatly on the pommel and cantle of his saddle, and riding on his well leg all the way over the Lolo Trail.

There also seem to have been desertions from the Nez Perce side during the Clearwater fighting. Alikkees [Hair Cut Short] (known as Alec Hays), a creditable fighter, stuck no longer than this two-days' battle. Allahkoliken [Buck Antlers] became scared and ran away the first day and joined the Christians.

---

[28] The story among the whites was that Albert received his wound as he dashed across the battlefield; whether from Indian or soldier gun was undetermined. In any case, his wound did not stop his fighting that first day's battle. Joe Albert went through the war to the final surrender, and in addition to this wound, which was not healed, he received a hip-and-thigh shot in the Canyon Creek fight, which prevented his escape to Canada. Exiled, he with a few others, escaped during the darkness of night, and rode back to Idaho where he died in 1929 (not 1933 as stated in *Yellow Wolf*, p. 181).

The Second Day of the Battle

Daybreak, on the morning of the twelfth, found the troops hurrying to their rifle pits, constructed during the darkness of the preceding night. Breakfast was to be served on the field.[29] Lieutenant Bailey was making the rounds of the immediate pits to ready the occupants for a general charge, contemplated for a later hour. Quoting from his manuscript:

The firing was much lighter as I went from company to company, and I was greatly assisted by Lieutenant Charles F. Humphrey, 4th Artillery, who was cool as everyday all through the battle, and he insisted on my going back to headquarters where the packsaddle barricade was, to get some coffee, as we had had nothing since commencing the fight, but I asked him to go; and at last he solved the problem by drawing straws; I won and went back to find about all the officers there.

No one was ready, however, to go out and help in arranging the troops for the charge, so Humphrey and I did it alone.[30] When approaching the trench of Captain J. A. Haughey and Lieutenant E. E. Eltonhead, they yelled at me, "Lie down!" as I was "drawing fire." But I was inconsiderate until a bullet struck the top of their little trench a few inches from the Captain's head and my ankles, when I stooped and dodged away. They stuck to their trench all through, and certainly looked very sweaty and dirty.[31]

---

[29] *Rep. of Sec. of War*, 1877, I, 122; *Nez Perce Joseph*, p. 162.

[30] That Bailey was piqued at what he felt was his commander's partiality toward certain of his subordinate officers, is clearly evident where he recapitulates. "I feel it just to add to my previous testimony, that most of the officers were, as I have said, away back at the General's headquarters at the time . . . among the piles of packsaddles and bundles, comparatively sheltered, while the bare ground of battle was dangerously exposed at every moment, especially when I had to go along from pit to pit to extend the skirmish line for the final charge, and where I failed to get those officers to help. . . ."

[31] Colonel Bailey gives an account of this in *Northwestern Fights and Fighters*, p. 162. Both officers were breveted for gallantry in the Clearwater Battle.

Nez Perce Fortifications

The Nez Perce stronghold boasted no trenches or excavations of any nature, but stones from the field had been roughly piled to give some protection. Citing Bailey on this, "The little stone forts you speak of seemed to be all built of boulders or cobble on the surface of the rocky ground. Such was the one where I saw the Indian with the shell hole in his forehead." Near the center of the field north and south, and in close proximity to its eastern border, stood a solitary pine tree. Less than fifty feet from this tree, paralleling the line of battle, and not over forty yards from the nearest soldier defense, was the boulder or cobblestone rifle pit here mentioned by Bailey, in which lay the dead Indian. This warrior, according to Chief Peopeo Tholekt (who was in the battle despite a leg wound received when Captain Whipple raided the Looking Glass village), was Lelooskin. This fine-looking young man was supposed to have been shot from the lone pine tree.[32]

On a visit to the field, a fairly well preserved shelter of boulders was pointed out to the writer by the Indians, in a shallow draw at the most southeastern angle of Nez Perce defense. This post was held by the flower of the Nez Perce warriors from the bands of Chiefs White Bird and Toohoolhoolzote. Here fought the "Three Red Coats," Wahlitits, Sarpsis Ilppilp, and Tipyahlanah Kapskaps, when not

---

[32] Sergeant Schorr, when questioned about this replied, "No! I did not see this Indian shot from the tree. It was when we made the final charge, near noon of the second day's battle that I saw him. He was lying about forty feet from the tree, as if he had been trying to get away from there. A truly splendid young warrior, he was the only dead Indian that I saw anywhere on the battlefield.

"He was not shot from the tree by cannon fire. That I know for a certainty. I do not know that anyone saw him fall from that tree, which I understood had drawn the fire of some parts of our battle line. An Indian was supposed to have been seen in its branches."

engaged as horsemen. They were supported by the redoubtable Pahkatos and two other men of equal bravery, Witslahtahpalakin [Hair Cut Upward] and Alikkees. The dislodged boulders of this barricade were replaced by our party, the Indians manifesting great solicitude for its preservation. They expressed regret that the marker placed by the Chief Joseph Memorial Association at the river highway could not have been set at this particular point.

From this point we traced well-defined rifle pits stretching west along the timberline skirting the south side of Battle Ridge proper. The pits were scattered among the numerous large boulders with no sign of excavations. Their splendid preservation can be traced to the unfitness of the land for cultivation and to the interest of the warriors in preserving them, and their number showed that the warriors had greatly strengthened their position during the night following the first day's battle.

Near the western extremity of these crude barricades, and slightly below them, just within the timberline and under a natural cliff of a few feet in height, was still (1935) to be seen the renowned "smoking lodge."[33] It was here that some of the older men, Husishusis Kute, Weyato Kakin, Helam Kawot, Two Moons, and others smoked and counciled while the battle raged. Aside from the shelter of the timber, it was well protected by a rude, though effective circular stone wall joined to the cliff. This formed a barricade three or four paces across. It marked the extreme western bounds of the Indian defensive line. This "smoking lodge" was respected by the Indians while it was a retreat for the old men only, but fell into disrepute when it became a refuge for the young men shirking the battle zone.

---

[33] See *Yellow Wolf*, p. 92.

The Nez Perces Quit the Fight

The Indians strengthened these fortifications as the troops were being readied for a proposed early-morning assault on the Nez Perce position, although actually this charge was not launched until mid-afternoon.[34] Howard's forces were to be helped in this undertaking by developments taking place among the Nez Perces during the interval. That events were not moving smoothly is revealed in the narratives of some of the warriors. Roaring Eagle states briefly:

> For a sun and a half we held the soldiers, then gave way because many of the warriors hung back from fighting. They argued, "No use fighting when soldiers are not attacking our camp."
>
> We then hurried from the ridge, down to the camp then on into the canyon. All retreating to the Clearwater near Kamiah. I left a few horses and do not know what became of them.

The doughty Two Moons tells the sad story in a breath, "Next morning was more battle until we made retreat, the soldiers pursuing."

The grim Husis Owyeen summarizes in two statements. "Two days we stood against the troops, and then retreated down to camp, the soldiers in pursuit. The camp broke and we rode into the hills. . . ."

Chief Peopeo Tholekt says of the break and retreat:

> That was the last I saw of Battle Ridge. Everybody was running, some leading, some falling behind! All skipping for their lives, for the camp! Every warrior, afoot or who had a horse strong enough to carry him, hurried from the ridge. They followed the families, the moving camp, guard-

---

[34] *Rep. of Sec. of War*, 1877, I, 122.

ing them from the pursuing soldiers. The cannons boomed and the Gatling gun rattled, sending out shot after shot after the fleeing families. . . .

Five Wounds, their recognized battle leader—now wounded in his right hand—soon realized that further resistance was useless, hence the startling announcement of retreat from the field. Wottolen, one of the older warriors, gave a more complete picture of the situation.

The fight was quit for a reason!

Wahchumyus, Pahkatos, Teeweeyownah [Over the Point], Sarpsis Ilppilp, Wahlitits, and Tipyahlanah Kapskaps were in one place. Teeweeyownah said to us older men, "Get ready! Let the young men mount their horses! We will go mix the soldiers! We will make a desperate fight!"

But there were cowards who refused. Teeweeyownah made to turn their horses loose. He told the Indians, "You go too often to camp! You are here to fight!"

Some got mad. They told Teeweeyownah, "You have no right turning our horses loose!"

Teeweeyownah then said to the brave men, "Let us quit the fight!" Then he turned to the other men and spoke to them, "You cowards! I will die soon! You will see hardships in bondage. You will have a hard time. Your freedom will be gone. Your liberty robbed from you. You will be slaves!"[35]

---

[35] See *Yellow Wolf*, pp. 171, 192, for the climax in the career of this fearless warrior. In confirmation of Wottolen's story are the following corroborations gleaned from various warrior sources. Teeweeyownah, who was a member of Chief White Bird's contingent, left the band of the best warriors and went among the rifle pits along the south side of the field. The men were at "Smoking Lodge," sitting around smoking. He upbraided them for not helping in the fight. They would not listen to him. He went the rounds and returning found the men still sitting comfortably, and still smoking. He scolded them more severely than ever, but to no purpose. Seeing their horses tied in the woods just below them, he went and untied them to take them away. They had been riding back and forth to camp. He would stop that! They got mad and upbraided him for bothering their horses. They said that he had no right to their horses. Teeweeyownah told them that if they were not going to fight, all had better quit and go to camp. This did no good. They answered, "All right." Teeweeyow-

The leaders then left the fighting, the cowards then following after. I did not know this and was left behind. I could hear shots from but one gun and I hurried to see what was wrong. I found only Yellow Wolf, all others gone. It was his rifle I heard. I called him, then thought to save myself.[36]

I saw soldiers starting on charge. I ran, but not swift as in other snows. It seemed a long stretch across that Battle Ridge. My breath began growing short. Bullets raised dust about me, but I could not make hurry.

I reached a lower flat from the battlefield. Rifle balls, still followed me, but I could run no more. I was now walking. Different noises seemed passing my ears. I looked back. Only soldiers seen. I came out on a long-like ridge; soldiers still shooting from upper ground. Their charge seemed checked! Some brush and maybe they were scared of ambuscade? Then I heard officers calling orders, the bugle, and soldiers cheering. I tried no more running. I had promise from my *Wyakin* that no bullets would hit me.

I now saw a white horse coming toward me. Coming slowly, loping an easy gait. Not a large horse, only medium size. When close, I recognized the man. He called to me, "I will ride by you, jump on behind me!"

Passing me, I reached him my gun. He took it, but did not stop. A short distance away, he turned and, sliding to opposite side his horse, came back at a gallop. I moved in the same direction, and as he passed, I caught the saddle horn and leaped up behind him. The horse running helped lift me. Bullets sang about us, but we went swiftly out from there, escaping with our lives.

The man on the white horse, who faced danger to save me was Weeahweoktpoo, my cousin. Afterwards he became Rev. William Wheeler, Presbyterian. He died at Lapwai. Yes, he was in exile.

---

nah returned to Wahlitits, Sarpsis Ilppilp, Rainbow, Five Wounds and Strong Eagle, and said, "Let's quit and go to camp!"

They did so, the cowards following after them. The soldiers, seeing this, became brave and made a charge. Part of the camp was left standing, so closely did the soldiers press. Before this happened, Rainbow had proposed that all the warriors mount and stampede towards the soldiers and fight it out hand to hand at close quarters. This they would not do, and the real fighters, growing discouraged, left the grounds, losing the battle.

[36] *Ibid.*, p. 96, for Yellow Wolf's account of this incident.

Both interesting and instructive is the description of the Indian retreat as it was experienced by Eelah-weemah, then an intelligent lad of fourteen years:

The second real battle took place near Peeta Auuwa, mouth of the canyon where our camp stood on the Clearwater River. I was one of the orderly boys carrying water to the warriors fighting on a big flat at top of the hill. The soldiers and Indians were not far apart. Perhaps quarter-mile, when I got there just before noon. The Indians had places circled with boulder rocks where I struck them. One such place was half size this room (12x16 feet). [This was the "smoking lodge."]

A lot of warriors were there; and they said to me, "While you are up here you can stay and see for yourself." I got in this walled-up hollow, and after a time raised up and looked across to where the soldiers were. They fired the big gun many times. I got scared and ready to run. One warrior, I do not know which one, called out, "Soldiers coming close! We must do fighting here." When the cannon-guns belched, rocks were showered and limbs of trees cut down. Smoke from that gun was like grass on fire. My near-brother Tumsuslehit [Rosebush], a warrior, said to me, "You better run now!"

I jumped out from there and ran! Soldiers must have fired at me, for bullets sang by but none touched me. Reaching my horse, a gray cayuse, I sprang on him and made for camp. When about half mile of home I heard someone say, "Indians are running from the battle!"

The foremost reaching camp told the women that they better rush to the brush. In about fifteen minutes I saw soldiers coming in sight down the bluff and hillside. They began firing across the river among our tepees. A few horses were hit but no Indians killed. We hurried packing, getting ready to move; the bullets falling around.

The Indians were now running their horses for the mouth of the canyon, leaving most of the tepees and other material. No time to save only a part of the camp. It was wild hurrying for shelter of the canyon hills.

I saw the last of the warriors galloping down the hills, but not my father. Everybody was passing me, but I did not go. There were just ten men behind me when I saw my father coming. He called to me, "My son! What you doing here?"

" 'Cause, father, I am waiting for you!" I answered.

Our race for the canyon now began. The soldiers coming where they could fire, one of those big cannon-guns sent a ball into the air. I was riding to left of father but I changed to his right. Soldiers were firing just as often as they could, and I saw my horse was stopped from running. My father missed me and looking back, he called to me, "Your horse is shot!"

My horse was shot through the left shoulder, the bullet coming out at the breast. I jumped from the saddle, and made for a draw close by, as one of our men showed up. It was my brother-in-law, Alahmoot [Elm Limb]. He gave me a horse he was leading. I pulled the saddle from my crippled cayuse and threw it on this new one. In mounting the saddle turned and I came off. My brother-in-law sprang down and drew the cinch and with him and my father, I rode away from those soldiers. We were soon in the hills where their shots could not reach us.

This was all that I saw of fighting of that day, the second real battle. I have told you the facts of what I saw of General Howard's war.

The Nez Perce Commanders

In the Clearwater battle, as at White Bird Canyon, Chief Joseph has been credited with the supreme command. Conspicuous as a diplomat, he was accorded genius on the field of battle by General Howard. Nothing could be further from actuality. While there was no commander among the Nez Perces, there were leaders; and as such in the Clearwater fight, stood the seasoned warriors, Five Wounds and Rainbow. But their plans and undertakings embraced no element of coercion. Participation was wholly voluntary. In the battle each of the five separate bands was under its own recognized chief with the exception of the Wallowa, Joseph's band, which was led by Chief Ollokot.

In the Nez Perce society, the laggards in battle, the despised cowards, were tolerated and permitted to live their own lives. Interpreter Hart explained, "It was customary in warfare, that the chief could not order any particular warrior out on scout duty. He must go of his own free will as a volunteer."

Essentially, this rule was enforced. A scout might be designated or selected because of his judgment, bravery or ability, and his selection was regarded as a mark of honor, but a chief, under the recognized laws of tribal government, did not have the arbitrary power to demand any particular action of a warrior. The sway of a chief was limited and was more advisory than mandatory; and if his demand entailed injury or loss of life to his followers, he was open to censure and even to forfeiture of leadership.

The Indians call little attention to the head chieftancy in the first stages of the war. While it is known that Chief Looking Glass joined the patriots early at their camp on the Clearwater, no mention of his taking any part in the battle was made by any of the Nez Perces.[37]

---

[37] The only hint of his possible presence is found in an interview granted by Private John Lynch of the First Cavalry to the author.

"At the battle of the Clearwater, it was sharpshooting on both sides. Our skirmish line was drawn out over two miles in length, and we seldom saw an Indian. One of them, from some vantage ground we could not locate, directed the fire of the warriors to telling effect. When the sun's rays flashed by that mirror would strike a certain point of our line, you would hear the warning cry go up, "Look out there!" as a hail of bullets raked that particular place. I had never seen the heliograph before, and that Indian, supposedly Looking Glass or one of the other leaders, handled the instrument most skillfully. . . . I do not know that he covered the entire battle line. Possibly not, could not.

"The Nez Perces were fine marksmen. I saw one man shot through the heel as his foot became exposed for an instant above the trench rim. [See *Rep. of Sec. of War*, 1877, I, 133, 'Thomas Burns, Corporal, E, Fourth Artillery; conical ball; left foot; flesh wound.'] A sergeant lost an eye, destroyed without a skin break. He continued with the command, wearing a green patch over the wound. One soldier displayed a freakish bullet mark. The ball had struck just above the right ear, traversed the contour of the skull to his left ear, leaving a

Disastrous as the defeat proved, it would have been more severe, possibly fatal, had not Chief Joseph, discerning the inevitable, hurried from the field warning the camp to pack for immediate flight.[38] And strange as it may seem to many, this is the only mention the warriors made of Joseph in connection with the Clearwater fight.

The Final Attack

It is questionable what would have happened to the belated assault on the Nez Perce position if the original plan for an early morning diversion had been executed by the troops. Colonel Bailey speaks of the enemy fire growing lighter as the day advanced,[39] coinciding with the developments the Nez Perces have suggested as the reason the field was abandoned by them. The warriors' withdrawal was made in complete ignorance of the pending enemy onslaught. Nor were the troops ready when the order to advance eventually came. Some of the cavalry horses were still unsaddled.[40]

That the officers were not anxious to charge the

---

seared blackened and hairless trail along its entire course. That soldier was rendered *hors de combat* for a long time, knocked entirely senseless.

"We had some casualties, heavy enough for whatever damages we inflicted on the Indians. I do not know that any of them were killed. They sustained some loss of equipment, and there was some slight execution among the horse herd from the howitzer fire."

Strange as it may seem, no warrior interviewed could throw the least light on the heliograph story. Colonel Bailey, then a second lieutenant, wrote in response to a query:

"I have heard of the Indian mirror flash signals, and may have seen such flashes. . . . The Indians, during some of the time, rode around, while yelling, at the head of the ravine, and flashes might have emanated from their equipment or rifles. They could have seen our men from that place at least in part."

[38] *Yellow Wolf*, p. 97.

[39] Colonel Bailey's manuscript, McW NP 30½, p. 17.

[40] *Rep. of Sec. of War*, 1877, I, 123; *Nez Perce Joseph*, p. 164.

Nez Perce stronghold is amply indicated in Colonel Bailey's memoir which reads, "When I was given the order to extend the men in skirmish line for the final charge, I asked several officers at Headquarters to go with me, or asked them if they would go, and all had some reason for not going at that time, and only joined later about the moment of making the charge...."[41]

It was midafternoon when the troops' advance was launched hard on the heels of the voluntary evacuation of the warriors. Of the attack General Howard writes, "For a few minutes there was a stubborn resistance at Joseph's barricades; then his whole line gave way."[42]

This stubborn resistance mentioned by Howard must be attributed to but two rifles handled by warriors Wottolen and Yellow Wolf, as Wottolen has so vividly shown. Colonel Bailey, among the most active officers of the command, is silent as to any resistance at the enemy barricade. His sole depiction of the charge and pursuit to the river's brink, is contained in a one-sentence paragraph, which reads, "On the 12th came the general charge which swept the foe down that ravine which had brought most of them up on our bare field, and the rout was rapid and complete, and I saw one chief lose his fine head feathers as they caught in a branch of a tree in the ravine."[43]

Casting up, the vaunted, gallant charge was probably successful only because the warriors had already

[41] Colonel Bailey's manuscript, McW NP 30½.

[42] *Nez Perce Joseph*, p. 164. See above pp. 317-18.

[43] Diligent inquiry among the warriors failed to reveal where a solitary war bonnet was sported by any warrior throughout the entire war. The feathers seen by Colonel [then lieutenant] Bailey were evidently a challenge tuft, worn by some young brave aspiring to fame in battle. The loss of his feather talisman augured ill for the loser.

decided to abandon the ground. And the Nez Perces retreated across country to the Clearwater near Kamiah where they made camp.

Plunder!

The foot soldiers were carried across the Clearwater by the cavalry but pursuit of the fleeing Indians was soon abandoned, and attention turned to plundering and destroying the deserted camp. Of the village and of its destruction, Colonel Bailey writes:

> The Indian camp appeared to have been their home for a long long time. The order was, "Burn everything!" The packers and citizens (for it was marvelous how many citizens seemed to arrive), showed us how to find the caches or underground storages, by prodding with our ramrods. It was a wonder to see the tons and tons of flour and other foods, and fine Indian goods, mostly burned. There was gold dust, jewelry, and fine silver tableware, some of which I judged dated from an early Hudson's Bay period. All this being brought to light, the packers and citizens helped themselves, while I tried to get a few things as souvenirs, but as fast as I got a little bundle, someone took it as I was looking after the troops.[44]

> Later an echo of this plunder came when our pack trains were attempting some of the false Indian trails on steep mountain sides, and in one place I saw six of the overloaded mules slip and go wheeling down, down several hundred feet, with a spurt of flour at every turn, no doubt breaking the packers' hearts, for our regular fare was only two meals a day, the Civil War kind of hard tack and unwrapped bacon and black issue coffee, all made delicious by unexampled mountain marches.

> We remained at the Indian camp for the night.

---

[44] Colonel Bailey adds, "I saved a few and sent them to Fort Lapwai by pack train going under escort for supplies. Later some of them were loaned to the Military Service Museum at Governor's Island and were mostly lost sight of during the World War. A very few are now in the Allen County, Ohio, Memorial Building at Lima, Ohio."

Casualties

General Howard's casualties in the Clearwater Battle were thirteen killed and twenty-seven wounded, two of them fatally.[45] Nez Perce casualties as listed by Yellow Wolf and verified by other warriors, included killed: Wayakat [Going Across], Yoomtis Kunnin [Grizzly Blanket], Heinmot Ilppilp [Red Thunder], Lelooskin [Whittling], totalling four. The bodies of Wayakat and Lelooskin could not be reached, so were left where they fell. The wounded were Kipkip Owyeen [Wounded Breast]; Pahkatos Owyeen [Five Wounds], shot in the right hand; Old Yellow Wolf, head wounds; Elaskolatat (known as Joe Albert), leg wound; Howwallits [Mean Man], injured by cannon fire at the camp, totaling five.[46] Yellow Wolf, who was twice wounded in the fight[47] did not include himself in his listing, which brings the number of wounded to six. Wounded Breast was the only one seriously struck and he did not quit the fight.

---

[45] *Rep. of Sec. of War*, 1877, I, 124.

[46] See *Yellow Wolf*, pp. 98-100. General Howard's report read, ". . . I reported at the time fifteen Indians killed and a large number wounded.

"After that, 8 dead were found on their trail, of those who died of mortal wounds, making for this battle 23 warriors killed; and there were at least twice as many wounded. Twenty-three prisoners, warriors, and 17 women were subsequently secured in the pursuit." *(Rep. of Sec. of War*, 1877, I, 124.)

Then later he said, ". . . They had twenty-three killed, about forty wounded, many of whom subsequently died, and some forty that fell into our hands as prisoners." *(Nez Perce Joseph*, pp. 166-67.)

That the Nez Perces would leave eight dead warriors along the trail of their unpursued retreat is completely without precedent in the annals of the conquest of the American Indian. From the eastern seaboard to the Pacific, from the Great Lakes to the Everglades, there was an immutable law that the body of a fallen warrior was not to be left for defilement by enemy hands, if within human power to prevent it.

[47] See *Yellow Wolf*, p. 96.

Howard's Success and Public Opinion

Accompanying Howard's supply train was Captain Keeler of General McDowell's staff who witnessed the closing scene of the Clearwater Battle. He lost no time in getting the following dispatch on the wire:

> Have been with General Howard in the battle of today, which he reports in detail. I consider this a most important success. Joseph is in full flight westward. Nothing can surpass the vigor of General Howard's movements and action.[48]

This wire did not reach its destination until the fourteenth, on which date the following was sent him from the headquarters of the Division of the Columbia at Portland,

> See Associated Press dispatches which state General Howard's removal under consideration by cabinet.[49]

On this same date, General Howard wired General McDowell fully of his Clearwater victory, declaring in part,

> The Indians fought as well as any troops I ever saw, and so did ours, not one man failing in duty....[50]

To army heads sorely perturbed over the Nez Perce situation these telegrams were welcome news when they reached headquarters two days later. General McDowell revealed his elation in his reply to General Howard which reads in part:

---

[48] "Keeler to McDowell, July 12, 1877," in "Claims of the Nez Perce Indians," *Senate Executive Document No. 257*, 56th Cong., 1st Sess., p. 37.

[49] "Wood to Howard, July 14, 1877," *ibid.*, p. 39.

[50] "Howard to McDowell, July 14, 1877," *ibid.*

The Nez Perces fought from behind these rock shelters at the battle of the Clearwater. They were still in position in 1928